HOME REPAIR

A
Minimal Maintenance Manual

HOME REPAIR

A
Minimal Maintenance Manual

FOR
THOSE
WHO
HATE
TO
BUT
HAVE
TO
$

GERSHON J. WHEELER

RESTON PUBLISHING COMPANY, INC., RESTON, VIRGINIA 22090
A Prentice-Hall Company

Library of Congress Cataloging in Publication Data

Wheeler, Gershon J
    Home repair: a minimal maintenance manual.

    1. Dwellings—Maintenance and repair. 2. Do-it
-yourself work. I. Title.
TH4817.W48   643   73-9534
ISBN 0-87909-341-2

© 1973 by
Reston Publishing Company, Inc.
A Prentice-Hall Company
Box 547
Reston, Virginia 22090

10 9 8 7 6 5 4 3 2

Printed in the United States of America.

Preface

If you rely on professional help to keep your home in top condition, it can cost you a small fortune in repair bills. If you try to do everything yourself, you won't have time for anything else, and it may still cost you a fortune for tools and materials. The purpose of this book is to show you how to save money and time on home maintenance and repair. For some tasks it pays, both in time and money, to call in professional help, and these are clearly indicated. For repair jobs you should tackle yourself, detailed explanations are included, as well as instructions for routine maintenance that will prevent most of the damage that can occur in a home. With a minimum of effort and a minimum expenditure for tools and equipment, you can have more time and money to enjoy your home.

Gershon J. Wheeler

Contents

1

When To
"Do-It-Yourself"

This book is for the vast majority of men and women who recognize that fixing things around the house is *not* fun but is simply something that has to be done. Whether it's a simple job like changing a burned out fuse or a major job like painting the whole house, it is still a *job* and not something that you would do for fun or enjoyment. If you are one of that rare breed who loves to tinker, and you are never happy unless you have a tool in your hand, this book is not for you. Or, if you can afford to move your family into a luxury hotel for three days while a corps of professionals paints your house, you don't need this book either.

This book, then, is for those of you who fix things around the home because you have to in order to save money, or because it is impossible to get a repairman. In these pages, you can learn how to do a job with a minimum of effort even if you have a minimum of expertise. You will be able to save money without having to spend a king's ransom on tools to do the work. You might not enjoy doing the work, but there is always a sense of satisfaction when a task is completed, especially when you think of it in terms of the money saved by doing it yourself.

Even if you don't know anything about repairs and maintenance and have never handled a tool, you *can* do most of your own repairs. Furthermore, you can do as good a job as a professional although it will probably take you longer to do it. This may seem paradoxical in these days of specialization, when professionals themselves limit their work to their own specialties. How can you be expected to do carpentry, plumbing, painting, and everything else, when a professional worker restricts his work to one specialty? The answer is *time* rather than knowledge. When a man is a professional painter, for example, he has learned to paint rapidly and efficiently by constant practice. He could do carpentry and electrical work if he had to, but at a slower rate than a professional carpenter or professional electrician. Consequently, he could not compete in price. By sticking to one specialty, the professional worker realizes the greatest return for his labors. When you do your own work, even reluctantly, you will probably be much slower than a professional worker, but the skills and knowledge needed to do the job well are easily acquired, and the finished work can be quite professional in appearance and durability.

There just aren't enough professionals to take care of all the repair work needed, and you must do some work yourself if you want it to get done. Manufacturers of building supplies recognize this problem and have developed lines specifically for the use of the amateur handyman or the average homeowner, such as paint rollers, prepasted wall paper, snap-on electrical devices, and do-it-yourself kits for almost every home repair job. These materials are available in hardware stores and mail-order houses. With each kit or each material, the manufacturer has furnished step-by-step instructions, so that the homeowner can do a satisfactory job even if he has never undertaken the specific task before. These special materials sometimes are competitive in price with the materials used by professionals, but even if they occasionally cost more, it pays to use them, since they simplify home repairs and maintenance.

Knowing *how* to do a job is only part of the problem. It is also important to recognize *what* has to be done and *when* it should be done. Even if you don't do your own repair work, knowing *what* has to be done will prevent your being charged for unnecessary jobs by less competent or unscrupulous repairmen.

Some repair jobs are emergencies which must be attended to at once. For example, if your oil burner fails during the winter, it must be fixed or you will freeze. Similarly, a broken water pipe, a leak in the roof, a broken front-door lock, or a gas leak must be taken care of immediately. In each of these situations the question of *when* never comes up. The job must be done at once. You may tackle some of these repairs yourself, but even if you don't, you ought to know what has to be done. For example, if the oil-burner failure is caused by a defective thermostat, you wouldn't want a repairman to install a whole new motor.

Another type of repair situation is the fault which you can live with for awhile, but which poses no immediate danger. For example, someone has banged open a bathroom door, causing the knob to make a dent in the plaster wall. Someday you plan to fix it, but the dent is not that bothersome, especially since it's in an out-of-the-way location. A faucet dripping slightly is also not too disturbing (although it really should be attended to, since it will only get worse if left alone). Torn wall paper, scratched floors, a broken bedroom lock, and similar defects fall in this category. In many cases, they are ignored until the owner wants to sell the house, at which time he spends a considerable amount of time or money fixing everything he can. If he had fixed these defects earlier, he would have had the pleasure of having things in proper shape. Perhaps, too, he would have enjoyed the satisfaction of fixing them for his own use instead of being irritated at having to fix them for someone else's pleasure.

Preventive maintenance is a third type of repair situation. Typically, an easily installed doorstop in the bathroom would have prevented the dent in the wall caused by the doorknob. The outside of the house especially should be checked periodically, and paint applied, shingles fixed, and stucco patched as needed to prevent the elements from causing damage. Again, as this type of repair is usually not urgent, you can approach these tasks at your leisure, but they should be done. Through regular and proper preventive maintenance, you will avoid most of the emergencies that can arise around the house.

One approach to nonemergency repairs and preventive maintenance is to make a list of repairs and checks which can be made at your leisure. Every time you notice a defect, however slight, add it to your list. As you fix something, cross it from the list. The advantage of the list is that it reminds you of jobs similar to the one you're doing, so that with certain tools and materials already in your hands, it is easy to take care of more than one job. Set aside one day a month for tackling some repairs. Don't be discouraged if the list never gets shorter.

Assuming you determine that a repair job is necessary, can you save money by doing it yourself? On small jobs that can be done relatively quickly and easily, there is no question. You should do it yourself, and the savings can be tremendous. On a percentage basis, the amount saved by tackling a large task such as an outside paint job or roofing is small, but on a small job, your cost is usually pennies plus your time. Your savings on the myriad of small jobs you do yourself around the house will more than pay for the occasional big one requiring professional help. Big jobs you do yourself can save you money, but not always. Some remodeling jobs, such as installing built-in shelves across a living room wall are easily done, and you can save by doing them yourself. Others, such as installing a new flight of stairs, are too complicated, and the potential savings is offset by the potential risks involved. Before undertaking any large job yourself, you should in effect ask yourself many questions.

In the first place (and this applies to small jobs as well as large), does the required work come under any sort of guarantee? For example, a roofer usually guarantees the roof against leaks for a specific period of time. Oil burners, gas furnaces, water heaters, and all appliances generally have guarantees ranging from three months to ten years. Floor coverings such as linoleum, tile, or wall-to-wall carpeting also are guaranteed. In fact, most professional workers guarantee their work, either expressly or implied. If there is a guarantee covering the needed work, the decision is simple. *Don't* do it yourself. Let the guarantor do it. This may be important, since if you try to fix it yourself, even if you do so successfully, you may void the guarantee.

Most of the work that should be done around a house is not covered by a guarantee. When you decide that such work must be done, you must also decide whether to call a professional or do it yourself.

You don't have to like doing it. You can do an excellent repair job and dislike every minute spent working on it. However, there are some jobs which are definitely not for the squeamish or fastidious person. Delving into an oil burner is dirty work; so is cleaning a septic tank. If undertaking this type of job would make you *sick*, don't do it. There's no sense in saving dollars on repairs and then spending them for medicine. If heights make you dizzy, don't tackle roof work or anything requiring climbing long ladders. In general, however, if you want to save money, you won't let a mere dislike of the work keep you from tackling a job.

Do you have the necessary knowledge and ability to do the work? Yes, you do! The new do-it-yourself materials are easy to use and are accompanied by very simple instructions. In addition, practically all the home-repair jobs you are likely to meet are discussed in detail in this book, with simple step-by-step instructions and short-cuts. In other words, don't let fear of botching a job prevent you from tackling it. However, before starting on a type of repair which you have never tried before, make sure you read *all* the instructions, including the precautions you must take to prevent possible damage. These precautions may be obvious, such as wrapping cloth around a nut on a chromium fixture before applying a pipe wrench, to prevent marring the finish. Nevertheless, chromium fixtures have been marred by amateur repairmen who didn't take the time to think or read all the instructions. On a more serious level, precautions are necessary to prevent lethal damage when working with electricity or gas lines. However, with proper care, these are among the simplest repairs in the house. For example, if a pilot light goes out on a gas range or gas furnace, it is a simple matter to light it again with a match. *But read the instructions first!* If there is an odor of gas, don't strike a match, or an explosion might result. The instructions tell you how to shut off the gas and to wait until the escaped gas has dispersed before trying to relight the pilot. Information is also included on how to adjust the flame so that it stays lit. In summary, then, don't be afraid to tackle a job because you have never done it before, but read all the instructions first.

Even if you know all the precautions which must be taken, you must maintain a sense of safety and caution when doing any repair work. Can you be careful? Of course you *can*, but if you find it hard not to be impulsive, you should consider carefully the possible difficulties that might arise on a job. The precautions necessary for each job are described in this book, along with the step-by-step procedures. *Read them!* An example will illustrate the potential difficulty. You may have to string electrical wires in an unfinished attic — a relatively simple job. If you step between the beams, however, you may be putting your whole weight on the plaster ceiling of the room below, and thus make a hole in the ceiling. In the description of the wiring procedures, there is a warning to be careful and step only on the beams. But what if you don't read it? If you are safety-minded, you will ask yourself what can happen or what can go wrong.

Safety should be your prime consideration in everything you do about the house. Sometimes, unfortunately, there is no way for a book like this to warn against all dangers. For example, a government booklet on stain removal indicates that gasoline may be used to remove grease stains. However, what it fails to say is that gasoline is dangerous if used indoors. For example, if you use gasoline to remove a grease stain from kitchen linoleum, the fumes may be ignited by a pilot light in the gas range or even by a spark in the motor of an electric refrigerator. In addition, gasoline fumes are toxic if inhaled. If you think "safety," you will automatically avoid using gasoline or any other flammable solvent.

If you have ever bumped your head on the edge of a door in the dark, you know how painful and serious this type of accident can be. Yet *it should never happen.* Doors should be either *wide open* or *closed tight.* When a door is wide open, you won't bump into it. When it is closed, your first contact with it in the dark will be with your hands held in front of you. This is not painful. But if a door is left partly open, as you approach it in the dark, one hand can pass on each side of it, and then your head makes contact with the edge. The solution to such a problem is simple, once you realize that you want to avoid bumping into a door in the dark. Carry the idea further. What should you do to avoid bumping your shin on a footstool? Upsetting coffee cups on a bridge table? If you anticipate the problem, you know the solution, and that's what safety engineering is all about.

Don't try to do too much. Every winter the papers are full of stories of people who had heart attacks shoveling snow. Again, it shouldn't happen, and it won't happen to you if you work within your limitations. If you are tired, *stop.* This applies whether you are shoveling snow, driving nails, painting, or doing any kind of physical work. There is also a mental or emotional strain in doing something you dislike to do. If you hate to paint, you can get a heart attack from forcing yourself to do it. So don't do any job you find too distasteful. Hire the professionals for these, and save money in other ways.

In addition to pacing yourself on the job, you should also learn how to handle materials and lift heavy objects safely. A back sprain or a hernia can result from lifting a load that is too heavy or from lifting any load improperly. Learn to lift with your legs rather than your back. Bend your knees to get down to the load, but keep your back straight and perpendicular to the ground. Get a firm grip on the load and lift it by straightening your legs. If it is too heavy, do not be tempted to bend over it and lift it with your back muscles. When lowering a heavy object, reverse the procedure and again use your leg muscles, not your back.

Whenever you exert force, think of what might happen if the object you are working against should suddenly yield. If you are tugging at a drawer or door that is stuck, make sure that your feet are so placed, that if it gives, you won't fall backward.

When handling glass, wear gloves. The edge of a sheet of glass is very sharp and can cut from the weight of the pane on your fingers. When handling an object with sharp edges or any sort of protrusions, move it slowly and make certain that it does not bump against anyone or anything.

You can learn what to do in case of fire, but the best thing to learn is how to prevent fires. Fires can start from defective electrical installations, from improper storage of combustible materials, from chemical vapors igniting from a spark, as well as from careless use of matches and cigarettes.

If your house is properly wired and fused, there should not be much danger of fire of electrical origin. An overload will blow a fuse. But don't try to bypass a fuse with a penny or piece of aluminum foil. You will have the electricity working again, but you are no longer protected, and an overload then can start a fire. Even with a properly wired home, you must be careful with your extension cords. If you run a cord under a rug, under a door, or in any area where it can be stepped on or abraded, you are inviting trouble from fire.

Combustible materials should be stored in closed metal or glass containers to prevent spontaneous combustion. Dirty rags, especially those used to wipe oil or paint, are especially susceptible. Old newspapers should be piled in well-ventilated areas. Flammable chemicals should be stored in sealed containers and labeled with a warning that they are flammable. Try to avoid using flammable cleaning agents, since adequate nonflammable cleaners are on the market.

When using a flammable chemical, work in a ventilated area away from sources of heat or fire. Note that a gas pilot on your kitchen range can ignite vapors from a volatile liquid; so can a spark in the motor when your refrigerator starts.

Cigarettes can start fires. The precautions are obvious, except that people die every year from fires caused by smoking in bed. *Never smoke in bed.*

If a fire does start, don't panic. Water can be used on ordinary fires of wood or paper but never on an electrical fire. For electrical fires, first shut off the electricity and then smother the fire with a suitable chemical. Carbon tetrachloride fire extinguishers are excellent for electrical fires and fires in your car. Ordinary baking soda is also effective and safe. Pour it on freely or just drop a 1-pound package of baking soda on the fire. The fire will burn the paper package, and then the soda starts to work by emitting carbon dioxide, which smothers the fire. Incidentally, baking soda is excellent for putting out cooking fires. If your steak catches fire because it is too close to the burner, smother the fire with baking soda, and then wash off the soda. The steak will not be damaged.

Many of the paints, cleaning agents, and caustics in the average home are poisonous, and some are even dangerous to inhale. As a first precaution, such dangerous materials must be labeled to indicate the risks and then stored so that children cannot reach them. Many of these materials are also volatile, and their fumes are flammable. When handling any of these, consider the fire precautions just discussed.

When pouring any liquid from a large metal can and especially when pouring dangerous chemicals, you must take care to avoid splashing. The proper way to prevent splashing is to pour with the spout at the top of the can. If you try pouring with the spout at the bottom, the liquid runs down the side of the can and also flows unevenly because air entering the can blocks the flow.

When handling caustics or irritating paint thinners or paint removers, wear gloves. For most materials, rubber gloves are satisfactory, but when using rubber solvents, wear plastic gloves. To avoid inhaling dangerous fumes, wear a mask; to protect your eyes, wear safety glasses; and to protect clothing from caustic solutions, wear a rubber apron. Even if you are protected, use these materials only in well-ventilated areas, preferably outdoors.

How much is your time worth? If the work necessary in the home keeps you from some other remunerative job, it is hardly a good idea to do it yourself. For most jobs you will take much longer to do the work than a professional, because you may perform the specific task perhaps once a year, whereas he does it every day. Thus, the money saved, though appreciable, may represent a discouragingly low hourly wage for your efforts.

Do you have the tools to do the job? If the work requires a special tool which is expensive, it may be cheaper to hire a professional, especially if the opportunity to use the tool again may be remote. However, in most cities tool-rental agencies offer many special tools rentable on an hourly basis. By careful planning special tools can be rented inexpensively. The work can be carried to the point where the special tool is needed, and then it can be rented, used immediately, and returned. Hand tools, however, are relatively cheap and will be used frequently. You will need a few basic tools, described in Chapter 2, but you should not spend a fortune on tools, as that would defeat the primary purpose of doing your own work. When figuring the savings on a job, consider the cost of additional tools, whether bought or rented, as part of the cost of the job rather than as capital equipment. The point is that you may never use the bought tool a second time, but, if you do, it will lower the cost of the next job.

Before deciding to do a large job yourself, ask yourself what the true costs of the work are. Include *all* the materials to be used. For example, if you are going to paint, you will need paint thinner, sandpaper, putty and a putty knife, a drop cloth to protect rugs and furniture, and cleaners for brushes and rollers when the work is done. The cost of each of these alone is negligible, but the sum may well be appreciable. In addition to the materials and tools, you should consider other costs that you incur that have nothing to do with the job. An example will make this clear. Two neighbors living in similar ranch-style (one-story) homes decided that their houses needed painting. Mr. A chose to have a professional painter do his house, while Mr. B thought that he and his wife could do the job and save money. Mrs. B worked a few hours during the day, and Mr. B joined her when he came home from work each day, and together they finished the job in two *weeks*. The professional painter finished Mr. A's house in two and a half *days*. Mr. A paid the painter $100 more than Mr. B spent on all the materials. Did Mr. B save $100, even forgetting the two weeks of inconvenience? Not really. In the first place, Mr. B drove to several paint stores before he selected the paint he wanted, whereas Mr. A's painter brought sample cards to Mr. A's home for inspection. Mr. B didn't figure the cost of gasoline in his car. But more important, on many occasions during the two weeks, Mrs. B was too tired to prepare dinner, so Mr. and Mrs. B ate out in a restaurant. Mr. B was understandably reluctant to discuss how much he spent on restaurant meals during this period. This doesn't mean that it is necessarily cheaper in the long run to call a professional painter. It does indicate that you should consider all possible expenses, including medical bills if you get hurt, before you tackle a large job just to save money.

To summarize, because professional workers charge high minimum fees for even the simplest jobs, you can indeed save money by doing much of the work yourself. You can also keep thing in good repair so that major problems are infrequent. You may feel that it's not worth calling a repairman to fix a minor defect that you can live with, but if you can fix it yourself, you don't have to live with it. Most important, since you are working on your own home, you have an incentive to do the job well and will frequently put in the extra care to do an excellent job; the professional, on the other hand, may simply be interested in doing an adequate job and getting on to his next assignment. There is a great deal of satisfaction in a job well done, and perhaps you won't be so reluctant to attempt the next repair.

In the pages that follow you will find step-by-step directions for doing practically all the repair and preventive maintenance work needed in a house, as well as simple remodeling. Most of the jobs are simple ones which you can tackle without qualms. Where a particular task requires extra care or experience, the precautions necessary are listed as well as a recommendation as to whether to tackle it yourself or to call a professional repairman. Complete descriptions are included even for the jobs requiring professional expertise, because usually you can do much of the preliminary work yourself, calling in a repairman to finish the work later. Also, in some areas different types of repair jobs are seasonal, and in an off-season you may be able to hire a professional to work *with* you on a job. Then you can do the simple work, allowing him to concentrate on the operations needing special ability. By doing all the simple jobs yourself and a minimum amount of preventive maintenance, you can save enough to pay for your vacations.

A few words of caution are necessary concerning the hiring of professional workers. Too often a homeowner is approached by an unscrupulous painter, for example, who offers to paint the house at a tremendous bargain. If the work is done, it might wash off after the first rainstorm, and the homeowner will find that the painter's card lists a fictitious name and address. You can hire home-maintenance or home-repair service for any job in the house, but you should know something about the firm or person you are hiring. It should be a reliable firm that will be in business when you need them. After all, what good is a five-year guarantee from a company that lasts only six months?

Contrary to popular belief, most service businesses do *not* do excellent work, because they find it difficult to attract competent help. You may have to hire a professional worker, because the job calls for special equipment or because the job is dangerous, but chances are that the man who comes to do the work is not an expert, unless you are careful in your hiring. In general, the best service is provided by professionals who *own and operate* their own businesses. Even here there are differences in quality of work and expertise, but at least they don't depend on inexperienced help. The best check on a service is a list of recommendations from satisfied customers.

Tools
And How To
Use Them

You need very few tools to keep a house in good condition. A complete, well-equipped workshop is an unnecessary expense, since you would be unlikely to use most of the tools in it. A better plan is to start with the few basic tools used on the most frequently occurring house repairs and to add other tools as they are needed. In this way, your initial investment is low, and the additional tools can be charged off against the cost of the jobs on which they are used. Also, this approach solves the gift-giving problem for others who might wonder what to give you for a bithday or Christmas present. With the help of a few well-placed hints, you should be able to get as gifts tools which you would like to have but don't feel you can afford or can justify buying.

For the few basic tools you need, it pays to buy good ones, but keep your eye out for cheap bargains, too. Most discount houses and auto-supply stores occasionally try to get rid of their remaining odd tools by selling them at bargain prices. If you see something you can use, buy it. Cheap tools can be banged around without qualms, and you can throw them away when they break, without worrying about cost. You can use them whenever you might not want to use your good tools. Thus, you'll feel better using your good screwdrivers only to drive screws and using a cheap screwdriver to pry open the lid of a paint can, for example.

2-1. HAMMERS AND NAILS

One of your basic tools is a claw hammer, and you should buy a good one. There are two types available, as shown in Fig. 2-1. The curved claw hammer, shown in Fig. 2-1(a), is better for pulling nails out. The straight claw hammer, shown in Fig. 2-1(b), is used for splitting boards and for prying wooden boxes apart. As there is little need for a straight-claw hammer for home repair, you should choose one with a curved claw.

The hammerhead may be cast iron or forged steel. Cast iron breaks easily, so you should avoid this metal. The handle may be wood, plastic, or steel. All are satifactory, but if a hammer is stored in an area which may be subject to dampness or excessive heat, a wooden handle might loosen. A good metal-handled, claw hammer is shown in Fig. 2-2.

Hammers are rated according to the weight of the head. If you never used a hammer, you might want a comparatively lightweight

15

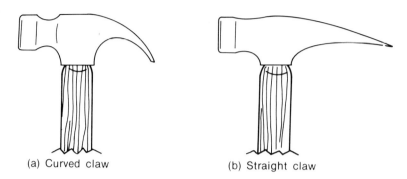

(a) Curved claw   (b) Straight claw

FIGURE 2–1. Claw Hammers.

head to start, 10 or 12 ounces. After you are accustomed to swinging a hammer, you should get a heavier model. The 16-ounce hammer shown in Fig. 2–2 is suitable for most jobs around the home. The lighter hammer is still useful for light work, such as driving tacks or glazier's points, or hanging pictures.

Besides the claw hammer, there is a wide variety of special-purpose hammers, such as tack hammers, which are magnetized to hold tacks, plastic hammers for working on delicate surfaces, metalworking hammers, heavy sledges for driving drills into masonry, and others. You don't *need* any of these for ordinary home repair and maintenance. If you decide to tackle a special job where a special hammer would be helpful, then buy it and consider its cost part of the cost of the job. For example, a tack hammer would be more useful than a claw hammer when upholstering a living-room set, and its cost is negligible compared to the cost of the materials used.

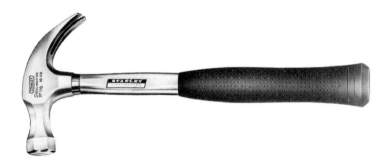

FIGURE 2–2. Hammer. Photo Courtesy of Stanley Tools,
Division of The Stanley Works.

A hammer has many uses around the home. You will use it to drive nails and also to pull out nails that you didn't drive correctly. In addition, you may use it with a chisel to fit a lock in a door .or to make a furniture joint. You will need it to drive points when putting glass in a window. You can put a right-angle bend in a piece of metal by holding the metal in a vise at the bend line and tapping it gently with a hammer.

For most applications, the hammer should be held at the end of the handle. Beginners sometimes make the mistake of holding the hammer at about the middle of the handle, but the farther your hand is from the head, the more force you can deliver with each blow. If you are using a heavy hammer for light work, such as driving tacks, you may not want to deliver the maximum force available, and in that case you would deliberately "choke up" on the handle to decrease the force at impact. It would be better to use a lighter hammer and hold it at the end, but if no lighter hammer is available, the short grip on a heavier hammer can be used.

To drive a nail, grasp the nail between the thumb and forefinger of one hand, and hold the hammer in the other. First, *tap* the nail so that it stands unsupported. Then remove the hand holding the nail and swing the hammer with harder strokes until the nail is driven into the wood or other material. Keep your eye on the *nail* as you do this, and you will be surprised at how easy it is to drive the nail in straight. If the nail begins to move off the perpendicular, you can straighten it by tapping it on the side to straighten it up again. If you bend the nail, remove it as described below, and start again with a new one. A word of caution: When starting a nail, hold it close to its head rather than at the surface of the wood. If you miss the nail and hit your fingers, it will hurt, but not seriously. On the other hand, if your fingers are near the surface, they can be squashed between the hammer and the wood.

A professional carpenter can drive a 2-inch nail with one tap and two strokes. After the tap, the hand which held the nail moves to his pocket and brings out another nail during the time taken to make two strokes, so that the hammering is almost continuous. Don't expect even to approach this kind of efficiency. You're not being paid by the hour to do the job. Be satisfied if you can drive a nail straight into a horizontal or a vertical surface.

As you drive the nail, the handle of the hammer should be parallel to the surface of the wood. On the last stroke, the hammerhead will then hit the nail squarely and will not mar the surface. The face of the hammer has a slight crown so that the perimeter of the face will not gouge into the wood when the nail is driven home. If the hammer is tilted, the perimeter will hit the wood before the nail is all the way in and mar the surface. An exaggerated view of this is shown in Fig. 2–3.

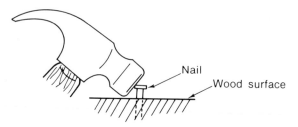

FIGURE 2–3. Gouging.

A handy accessory which you will need is a *nail set*. This is a short, solid-metal rod, tapering to a blunt point at one end; it is pictured in Fig. 2–4. You can use the nail set to finish driving a nail when you are afraid of marring the surface. When the nail is almost all the way in, hold the nail set with its tapered end on top of the head of the nail and hammer on the head of the nail set. This drives in the nail with no danger of the hammerhead hitting and marring the surface. The nail set is used also to drive nails slightly below the

FIGURE 2–4. Nail Set. Photo Courtesy of Stanley Tools, Division of The Stanley Works.

surface. Then the hole can be filled with putty, covering the head of the nail, and when the surface is painted, it is completely smooth, with no indication of the location of nails. In a pinch you can file off the point of a spike and use it as a nail set, but a good nail set is very inexpensive and is well worth having.

If you nail two boards together, you can improve the holding power by *clinching* the nails. This means simply bending the end of the nail after it is driven all the way through both boards, as shown in Fig. 2–5. The nail should protrude at least 1 inch, preferably nearer 2 inches. The end of the nail is struck at an angle, bending the nail until it lies flat on the surface. The nail should be clinched so that it is parallel to the grain in the wood. The point of the nail should be driven below the surface, either by giving it a strong rap or by using a nail set.

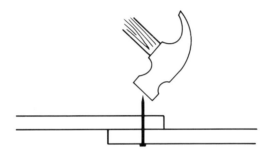

FIGURE 2–5. Clinching.

It is sometimes necessary to fasten a piece of wood at right angles to another where it is impossible to drive a nail straight into the end of the perpendicular member, as, for example, to fasten a stud in the wall of a house to a supporting beam. The method used is called *toe-nailing* and is illustrated in Fig. 2–6. The nails are driven into the vertical member or stud at an angle so that they penetrate into the horizontal beam. As you strike the nail, the stud would tend to move to the left from the blows. To prevent this, the stud should be held firmly in place, for example, by putting your left foot against it while nailing or by using a length of board as a wedge to prevent this movement. The joint can be strengthened by first bending the point of the nail slightly before toenailing it. The nail then follows a curved path and is more difficult to remove.

When a nail is driven close to the end of a board, it may split the wood, as shown in Fig. 2–7. As the nail is driven in, it pushes aside the fibers of the wood, and this causes the split. Splitting can be

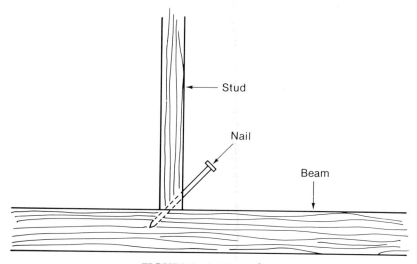

FIGURE 2–6. Toenailing.

prevented by blunting the point of the nail, either by filing it, or by hitting it with a hammer. The blunt nail then acts as a punch, pushing fibers before it, instead of pushing them aside. Special blunt nails are available, for use in applications where splitting might occur. You can also prevent splitting by drilling a small hole first before driving in the nail.

Splits may also occur in a board if adjacent nails lie on the same grain line. To avoid this, it is common practice to stagger nails along a board. Staggering nails also makes a stronger joint than having all nails on one line. Another way to strengthen a nailed joint is to drive nails in at an angle instead of perpendicular to the surface, alternating the direction of the nails along the line.

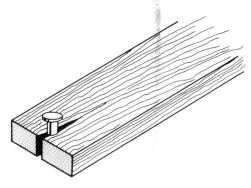

FIGURE 2–7. Split Near End of Board.

The claw end of the hammer is used to pull out nails. On a good hammer, the claw is machined to a thin edge so that it can be slipped under the head of a nail that barely protrudes from the surface. In addition, the inner edges of the claw are sharp so that they can grip the body of a nail, without depending on the head for holding.

When pulling a long nail, you should take pains to have the nail move out perpendicular to the surface. As you pull the handle, the nail will move straight out of the wood until it is exposed about $\frac{1}{2}$ inch, as shown in Fig. 2–8. If you continue to pull, the nail will start to bend over in the direction of the pull and will be difficult to remove. Also, the edge of the face of the hammer will dig into the surface and mar it. To prevent both from happening, you should place a block of wood under the hammerhead after the nail is part way out, as shown in Fig. 2–9. The block increases the leverage on the nail, helps pull the nail straight, and keeps the hammer face from marring the surface. A block is not necessary when pulling a short nail.

If a nail that is driven all the way in must be removed, you will not be able to get the claws under the head. You may be able to pry the boards apart slightly with a screwdriver or hit the nail on the point to start it (if it protrudes from the other side). If not, you will have to use a screwdriver to pry under the head of the nail and lift it enough to get the claws under it. This will mar the wood, but you have no choice. You can always repair the damage afterward with some sort of wood filler or wood paste.

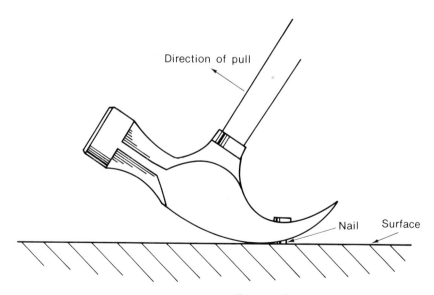

Direction of pull

Nail   Surface

FIGURE 2–8. Pulling Nail.

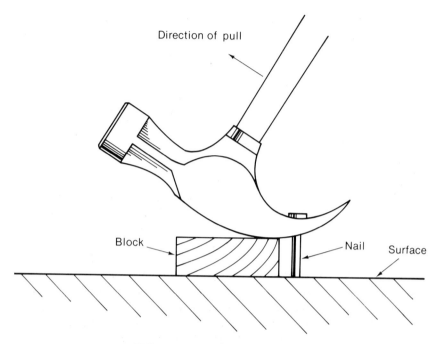

FIGURE 2–9. Block for Leverage.

There are literally hundreds of different kinds of nails, and each type comes in a wide range of sizes. Nails are used throughout the home despite the fact that screws have greater holding strength. The reason is the relative ease of driving a nail as compared to turning a screw. Although special nails have been designed for different parts of the house, the amateur handyman would find it impossible to keep a supply of each type on hand. Instead, he should concentrate on a few types which are applicable to many jobs.

A few popular types are shown in Fig. 2–10. These represent only a small portion of the large variety of nail types, but they can be used for most of the repair jobs in the home. Each type illustrated comes in many sizes, sometimes designated in terms of "pennies." Rather than try to remember these designations (as, for example, that a 6-penny common nail is 2 inches long, while a 20-penny nail is 4 inches long), just think in terms of length. If you need a 2-inch nail, ask for a 2-inch nail, and let the hardware dealer tell you the penny size. Nails are sold by the pound, so that 1 pound of 3-inch nails will contain fewer nails than 1 pound of 2-inch nails of the same type, although they may sell at the same price per pound. The lengths corresponding to various penny sizes and the approximate minimum

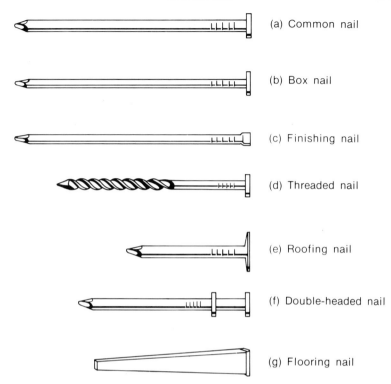

(a) Common nail

(b) Box nail

(c) Finishing nail

(d) Threaded nail

(e) Roofing nail

(f) Double-headed nail

(g) Flooring nail

FIGURE 2–10. Types of Nails.

number of nails per pound for three popular types of nail are given in Table 2-1.

The most popular type of nail is the *common nail,* shown in Fig.

Table 2–1

Penny Number	Length	Number per Pound (Minimum)		
		Common	Box	Finishing
2	1	850	1000	1300
3	1¼	550	600	750
4	1½	300	400	500
5	1¾	250	350	450
6	2	150	200	250
8	2½	100	130	160
10	3	65	90	110
12	3¼	60	80	100
16	3½	45	65	85
20	4	30	50	60

2-10(a). The *box nail*, shown in Fig. 2-10(b), is similar but is thinner for the same length. Since nails hold by friction, the larger the surface area of the nail, the better the nail will hold, so that, in general, a common nail will hold better than a box nail of the same length. In addition, small ridges near the head of the nail increase the holding power. Box nails are used in light applications where the heavier common nail may split the wood. Rather than trying to remember a set of rules with numerous exceptions as to what type of nail to use, rely on your hardware dealer. He can tell you what type and size to use for specific applications.

The harder it is to drive in a nail, the better the nail will hold. Since it is more difficult to drive a nail into a hardwood like oak than into a softwood like pine, hardwoods hold nails better. Hardwoods, however, are more likely to split when a thick nail is driven into it. Nails can be driven into hardwoods more easily and with less risk of splitting if they are lubricated. A professional carpenter sometimes drills a hole about 1 inch deep and $\frac{1}{4}$ inch in diameter in the end of the handle of his hammer and fills the hole with beeswax. When nailing into hardwood, he first sticks the nail into the beeswax to lubricate it. Ordinary soap is also a good lubricant, and you can drive nails more easily if you first draw each nail across a bar of dry soap. Soap, however, may cause the nail to rust and should not be used in permanent installations. Any wax is satisfactory.

Both the common nail and box nail have large heads which may be unsightly. Where a less conspicuous head is required, finishing nails, shown in Fig. 2-10(c), are used. The diameter of the head of a finishing nail is barely larger than that of the nail itself, and it can be driven completely into and below the surface with a nail set. The head can then be covered with putty or wood filler, and when the surface is painted, there is no indication of the location of nails.

Many ways have been devised to increase the holding power of nails. Some nails are coated with a hard glue which melts when the nail is driven and then quickly dries again, making the nail almost impossible to pull out. Coated nails should be used only by an expert, however, because they leave no room for errors. If a coated nail is driven part way, it becomes permanently fixed in place and can neither be driven further or removed.

Increased holding power can be obtained from *threaded nails* or *screw nails*, shown in Fig. 2-10(d). There are two basic types—one having a real screw thread and the other a set of annular rings. The annular rings may have their axis along the nail or they may be tilted at a helix angle. When a threaded nail having a real thread is driven, it rotates like a screw and spirals into the wood. It holds more like a screw than a nail. When an annular ring nail is driven, it does not rotate, but the wood fibers press into the spaces between the rings, increasing the holding power. Threaded nails are more expensive per pound than common nails, but there are more per pound. In addition, the increased holding power of each nail enables you to use fewer nails to get the required strength.

The *roofing nail*, shown in Fig. 2-10(e), is a short, stubby, *galvanized* nail with a large head. Its name indicates its application.

The *double-headed nail*, shown in Fig. 2-10(f), is used for temporary structures which will be taken apart. Typically, cement forms are usually built with double-headed nails. When the cement has hardened, the nails are pulled and the forms removed. The nail is driven in up to the first head, and the protruding second head can easily be grasped with a claw hammer for removal. These nails can also be used to support heavy objects on a wall.

The *flooring nail* in Fig. 2-10(g) is illustrated as a special nail for a specific application. It requires a great deal of skill to drive these nails at the proper angle into floors, and thus you will probably never use them. They are shown here only as an example of the wide variety of nails available.

The roofing nail mentioned above is *galvanized*, that is, it is coated with zinc to prevent rust. All nails used on the exterior of the house must be rustproof. Sometimes an excellent paint job can be ruined by nails rusting in the walls. Nails should be galvanized or made of aluminum. Aluminum nails will not rust, but they are softer than steel and must be driven carefully to prevent bending.

2-2. SCREWDRIVERS AND SCREWS

Screwdrivers are used more than any other tool around the house, and you can't have too many of them. Since they come in hundreds of sizes and shapes, you could easily go broke if you tried to own one for every contingency. You should begin with only two or three *good* screwdrivers and add special ones as needed. If you see screwdrivers for sale at bargain prices, don't be afraid to buy a few in odd shapes or sizes. For many applications you don't *need* a good screwdriver, and for some jobs you won't *want* to use your good tools, so it pays to have a few cheap ones around.

A typical well-built screwdriver is shown in Fig. 2-11. The blade or metal part is made of a steel alloy and is strong enough to be used as a lever without danger of bending. The metal extends into the handle far enough to ensure a firm grip which won't

FIGURE 2–11. Screwdriver. Photo Courtesy of Stanley
Tools, Division of The Stanley Works.

loosen.   The handle itself is made of a tough plastic which can be
hit with a hammer without breaking.   The tip of the blade is *square;*
that is, it is flat across the blade and the bevels are not rounded.   The
handle should not be round, or, if round, it should be fluted so that
it can be gripped without slippage on tough jobs.   In order to select
screwdrivers intelligently, you should know something about screws.
Screws are available with two different kinds of heads, as shown in
Fig. 2–12, and therefore you will need screwdrivers for both types.
The slotted head in Fig. 2–12(a) is the more familiar and takes the
common flat-bladed screwdriver.   The recessed or Phillips head,
shown in Fig. 2–12(b), is used on many electrical appliances and on
some furniture.   The Phillips screwdriver has a blade especially shaped
to fit into the recessed head of these screws.   In Fig. 2–12, the screws
are shown with *flat* heads.   Other commonly available head shapes
are *round* and *oval.*   These head shapes are shown in Fig. 2–13.   Flat-
headed screws, shown in Fig. 2–13(a), are used where it is necessary
or desirable to have the screw head flat or below the surface of the

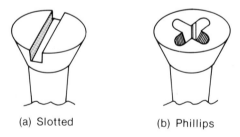

(a) Slotted   (b) Phillips

FIGURE 2–12. Screw Head Openings.

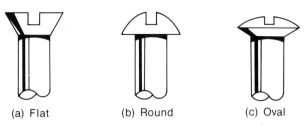

(a) Flat   (b) Round   (c) Oval

FIGURE 2–13. Screw Heads.

material.   The hole must first be countersunk; that is, a recess is drilled into the surface to accomodate the head.   Round or oval heads usually project above the surface.   As indicated in the figure, the oval head protrudes less than the round.   But the hole for the oval-head screw must also be countersunk, whereas no countersinking is required for the round head. All three head shapes are available in Phillips screws as well as slotted heads.

The parts of a screw are indicated in Fig. 2–14.   Between the head and the threaded portion there is a section called the *shank*, which is *not* tapered. The diameter of the screw is simply the diameter of the shank.   It is usually specified in a numbered series, from #0 to 30.   The length of a screw is the length of the portion which normally goes below the surface.   For the round-head screw, shown in Fig. 2–14(a), it is the length of the shank plus the thread. For the flat-head screw, shown in Fig. 2–14(b), it is the overall length, as the whole head normally goes into the material.   For the oval head, shown in Fig. 2–14(c), it is the length from the beginning of the tapered portion of the head to the tip of the screw.   Screw lengths range from ¼ inch to about 4 inches.   If you have to buy screws, plan to have the threaded portion extend about two thirds of the way into the second board.   For example, if you were using screws to fasten a ½-inch board to one 1½ inches thick, you would want the screw to go entirely through the ½-inch board and 1 inch into the other.   Thus, you would need screws 1½ inches long.   This doesn't

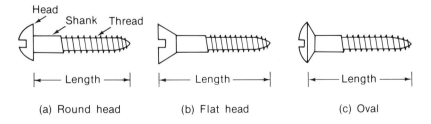

(a) Round head   (b) Flat head   (c) Oval

FIGURE 2–14. Parts of Screw.

apply if you are screwing a hinge to a door or in other similar applications. For most jobs just tell the hardware dealer where you will be using the screws, and he can advise you on proper length and diameter.

Screws may be made of almost any metal, and some plastic screws are also available. Steel screws are strong and cheap, but they may rust in a damp location. Stainless steel screws are rustproof, but are more expensive. When screws are used to join metal parts, the screw should be made of the same material as the metal or should be plated with that material.

The larger the diameter of the screw, the wider will be the slot in the head. Ideally, when you are driving a screw, the blade of the screwdriver should fit the slot, as shown in Fig. 2-15. This would mean that you would need a separate screwdriver for every different diameter of screw. In practice, you can use a smaller screwdriver in a large slot as long as the blade is not too free. If the blade is too small, it will tend to twist in the slot, chewing the edges. As long as you can turn the screw easily, don't worry about the fit, but do use the largest blade you have which will fit into the slot. If the blade is rounded from frequent use, it may tend to jump out of the slot. You can correct this by filing the end of the blade square if you have a file. If not, don't throw the worn screwdriver away. You can still use it to open paint cans, as a lever, or in other less glamourous applications, and someday you may buy a file for another job, and then you can square the end again.

In general, the longer the handle on your screwdriver, the more twisting force or *torque* you can exert. However, unless you have considerable practice, a longer screwdriver is more difficult to keep

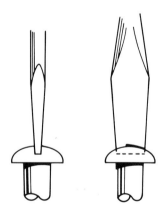

FIGURE 2-15. Correct Fit.

in the slot than a short one. A good size for your first screwdriver is about 7 inches in overall length with a blade about ¼ inch wide. You can add another about 8 inches long with a slightly wider blade. Note that the wider blade is used to drive larger screws, which are correspondingly harder to drive. Thus, the larger blade is used in a longer screwdriver to get additional torque.

Besides the screwdrivers for slotted screws you should have at least one Phillips screwdriver. These come in four sizes, #1, 2, 3, and 4, to handle all Phillips screws from the smallest to the largest. You can get by with a #2, which will fit practically all the Phillips screws you are likely to meet around the home. If you fix a lot of electrical appliances or work on your car, you may want a complete set of Phillips screwdrivers.

Other popular types of screwdrivers are shown in Fig. 2–16. The offset screwdriver, shown in Fig. 2–16(a), is used to reach into tight areas where there is no room to use even a short regular screwdriver. The stubby driver, shown in Fig. 2–16(b), has an overall length of about 3 inches. It is useful in cramped quarters and also wherever it may be difficult to keep the blade in the slot. Remember that a short screwdriver has less torque but can be handled more easily. The screwdriver bit, shown in Fig. 2–16(c), is used with a brace to exert extra torque on screws which are too difficult to drive conventionally. The stubby screwdriver is also available with a Phillips blade. You will probably find a stubby screwdriver for slotted screws useful, but

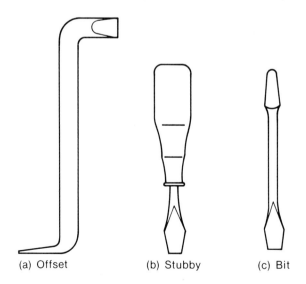

(a) Offset   (b) Stubby   (c) Bit

FIGURE 2–16. Screwdriver Types.

it needn't be of excellent quality. Buy one when you see it on sale. The offset screwdriver and the bit have less direct application in the home. Don't buy these unless you really need them.

WARNING: No matter what type of screwdriver you use, you must keep in mind that it can be a dangerous instrument. You don't have to be warned about a knife, because you know it is sharp and can cut you. However, since a screwdriver has no sharp edges, you may tend to be careless using it. As you drive or set a screw, you turn the screwdriver, but you also exert force in the direction of the screw by pushing the screwdriver to keep it in the slot. If the screwdriver slips out of the slot, it moves with great speed and force in the direction you were pushing it. If your other hand is in the way, you can get gouged much worse than you would from a sharp knife. Even if you take care to stay clear of a possible slip, your screwdriver can dig into or otherwise mar the surface of the wood you are fastening. If you realize and remember that this can happen, you will automatically take proper precautions to prevent it.

If you are setting a small screw in softwood, you can start it by making a slight indentation in the wood with an ice pick or awl. If you have no ice pick, you can use a nail. Tap it in slightly and then pull it out. Place the screw in the indentation and screw it in with a screwdriver. The thread will pull the screw into the wood as you turn the screwdriver, and the softwood will push aside as the shank of the screw is drawn in. Larger screws need *pilot holes* and *shank holes*. Also, if two boards are joined by a screw, a pilot hole is necessary in the lower board and a shank hole is needed in the board near the screw head, as shown in Fig. 2–17. In Fig. 2–17(a), a round-head screw is shown. The shank hole in the upper board is just large

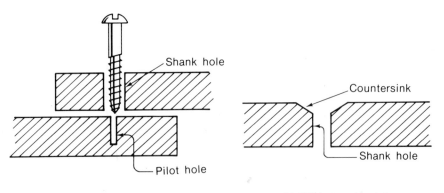

(a) For round head screw   (b) With countersink

FIGURE 2–17. Pilot and Shank Holes.

enough to pass the shank of the screw. The pilot hole in the lower board is smaller than the diameter of the screw thread, but enough has been removed so that the screw will cut a thread on the inside of the hole instead of just pushing the fibers apart like a nail. A pilot hole enables you to set a nail in very hard wood. Otherwise, as you turn the screwdriver (if you can), the screw would force the fibers apart and cause the wood to split. In Fig. 2–17(b), a countersunk shank hole is shown in the top board for a flat-head screw. A pilot hole is still used in the lower board, (not shown in the figure). Drilling the shank and pilot holes and making the countersink are explained in the next section.

In very hard wood, the screw can be set more easily if it is lubricated. As with nails, dry soap is a satisfactory lubricant. However, a soaped screw is harder to remove later. Also, the moisture in soap, even dry soap, may cause rust or corrosion on the screw. Ordinary wax or powdered graphite is better. In any event, do not use oil, since it will seep into the wood and stain it.

If a screw is withdrawn and replaced in the same hole a few times, it loses its holding power because of the wear on the threads in the wood. If you must use the same hole, you can replace the screw with a longer one for greater holding power. Alternatively, you can fill the hole with wood filler or a plastic plug and set the screw in the new material.

When you set a small screw in softwood, it takes very little torque. If you use a large screwdriver, you may exert too much torque, turning the screw after it is all the way in. This strips the thread in the wood and leaves nothing for the screw to hold on to. To avoid this, whenever a screw is going in easily, use the smallest screwdriver you can so that there is less danger of applying too much torque. Likewise, be careful to avoid stripping threads in soft metals such as aluminum when screwing machine screws.

If you have many screws to set on one project, you might consider buying a spiral-ratchet screwdriver, such as the one shown in Fig. 2–18. When you push down on the handle, the screwdriver blade revolves, exerting a large torque with little effort. Screws can be driven quickly and easily, but extra care is needed to prevent stripping the threads in the wood. The ratchet screwdriver is particularly useful for driving large screws into hardwood where stripping is unlikely and a large torque is needed. This type of screwdriver is a luxury, but it does simplify the work.

If you attempt to set a screw into the end of a piece of lumber, it will not hold as well as one set across the grain. The end fibers separate too easily and do not form threads readily. For increased holding, you can insert a *dowel* near the end of the board, as shown in Fig. 2-19, so that the screw bites into the dowel. A dowel is simply a short wooden rod. Drill a hole, just large enough for the dowel, completely through the board, and then glue in the dowel, cutting it off flush with the surface. Now the screw will go into the dowel and be held better than in the end fibers alone.

2-3. DRILLS

You may never have to drill a hole in doing repair or maintenance work around the home. However, if you do any extensive remodeling or even decide to change a lock in one of your doors, you will need some sort of drill. A drill is also necessary in furniture building and handy in many other applications which are not related to the house, such as repairing or building toys. In other words, you may not *need* a drill, but if you have one, you will find many uses for it.

Sooner or later you should acquire a bit brace, shown in Fig. 2-20. The chuck is adjustable and will take a variety of bits for drilling holes and other jobs. Make sure that you buy a good brace; a cheap one is false economy. The round knob should turn easily on ball bearings; the chuck should hold the bit centered automatically and should be capable of gripping drill bits with round shanks as well as

FIGURE 2-18. Ratchet Screwdriver. Photo Courtesy of Stanley Tools, Division of The Stanley Works.

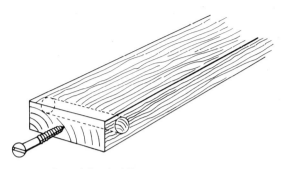

Dowel for holding power

FIGURE 2–19. Dowel for Holding Power.

those with square shanks; and the brace should have a heavy-duty ratchet for work in close quarters.

Some of the bits that are used with a brace are shown in Fig. 2–21. The twist drill, shown in Fig. 2–21(a), has a round shank of the same diameter as the cutting edge of the drill. It is used for drilling into metals and plastics. This type of bit is usually used in an electric drill or other drill which can be turned more rapidly than a hand brace. Twist drills are also available with a square shank for use in a brace. However, if you are careful to select a brace that will take a round shank as well as a square, you can buy round twist drills and use them with the brace and any other drill you happen to have. The auger bit, shown in Fig. 2–21(b), is specifically used for drilling in wood. It is available in hole sizes from about ¼ inch to 1⅛ inches in diameter. These sizes are numbered by sixteenths of an inch, so that a ¼-inch bit is #4 and a 1-inch bit is #16. Auger bits are about 6 inches long, but 18-inch lengths are available for special jobs. The long bits are expensive. Auger bits with adjustable cutters are used for larger holes; these are called *expansive* bits. Typically, an expansive bit is available which can be set for any size of hole from ⅞ inch to 3 inches in diameter. The auger bit has a small screw thread at the point. As the bit is turned, this thread pulls the cutter into the wood.

Other bits are available for purposes other than drilling holes. The countersink, shown in Fig. 2–21(c), is for countersinking screws. The screwdriver bit, shown in Fig. 2–21(d), is used to drive screws into hardwood or wherever the extra torque of the brace is needed. The reamer in Fig. 2–21(e) is used to enlarge holes that have already been drilled and to remove burrs from holes in metal.

The ratchet near the base of the brace can be set so that the brace will turn the bit in one direction only. When the brace is rotated in

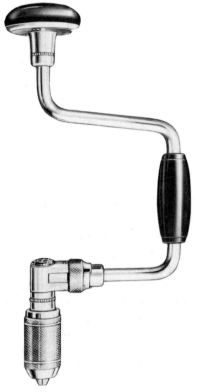

FIGURE 2–20. Bit Brace. Photo Courtesy of Stanley Tools,
Division of The Stanley Works.

the opposite direction, the bit remains motionless. This is useful
when the brace must be used in a place where the arm cannot rotate
360 degrees, such as when drilling a hole in a floor next to a wall.
The ratchet can be set to operate in either direction, so that the brace
can be used in close quarters to remove screws as well as to drive them.

To drill a hole in wood, first make a small hole in the surface.
Carpenters use a punch or an awl to do this, but you can use a nail
if you wish. A punch looks just like the nail set in Fig. 2–4, but it
has a sharp point. You place its point at the spot where you want the
hole and tap it with a hammer. An awl looks like a short ice pick.
If you have an ice pick, it will work just as well. The small hole is
a starting hole for the drill. Set the point of your auger bit in the starting hole and hold the knob of the brace so that the drill is perpendicular to the surface. Rotate the arm of the brace in a clockwise direction, and the drill will bite into the wood. *Do not drill all the way*

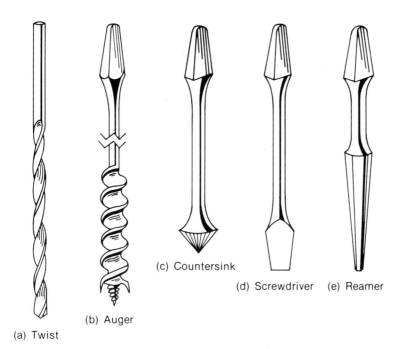

(c) Countersink

(d) Screwdriver   (e) Reamer

(b) Auger

(a) Twist

FIGURE 2-21. Types of Bits.

through, since the drill emerging from the other side will tear the fibers of the wood. If the hole must go all the way through the board, drill only until the point of the bit just emerges from the other side. Then pull out the bit and drill from the opposite side by inserting the bit in the small hole made by the point. It is important to keep the drill perpendicular to the surface, but you can do this easily if you keep your mind on it.

Another way to prevent fibers from ripping when you are drilling all the way through a board is to place a block of scrap wood against the board at the point where the drill will emerge. You will drill into the block (which you can throw away later), but it will hold the fibers in the main work. If you are drilling through a beam or stud in a house where you cannot get to the other side, just drill through without worrying. No one will see the torn fibers inside the wall.

When drilling pilot and shank holes for screws, each hole is drilled separately when they are in two different boards, as shown in Fig. 2-17(a). If both are in one board, as, for example, when screwing a hinge to a door, the order of drilling is important; refer to Fig. 2-22. If you use auger bits, then the bit is centered and pulled through by the thread on the tip. Now if you drill the pilot hole first, there will

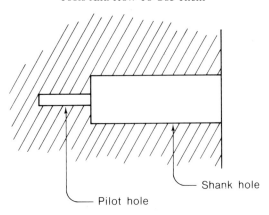

Shank hole

Pilot hole

FIGURE 2–22. Hole for Screw.

be nothing for the point of the shank drill to bite into, and you will not be able to drill the shank hole. Hence, you should drill the shank hole first to the proper depth and then drill the pilot hole (when using auger bits you can put an elastic around the drill as a depth indicator to make sure that you don't drill too far). However, when you are using twist drills, the tapered point automatically centers the drill in a smaller hole. In this case, you should drill the pilot hole first. In either case, if a countersink is needed, you can drill with a countersink bit after the other holes are drilled. Special bits are also available to drill screw holes. Each bit matches a particular size of screw and drills the pilot hole, shank hole, and countersink (if needed), all in one operation. These bits are not too expensive, and if you are going to set a large number of screws of one size, you might want to buy one to match the screw size.

You could spend a fortune on bits. As a start you might buy two particularly useful auger bits, a #6 and a #10 or 12. You may find a screwdriver bit useful, but if you wish, you can wait until you need one before you buy it. The same applies for a countersink, although if you have a countersink, you will use it. Expansive bits and extra long bits are expensive, so avoid them unless they are needed on a job. All the bits you buy for use with your brace should have square shanks.

The brace is turned by hand, and its speed is limited by how fast you can move your arm. It is especially useful for drilling in wood and wherever high torque is needed. For metals and plastics, the drill should turn much faster, so that a different kind of drill is needed. The hand drill shown in Fig. 2–23 uses twist drill bits and by means of gears rotates the bit much faster than the crank is turned. This drill

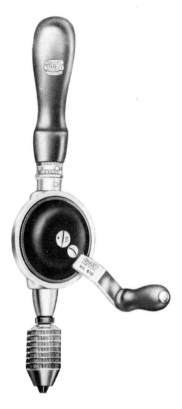

FIGURE 2–23. Hand Drill. Photo Courtesy of Stanley
Tools, Division of The Stanley Works.

can be used for drilling holes in plastic or soft metals. Cheaper models
use nylon gears. A hand drill is not essential, but you should own
an electric drill. This is the one power tool that you really must have.
Although it is not absolutely essential, you will find so many uses for
it that you will wonder how you ever got along without it. Electric
drills are designated by the size of the largest bit that they will take.
Thus a ¼-inch drill will take all bits from the smallest up to one that is
¼ inch in diameter. In practice a ¼ inch drill will take a bit slightly
larger than this so that you can drill a clearance hole for a ¼-inch bolt.
An expensive ¼-inch drill that sells for well under $10, but is adequate
for the home owner, is shown in Fig. 2–24. If you do not have a specific application in mind but want to buy an electric drill, you should
look for one similar to this. Make sure that it has a geared chuck, as
shown, and bears a UL label indicating approval by Underwriters'
Laboratories.

FIGURE 2–24. Electric Drill. Photo Courtesy of The
Black & Decker Manufacturing Company.

A ⅜-inch drill is generally more powerful and slower than a
¼-inch model. It can be used for tougher jobs, such as drilling in hard
metal or concrete. It is also heavier. More expensive drills have
additional features such as variable speed, reversible motor, and a
trigger switch. If you intend to do extensive remodeling, cabinet work,
or metal work, you will want a more powerful drill with all these
features and should buy a ⅜-inch drill.

The versatility of the electric drill is not limited to drilling holes.
It is essentially a portable electric motor, and many attachments have
been devised to utilize the rotary motion or convert it to linear motion.
Sanding wheels and buffers require high speed and thus perform better
with the faster ¼-inch model. Other attachments include a grinding
wheel for sharpening knives and other tools, hedge clippers, a rotary
saw, circle cutters, sabre saw, and many others. These are available
for both the ¼- and ⅜-inch drills. One accessory of special interest
to the home repairman is the water pump, illustrated in Fig. 2–25.
With this attachment plus an ordinary garden hose, you can use your
electric drill to pump water out of a flooded cellar or a clogged sink.

When you use an electric drill for a long period without interrup-
tion, it tends to get hot. If your drill gets too hot to touch, it needs a
rest. Heavy-duty drills have a fan for cooling, but this is usually

FIGURE 2-25. Water Pump Attachment. Photo Courtesy of The Black & Decker Manufacturing Company.

omitted on the more inexpensive, light-duty models. Just make sure that dirt hasn't clogged the vent holes on the drill, which would also cause overheating.

2-4. PLIERS

A pair of pliers is one of the tools you will use frequently and is, therefore, a must in your tool kit. In fact, most of the repairs needed around a home can be done with hammer, screwdriver, and pliers. Pliers are used for holding an object more firmly than you can hold it in your fingers or for exerting extra torque, as for example, to remove the cover of a bottle or small jar. They may also be used to hold a piece of metal which is being heated. Long, thin pliers are used to reach into confined spaces, to retrieve a dropped screw, for example. or to tighten a nut you can't reach with your fingers.

Pliers come in many sizes and shapes for specific applications. For general home repair, you will need a pair of *slip-joint pliers*, illustrated in Fig. 2-26. The serrated jaws provide an excellent grip, even on round pipes. The slip-joint feature enables you to grip larger objects

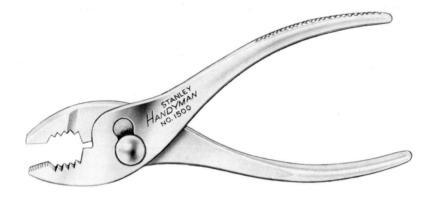

FIGURE 2–26. Slip-Joint Pliers. Photo Courtesy of Stanley
Tools, Division of The Stanley Works.

with the jaws almost parallel. If you use these pliers on smooth
surfaces which might be damaged by the serrations, it is best to
cover the faces of the jaws with adhesive bandages, as shown in
Fig. 2–27.

Special applications require special tools, and a large variety of
special-purpose pliers have been designed. Two are illustrated in
Fig. 2–28. In Fig. 2–28(a), the cutting head of *pincers* are shown. These
pliers are used for cutting wire or small nails. Some pincers have
the cutting edge on a diagonal instead of straight across the top.
Some pliers have a cutting edge on the side in addition to the regular
jaws. These are called *side-cutting* pliers. The long-nosed pliers

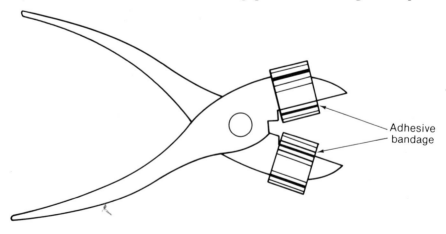

Adhesive
bandage

FIGURE 2–27. Pads for Pliers.

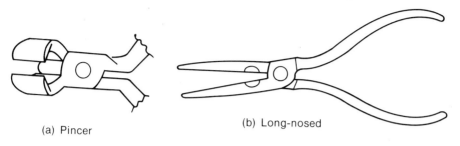

(a) Pincer

(b) Long-nosed

FIGURE 2–28. Special Pliers.

shown in Fig- 2–28(b) are especially useful in electrical work. Although they are not essential to home repair, you might want to add long-nosed pliers and some type of cutting pliers or pincers to your tool kit.

When using pliers, you hold the handles against the palm of your hand. One handle is held snugly under the thumb, and the next three fingers grip the other. The little finger is tucked between the handles and is used to force the pliers open. When the pliers are used just to get a firm grip on something and are not opened and closed repeatedly, the little finger remains outside the handle with the other three fingers.

2–5. WRENCHES

Wrenches are used to grip nuts or bolt heads firmly and to turn them with a larger force than would be possible with your fingers or a pair of pliers. Common types of wrenches which the home owner may find useful are shown in Fig. 2–29. The open-end wrench in Fig. 2–29(a) is the most common. The end slips onto a hexagonal or square nut or head of a bolt on which it is a close fit, and the nut can then be turned by rotating the arm. The box wrench shown in 2–29(b) is similar to the open-end wrench, except that it completely encloses the nut. If the opening is shaped to fit the nut, then different box wrenches would be needed for hexagonal and square nuts. Instead, the opening may have 12 teeth so that it can grip either a six-sided or four-sided nut. In both the open-end and box types, the two ends of each wrench fit different sizes of nuts, but several different wrenches would be required to take care of all sizes of nuts that you might find in the home.

The hex wrench shown in Fig. 2–29(c), is simply a solid rod with hexagonal cross section and a right-angled bend near one end. It is usually called an *Allen* wrench, which is a trade name. This wrench is used to turn screws which have a hexagonal opening in the head. These screws are used frequently in radios and electrical appliances. Hex wrenches are very inexpensive, and you can buy them as you need them.

Because so many open-end or box wrenches would be needed to handle all sizes of nuts, the homeowner should start with an adjustable open-end wrench, as pictured in Fig. 2–30. As its name implies, the opening may be adjusted to fit any size of nut up to the maximum width. Thus, one adjustable wrench replaces a whole set of fixed wrenches. The adjustable wrench is frequently referred to as a *Crescent* wrench. These adjustable wrenches are available from about 4 inches in length up to about 3 feet. A good size to get is one 6 or 8 inches long. The adjustable wrench does not grip as firmly as a fixed wrench and is somewhat bulkier, so you may want to add a few fixed wrenches later. If you have to tighten or adjust a fixed size of nut

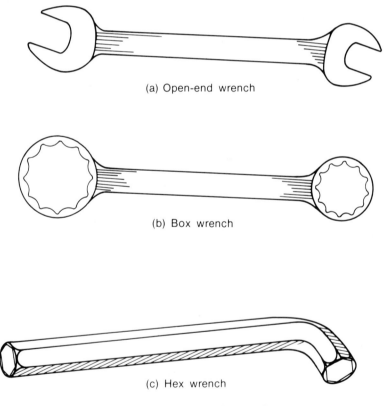

(a) Open-end wrench

(b) Box wrench

(c) Hex wrench

FIGURE 2–29. Types of Wrenches.

frequently, as, for example, on a bicycle hub, treat yourself to the proper size of box wrench or open-end model to do the job. You can get by with your adjustable wrench, however, and a better investment may be a second adjustable wrench large enough to fit your plumbing fixtures.

The *Stillson wrench,* or *pipe wrench,* illustrated in Fig. 2–31, is specifically designed for getting a firm grip on round objects, such as pipes. The grip tightens as the handle is moved in a direction to close the jaws. A ratchet-like action results, since the wrench releases its grip when the handle is moved in the opposite direction. You will need one Stillson wrench, about 1 foot long, for your plumbing jobs. You can also use this wrench on the hexagonal couplings on your plumbing as long as you take care to pad the teeth with cloth or cardboard to prevent marring the finish. To make the work easier, you should have two pipe wrenches, one to turn the section of pipe you want to remove and a second to keep the rest of the pipe from twisting out of shape. However, with care you can get by with one.

A *monkey wrench* is an adjustable wrench that looks something like a Stillson wrench but has smooth jaws. It is especially suited to home plumbing repairs, because it will not mar the finish when used on the hexagonal couplings in your plumbing. Also, it opens wider for a given size of wrench than the adjustable wrench shown in Fig. 2–30. Unfortunately, it is not always available. If you can find one, buy it instead of the larger-sized adjustable wrench. The ideal assort-

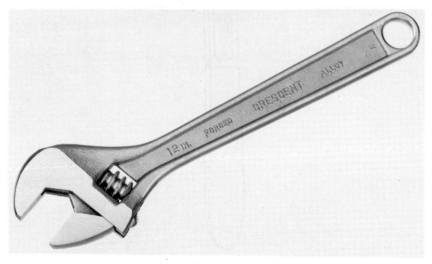

FIGURE 2–30. Adjustable Wrench. Photo Courtesy of The Cooper Group, Cooper Industries.

ment is one adjustable wrench, about 6 or 8 inches long, one monkey wrench, and one Stillson wrench.

    Whenever you use a tool, think of what could happen if it slipped. A wrench should always be pulled toward you, never pushed away from you. If you are pushing hard and the wrench slips, you will fall forward onto the work. If the wrench slips when you are pulling, you will not fall if your feet are properly positioned. Also, the opening of the jaws of the wrench should point toward the direction of the pull. This makes it less likely that the wrench will slip off. If you want to turn the nut in the other direction, turn the wrench over and place it so that you will pull, not push it.

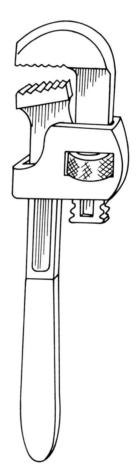

FIGURE 2–31. Pipe Wrench.

2–6. PLUNGER

The plunger, illustrated in Fig. 2–32, consists of a rubber cup at the end of a wooden stick. It is also called a *force cup* or a *plumber's helper.* You will need one to free clogged drains. You can wait until you need one, but as they are usually very inexpensive, you can afford to have one on hand.

2–7. SAWS

Although a *saw* is not essential for most home repairs, it is often useful. Certainly a saw is necessary if you are building shelves, making furniture, or doing even simple remodeling. In fact, *one* saw is not enough, but you don't have to own every type.

There are many different types of saws, each for a specific purpose. A few are illustrated in Fig. 2–33. The *crosscut saw*, shown in Fig. 2–33(a), is designed for cutting wood *across* the grain. The teeth are pushed out from the centerline alternately. A *ripsaw* also looks like the crosscut saw but has differently shaped teeth. The difference is shown in Fig. 2–34. The teeth of the crosscut saw, shown in Fig. 2–34(a), are uniform and beveled on both leading and trailing edges, so that the saw can cut when it is moved forward or backward. The ripsaw is designed to cut *along* the grain. The crosscut saw has 6 to 12 teeth per inch, the ripsaw only 4 to 6 teeth. In general, the more teeth per inch, the smoother will be the cut, but the saw with fewer teeth will cut faster because the teeth are bigger. A *backsaw* is a smaller version of a crosscut saw with as many as 32 teeth per inch. It is used for smooth work.

You can rip (that is, cut with the grain) with a crosscut saw, but you cannot use a ripsaw for a crosscut saw. Therefore, you should get a crosscut saw with about 8 points per inch for general all-around use. You won't really need either a ripsaw or a backsaw.

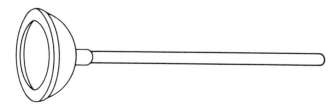

FIGURE 2–32. Plunger.

The *hacksaw,* shown in Fig. 2–33(b), is used primarily for cutting metal. You will *need* one. Blades are replaceable and are very inexpensive. Coarse blades have 18 points per inch, and fine-toothed blades have 32, with all sizes in between. The coarser blades are used on armored cable, pipes, and most metals. Finer blades are used on plastics and for smooth cuts on soft metals. Don't worry too much about tooth size, however, because a fine blade can cut through

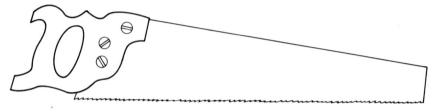

(a) Cross-cut saw

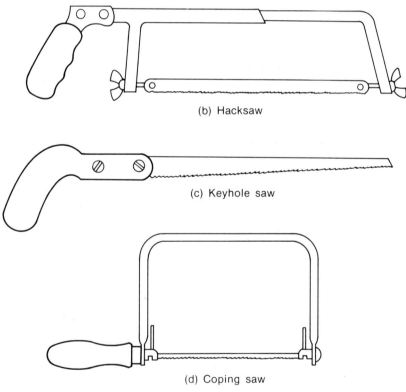

(b) Hacksaw

(c) Keyhole saw

(d) Coping saw

FIGURE 2–33. Saws.

armored cable, although it will take longer to do it than a coarse blade.
You don't need a large assortment of blades. Get a few in the 18 to 24
range and a few near 30. Incidentally, keep one of the fine-toothed
blades in your kitchen for cutting frozen foods.

When you put a blade in the hacksaw frame, the teeth can point
toward you or away from you. Either is correct. It is just a matter of
whether you prefer to cut on the forward or the backward stroke of
the saw.

The *keyhole saw*, shown in Fig. 2–33(c), is used for making cut-
outs. The saw is inserted in a small starting hole in the wood and can
then be maneuvered to follow the outline of the desired cutout. The
keyhole saw is fine toothed. A *compass saw* has a coarser blade and
tapers to a point but is otherwise similar to the keyhole saw. The
compass saw is used specifically for plywood. A special *all-purpose
saw* which resembles the keyhole saw has a metal handle and replaceable blades. Both fine and coarse blades are available, as well as blades
that will cut through metal.

The *coping* saw, shown in Fig. 2–33(d), is used for fancy cuts in
cabinet work. It can cut circles or right angles. The thin blade is held
in tension in a large metal frame, which causes blades to snap frequently.

If you have an electric drill, get a *sabre saw* attachment for intricate cuts. You can forget about the coping saw, keyhole saw, or compass saw, since the sabre saw does all the work with little effort.
Finally, if you see an all-purpose saw on sale, you should buy it, since
it can be used in a hurry for almost everything from pruning rosebushes
to cutting a bolt that is too long.

When you use a crosscut saw to cut firewood, you don't need a
guideline, since dimensions are not critical. When you are cutting
boards for shelving, furniture, or remodeling, however, it is important
that the cuts be straight and in the right place. First, draw a pencil
line for the direction of the cut. Hold the saw touching the line on
the scrap side and draw it toward you to make a starting cut. Use the
knuckle of your left thumb (if you hold the saw in your right hand) as

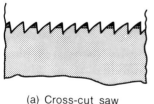

(a) Cross-cut saw

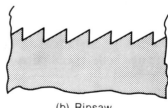

(b) Ripsaw

FIGURE 2–34. Teeth.

a brace against the saw until the cut is well started. Push the saw forward with the whole arm, exerting a slight downward pressure. At
the end of the stroke, pull the saw back with no downward pressure.
Keep your head above the saw, and it will tend to go straight. If it
wanders slightly from the line, you can bring it back with a slight
twisting action. If it strays far from the line, because you weren't
paying attention, pull out the saw and start again where it began to
stray. As you approach the end of the cut, support the scrap piece,
since it may fall off too soon and tear the wood. If the wood is green
or is otherwise hard to cut, rub paraffin on the saw to lubricate it.

2-8. PUTTY KNIFE

A putty knife is a specialized tool to spread putty when you are replacing glass in a broken window. It may also be used to spread wood
filler, tree seal, or any other viscous material. It should be wiped
clean after each use, since if the material hardens, it may be difficult
to remove later.

A putty knife is simply a metal blade held in a wooden or plastic
handle, as shown in Fig. 2-35. Make sure that the blade is firmly
fixed in the handle, since a blade falling out of the handle can be quite
annoying. If the blade is held in place by rivets or screws through
the handle, as in the knife in Fig. 2-35, it will stay in place. Beware
of knives with blades held in by friction alone.

2-9. CHISELS

Wood chisels are used to cut recesses for hinges, openings for locks,
mortises, dovetails, and other joints requiring removal of a rectangular
piece of wood. A wood chisel, as illustrated in Fig. 2-36, has a blade
with a beveled edge on one side only, held in a wooden or plastic handle. In use the chisel is held in one hand at the location where a cut is
to be made, and it is struck lightly with a mallet on the head of the
handle.

When cutting with a chisel, don't try to remove too much with
each cut. Like any knife, the chisel cuts best when it slides along the
wood instead of perpendicular to it. Specific instructions for positioning the chisel when cutting many types of joints are included in the
sections on joints in Chapter 7.

A *cold chisel* is a solid steel rod with one end ground to a sharp
edge. It is used to cut metal, masonry, or plaster. The chisel is held

FIGURE 2–35. Putty Knife. Photo Courtesy of Stanley
Tools, Division of The Stanley Works.

in one hand and is struck forcibly by a hammer held in the other.
You should wear a heavy glove on the hand holding the chisel to absorb the shock of the hammer blows and also in case you miss.

Chisels are designated by the width of the blade. You should have
a 1-inch chisel in your tool box and you may also find use for a ¼-inch.
Don't buy a complete assortment. Don't buy a cold chisel unless it is
needed for a specific job. Most homeowners never have occasion to
use one.

2-10. PLANES

A plane is used to smooth the edge of a board. Although it is an essential tool for a carpenter, the average homeowner will find it a luxury,
since he will use it infrequently. If you are building cabinets, you may
need a plane to fit drawers and doors, but you will not use it for normal
home repairs.

FIGURE 2–36. Chisel. Photo Courtesy of Stanley Tools,
Division of The Stanley Works.

Planes come in a variety of shapes and sizes, each designed for a specific task. When you have a need for a plane, get a *jack plane*, shown in Fig. 2-37. This can be used for most planing jobs around the home. When you buy a plane, ask the hardware dealer to show you how to take it apart and put it together and how to adjust the blade. The knurled wheel near the rear handle controls the depth of the cut by moving the blade in and out. When not in use, the blade should be retracted so that it cannot be struck accidently.

To use the plane, first adjust the blade so that it protrudes slightly. If you can see the blade when sighting along the bottom of the plane, it is out far enough. Make sure that the blade is parallel to the face. Grasp the plane with one hand on the knob and the other on the rear handle. Place the front of the plane on the surface to be smoothed with the blade just off the surface. Apply pressure on the knob and push the plane forward. As the plane moves forward, exert some downward pressure with the rear hand. When the front end moves off the other end of the board, release the downward pressure on the knob, but continue pushing downward on the rear handle until the blade moves off the end. Move the plane in long smooth strokes parallel to the edge being smoothed, but keep the plane at a slight angle to the direction of movement, as shown in Fig. 2-38. This gives a shearing action and results in a smoother cut.

FIGURE 2-37. Plane. Photo Courtesy of Stanley Tools, Division of The Stanley Works.

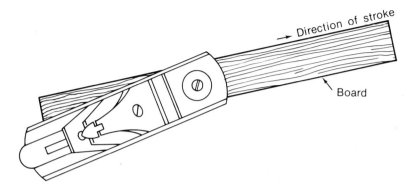

FIGURE 2–38. Position of Plane.

When cutting along the grain of a board, try to cut *with the grain,* as shown in Fig. 2–39. When you cut against the grain, the plane tends to catch or tear the wood. If the plane snags on the first cut, try reversing the direction of cutting. When cutting across the grain, as when smoothing the end of a board, the plane may split the end fibers as the blade moves off the board. For best results, do not plane entirely across the end of a board, but move the plane from each edge toward the middle.

2–11. VISE AND CLAMPS

Although not really a tool, a vise is usually seen on a home workbench. A good vise holds material firmly without marring so that it can be worked on without danger of slipping. In effect, it gives the worker a strong third hand. For the home workshop, a good vise is not a necessity, but if you have one, you will use it. If you have a permanent workbench, you should consider buying a vise which is to be permanently fastened to the bench with bolts or screws and which has a swivel base so that it can be turned to permit you to work on

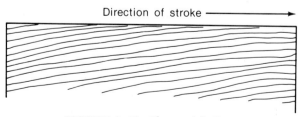

FIGURE 2–39. Plane with Grain.

the material from different angles. If your workbench is a kitchen table or other piece of furniture which is pressed into service when you need it, you can use a small clamp-on visc, like that shown in Fig. 2–40.

Clamps come in many sizes and shapes, but the two shown in Fig. 2–41 are of interest to the home workman. The C-clamp shown in Fig. 2–41(a), is available in sizes from 1 inch (maximum opening) to more than 1 foot. These clamps are inexpensive and very handy. You should have two or three in sizes from 3 to 6 inches in your kit. If you have them, you'll think of all sorts of applications for them. The hand-screw clamp, shown in Fig. 2–41(b), is capable of applying equal pressure over a large surface. It is especially applicable for holding glued wood surfaces together until the glue dries. You won't need this type of clamp unless you do some cabinet work. Buy it when you do need it, and then charge it to the cost of the job. The C-clamps are more versatile, and with a little ingenuity you can use two small C-clamps in place of a hand-screw clamp.

2-12. FILES AND RASPS

Files are used for smoothing, enlarging, sharpening, cutting, and a variety of other jobs, depending on the ingenuity of the user. Wood files are commonly called *rasps;* those used on metal are called simply *files.* The teeth are long parallel lines across the face at an angle of about 25 degrees. A second set of teeth may be added, also in parallel lines, crossing the first set at about 75 degrees. Files with one set of teeth are called *single-cut,* those with two, *double-cut.* Double-cut files cut faster than single-cut, but the single-cut leave a smoother finish for the same-sized teeth.

The smoothness of the finish obtainable with a file depends on the size and spacing of the teeth. Large teeth, widely spaced, give a rough finish, while small, closely spaced teeth leave a smooth finish. Files are designated according to finish in at least seven categories: rough, coarse, middle, halfway, bastard, second-cut, smooth, and superfine. The smooth and superfine files are usually single-cut, while the others are double-cut. Wood rasps are also available in different degrees of smoothness.

Files come in many shapes and sizes, as shown in Fig. 2–42. The face of a rectangular file is shown in Fig. 2–42(a). The point at the top is called the *tang.* The length should be chosen for convenience; about 10 inches is satisfactory for most applications. Various cross sections are shown in Fig. 2–42(b). Files come without a handle, but

FIGURE 2–40. Vise. Photo Courtesy of Stanley Tools, Division of The Stanley Works.

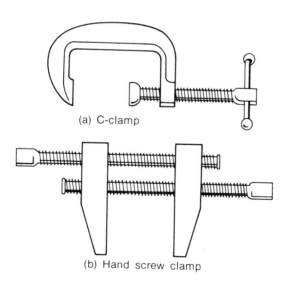

(a) C-clamp

(b) Hand screw clamp

FIGURE 2–41. Clamps.

a wooden or plastic handle, as shown in Fig. 2–42(c), can be purchased. This is pushed down on the tang when you wish to use the file. Files and handles are very inexpensive.

You will rarely *need* files for home repairs, but you can find many uses for them. Wood rasps are frequently used to smooth inside surfaces after making a cutout with a sabre saw or coping saw. This can also be done with sandpaper on a round block of wood, although it is easier with the rasp. A smooth file is useful for sharpening tools. A round file can be used to enlarge holes and smooth inside curved surfaces. A small bastard file can be used to enlarge the opening in a striker plate when a door has sagged slightly. Files are also valuable for removing rust, smoothing the end of a pipe or metal bar after hacksawing, cutting thin metal tubing, and many other uses. Since they are so useful and inexpensive, you should plan to add a few to your tool

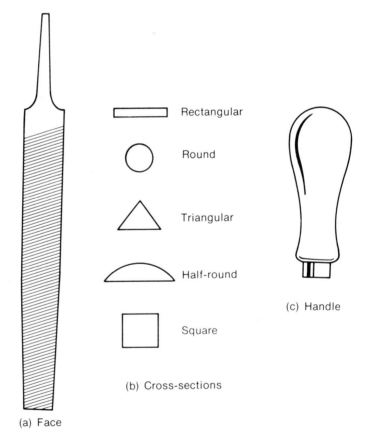

Rectangular

Round

Triangular

Half-round

(c) Handle

Square

(b) Cross-sections

(a) Face

FIGURE 2–42. Files.

collection. Make sure that they are of good quality. Avoid buying files from a collection of tools thrown together in a box, as is frequently done in special sales, because the teeth will be dulled from banging against other tools. To start, you should acquire a small smooth file for sharpening and a bastard file for general all-around use. Add others as the need arises.

When using a file, apply pressure on the forward stroke only, bearing down just hard enough to cut the metal. On the back stroke lift the file from the metal to prevent dulling the teeth, unless you are working on a soft metal such as copper. Small metal parts which need filing should be gripped in a vise.

When teeth of a file start to get clogged, you should clean them with a *file card*. This is simply a stiff wire brush designed specifically for cleaning files.

2-13. MEASURING AND MONITORING

Whenever material is bought or cut to fit, it is usually measured, and the home repairman must have some tools to measure the materials as well as the spaces in which they will be used. In addition, he will need implements to make sure that materials are installed properly. For example, floors should be level, wallpaper must be hung perpendicular to the floor, and studs and door frames should be vertical.

A very simple and satisfactory measuring device is the common *yardstick*, which many hardware stores and lumberyards give away free or for a few pennies. It is not a precision device, but most home repairs do not require precision. The yardstick is satisfactory for measuring boards for shelving, measuring floors for linoleum, and other similar tasks. A 6-foot retractable steel tape, pictured in Fig. 2–43, is more compact and more convenient for many jobs. Either the tape or the yardstick can be used for almost all your measuring requirements.

The *level*, shown in Fig. 2–44, can be used to determine if a surface is exactly horizontal or exactly vertical. When installing shelves for example, some form of level must be used to ensure that each shelf is horizontal. A level like that pictured in Fig. 2–44 is simply placed on the shelf, and the shelf is adjusted at either end to center the bubble in the level, indicating that the shelf is horizontal. In a similar manner, the level can be placed alongside a vertical line, and the other bubble will indicate if the line is exactly vertical. A plumb line can also be used to determine if a line is vertical. In a pinch,

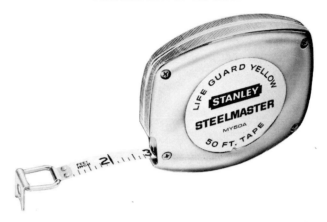

FIGURE 2–43. Steel Tape. Photo Courtesy of Stanley
Tools, Division of The Stanley Works.

you can use a piece of string with a weight on the end as a plumb
line. It should be accurate enough for your repair jobs, although not
really acceptable for new construction projects.

An instrument for determining if two surfaces are at right angles
to one another is a try square. This tool is simply a metal bar attached to one end of a wooden handle at right angles to the handle.
A more useful variation of the try square is the combination square
shown in Fig. 2–45. In addition to the right angle, there are two
surfaces at an angle of 45 degrees, and the handle (metal instead of
wood) can be slid to any position along the steel bar. The steel
bar is graduated so that it can be used as a ruler. This square also
has a level on one arm and a small scriber in the handle, which is
handy for marking a reference point on the material being measured.

FIGURE 2–44. Level. Photo Courtesy of Stanley Tools,
Division of The Stanley Works.

The level is adequate for most small jobs, although for long shelves it is better to use a large level, as shown in Fig. 2–44. The combination square is such a handy instrument that you should have one.

2–14. SANDPAPER

Sandpaper consists of a base material such as paper or cloth to which are attached grains of an abrasive material, called *grit*. When the grains are large and far apart, they dig more deeply. As the grains are brought closer together, the sanding becomes smoother. Ranging from the coarsest to the finest, grits are usually designated *very coarse, coarse, medium, fine,* and *very fine.*

Very coarse grit sandpaper is used to remove heavy coats of varnish or paint or for other extremely heavy sanding. Coarse is used to remove irregularities from wood, such as gouges and dents. Medium is used to remove small scratches from wood, rust from metal, and for smoothing after using the coarse grade. Fine is used for final finishing on base wood. Very fine is used between coats of varnish for an extra smooth finish. A variety of minerals are used for the

FIGURE 2–45. Combination Square. Photo Courtesy of Stanley Tools, Division of The Stanley Works.

different grits, but this should not concern you; just specify the grit you want. It is usually a good idea to buy a packet of assorted grits of sandpaper. This will be handy for most of your small sanding tasks. When you have a large sanding job, buy large sheets of the correct grit. WARNING: Do not use emery paper to sand parts of an electric motor or electric circuit. Emery dust is a conductor and can short-circuit the motor.

2–15. CARE OF TOOLS

Tools should be kept in good repair and ready for use. One major problem is protection from rust, since most of your tools contain iron or steel parts. If your tools are always stored in a warm, dry room, there is little danger of their rusting. However, if you store them in a cellar or garage, which might be cold or damp, you must take steps to prevent corrosion. The simplest method of preventing rust is to coat the metal parts of each tool with light machine oil. The oil coating should be so thin that it is barely discernible. One way of doing this is to make a pad of cheese cloth or a piece of an old bed sheet. Put a few drops of oil on the pad, and then wipe each tool with the cloth. Make certain that the tool is clean before you oil it. Be careful not to oil wooden or plastic handles, since an oily or greasy handle on a tool makes it difficult to use the tool properly. You can store the oil pad in a closed, fireproof can, such as an empty coffee tin, but make sure that the can is covered when the pad is in it. When you use a tool, you may wipe the oil off with your hands, but you can oil it again quickly if you wipe it with your oil pad just before you put the tool away. Paraffin is also a good protector from rust but is more difficult to apply. Do not use soap, since dry soap has a high water content and would only hasten rusting. Other substances that can be used to keep rust from tools are ordinary paste wax, petroleum jelly, or acrylic sprays. If rust does form on any tool, you can remove it with steel wool and a few drops of oil or with a commercial rust remover. After the surface is clean, apply oil or any other rust-preventive material.

Sharp edges and teeth on knives, chisels, files, saws, planes, and similar tools should be kept sharp. These tools are frequently dulled by banging against other tools in your tool kit. Thus, proper storage is important. If you want to store screwdrivers and pliers loosely in a drawer, they will not lose their effectiveness, but chisels and files could be dulled if kept in this manner. If you have a workbench, you can install a shelf with holes, as shown in Fig. 2–46, to store some of your small tools. Each chisel, knife, and file can be placed in a separate hole or slot in the shelf. Alternatively, you could simply drive nails into the back of the bench and space them to take the tools. Hardware stores also sell pegboards with hooks to take a variety of tools. If you are like most home handymen and don't have a workbench, you probably keep your tools in a toolbox or in drawers in a cabinet. To protect sharp edges, put each sharp tool in a separate plastic bag, or wrap it in cloth before putting it away.

Unless you are making repairs or remodeling every week, a workbench is a luxury. It's nice to have a proper workbench with all your tools arrayed each in its allotted space, but the truth is that for home repairs, most of the work is done where the fault occurs. This means that you must bring your tools to the location of the trouble. When you gather the appropriate tools and carry them to the spot where you are going to install an electric outlet, for example, you must still be careful to keep sharp edges from banging against anything that might dull them.

When you are through with a job, make sure that your tools are clean before you put them away. This is especially important when working with paint, putty, or other messy substances, but also be on the alert to wipe off mortar dust, wood chips on the blade of a

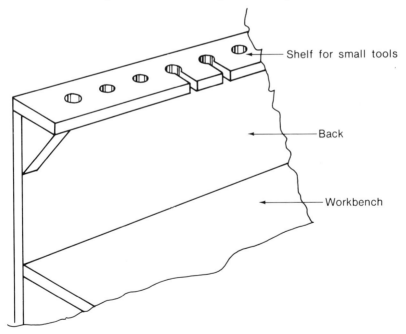

FIGURE 2-46. Tool Storage.

plane or teeth of a saw, and any other foreign matter. Saws especially may be stained by pitch in the wood, so the pitch should be removed before putting a saw away. Special pitch-removing chemicals are available in most hardware stores.

When a tool gets dull, it can be sharpened on a *sharpening stone.* The stone is made of an abrasive material and acts as a very smooth file. Other names for the sharpening stone are *hone, oilstone,* or *whetstone.* The blades of chisels and planes have beveled edges. The first step in sharpening a beveled blade is to remove burrs by placing the flat side of the blade against the abrasive stone and moving the blade in a rotary motion. Then the beveled edge is placed against the stone, as shown in Fig. 2–47, and again a rotary motion is used. A few drops of water or oil may be used on the stone to prevent the blade from getting too hot from the friction of the rubbing operation. When steel overheats, it may lose its hardness.

A jacknife or similar blade is also sharpened on a hone by stroking both sides of the blade against the stone alternately. The blade is moved along the stone as if it were cutting a thin film off of it. A knife can also be sharpened on a piece of fine sandpaper tacked to your workbench.

When the blades of tools become nicked, they should be reground on a grinding wheel. This is not simple to do. The blade must be held at the correct angle and just the right pressure exerted. The blade must also be cooled constantly, since the grinding wheel generates an excessive amount of heat. Since it is too easy to ruin a blade by improper grinding, it is best to leave this to a professional tool sharpener. Similarly, when a saw becomes dull, let a professional sharpen it and reset the points. However, inexpensive tools should not be resharpened. Dull hacksaw blades can be thrown away or saved in your junkbox for emergencies, as can dull files.

Hand tools can be dangerous just because you don't expect them to be. Proper care, proper use, and proper storage can do much to eliminate the dangers, in addition to increasing the life of your tools.

When tools are stored, you should be able to select any one tool without nicking your fingers on another. Sharp tools should be stored in separate compartments, with sharp edges shielded. Planes should have their blades retracted. Drills should be mounted in a drill index or rack or otherwise stored so that they do not bang against one another. Razor blades should not be left where they can cut someone reaching for another tool. Even tools without sharp edges can harm you if not stored properly.

A common mistake is to place racks too close together in a tool storage wall. When a tool is removed from the lower rack, you can bump your hand against a tool hanging in the upper one. Even a screwdriver or a pair of pliers in the upper rack can nick your hand if you are careless.

When carrying tools, make sure that sharp edges will not endanger you or anyone else. Think of what might happen if you tripped, and carry the tools accordingly. The best way is to carry the tools in a closed container, but even a tray is better than holding them in your hand.

2-16. POWER TOOLS AND SAFETY

Most home workshops have at least an electric drill, and some have a large assortment of electrically operated tools. Every power tool is potentially dangerous. Treat it with respect. The first consideration is proper clothing. Wear short-sleeved clothing that is snug. Loose clothing, such as a necktie or a flowing sleeve or sash can catch on a spinning axle and cause serious injury before you can stop the motor. Rings, bracelets, and wristwatches can catch on protruding parts and thus should not be worn.

Most power tools have guards of some sort. *Use them.* In addition, wear safety goggles to protect your eyes when working on a grinder, lathe, mill, or any tool which can eject metallic or wood particles. Moving belts are a hazard, and if possible you should enclose all belts with suitable enclosures to prevent contact with them.

Make sure that power tools are grounded to prevent electric shock. When the tools are installed, check the voltage rating to be

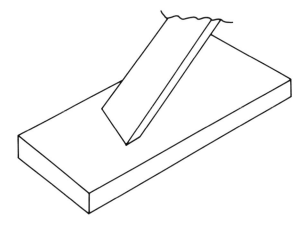

FIGURE 2-47. Sharpening Beveled Blade.

sure that it is correct. Mount switches so that they can be turned on and off without your reaching across the machine.

Always have the work firmly in place. Do not hold a piece of material in your hand when you are working on it with a power tool. A common and dangerous error is to hold a metal sheet in your hand while drilling into it with a bench drill. If the drill binds, the metal sheet starts to spin and can cut off a hand.

When you shut off a motor, wait until the machine stops before you do *anything*. Don't reach across the machine while it is slowing down. Don't brush sawdust off a woodworking machine until it stops.

Lock up power tools when not in use, especially if there are children in the house. This protects the children as well as the tools. If you can't keep the children out of the shop, disconnect the electricity to the outlets when the tools are not in use.

3

Home Maintenance

Home maintenance means keeping your house in good condition and taking steps to prevent damage. Houses don't last forever, and in fact, if a house is not maintained, it will deteriorate very rapidly. By anticipating trouble and strengthening the weak spots as they occur, you can do much to prolong the useful life of your home and avert many costly catastrophes.

Some things just wear out from constant use. Friction is the culprit. Motors in washing machines or oil burners eventually wear out. So does carpeting. But there are ways to minimize the wear so as to get a few more years of service from the motor or carpet.

Besides ordinary wear, in many homes people *abuse* rather than use at least a few parts of the house. For example, doors are banged open so that knobs crack plaster walls, grease is poured into plumbing, or electric lines are overloaded. Strictly speaking, avoiding abuse is not maintenance, but it reduces the need for repair and maintenance later.

Another source of damage in the home is the work of nature, such as rain, hail, snow, wind, extreme cold, or extreme heat. The damage may not be immediately apparent but can lead to an expensive repair job later. As an example, a severe wind can lift shingles on a roof to such an extent that after a few rainstorms a leak develops. Checking and refastening the shingles will prevent the leak and all the accompanying discomfort.

Insects and rodents also are potential threats to a house. Steps to prevent and control damage from these sources also come under the heading of home maintenance, since they are necessary to keep your home livable.

Maintenance, then, means keeping your home comfortable and preventing costly repairs by controlling wear, avoiding abuse, and anticipating troubles and correcting them before they become serious. *Complete home maintenance can be a full-time job.* Even if you had the time and money to spend all your days puttering around the house, you would not enjoy it. Consequently, you should not expect to do everything to keep your home in perfect condition. In the list of maintenance jobs in this chapter you will find some that are *necessary*. You should do these or have them done. Some are easy, and therefore you will probably do them, whether or not they are necessary. Some are difficult or dangerous, and although you may save money by tackling them, you may not think it worth the trouble or risk. In other words, perform those maintenance jobs that must be done and any others you can and want to do. Don't feel guilty about skipping the rest. You can't do everything.

3-1. HOW TO KEEP PIPES FROM FREEZING

When water freezes, it expands as it cools. If the water is contained in a metal pipe, the force of the expanding ice can crack the pipe. Then, when the ice eventually melts, water pours from the crack. If you live in a climate which has below freezing temperatures, you *must* take precautions to make sure that none of the pipes in your home will freeze. Note that this is not likely to be a problem with plastic pipe, since the plastic stretches when the ice expands. On the other hand, metal contracts with cold, so that the combination of expanding ice and contracting metal can cause cracks at only a few degrees below 32 degrees Fahrenheit (°F), the freezing point of water.

To prevent a pipe from freezing, simply make sure that there is no water in any pipe that may be exposed to temperatures below 32°F. If you are living in a house and maintaining a comfortable temperature there, all indoor plumbing is safely above the freezing point at all times. Your only concern is with outside faucets that are used, for example, to connect garden hoses to the water supply. The water in the pipe leading to an outside faucet can freeze, and the ice can extend in the pipe to a point inside the house.

To drain the water from a pipe leading to an outside faucet, first shut off the flow of water in the pipe by turning the control valve shut. The control valve is on the same pipe but inside the house, as shown in Fig. 3-1. The wheel on the control valve is turned clockwise to shut off the flow of water. Now the outside faucet is opened fully and the water should flow out, because the pipe leading to the faucet should be tilted downward toward the outside, as shown in exaggerated form in the figure. The control valve should have a drainage screw cap on the faucet side of the valve, and it also should be opened. This ensures complete drainage even if the pipe is not tilted correctly. After the water has run out of the pipe, the handle of the outside faucet should be turned slightly so that it will not be fully opened, and it should be left open all winter. In the spring, the outside faucet is closed, the drainage screw cap is closed, and the control valve is opened.

If it is necessary to have water available outside the house during winter, your home should have an antifreeze faucet, shown in Fig. 3-2. The handle of the outside faucet is connected by a long rod to the

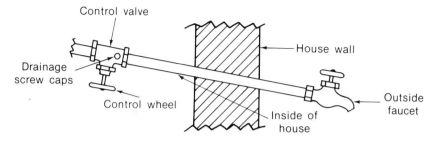

FIGURE 3-1. Outside Faucet and Connections.

valve inside the house. When the faucet is turned off, it closes this valve, and any water left in the pipe between the valve and the outside simply flows out of the faucet because of the downward tilt of the pipe. If your outside faucets are of this type, you don't have to worry about freezing pipes.

If you are leaving the house empty for any period of time, you have to be concerned about indoor pipes freezing as well as outside faucets. For short periods, such as a two-week vacation, you should leave the heat turned on low to keep the house at a temperature above freezing. The fuel cost is small compared to the trouble of draining all the water pipes. For long periods, such as when closing a summer cottage for the winter, you must drain all the water from the plumbing and heating systems, in addition to other protective measures discussed in the next section. Remember that during the winter, the temperature inside an unheated house is not very different from the outside temperature.

To drain the plumbing, first make sure that the main supply valve

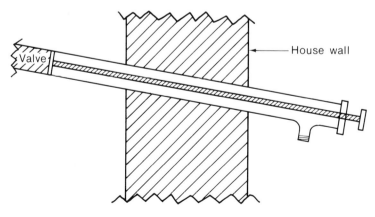

FIGURE 3-2. Anti-Freeze Faucet.

is closed. The water main is below the frost line so that you don't have to worry about that freezing. Now open all faucets in the house. This will drain all the water to the level of the lowest point in the water system, and this can now be opened to remove the remaining water. If there is no drain outlet in your system, you have to disconnect the supply pipe at its lowest point, which is usually at the main supply valve. If any pipes have loops or upward tilts, you must make certain that they are emptied. This can sometimes be done by blowing through the pipe, but preferably you should disconnect the section of pipe and pour out the water.

Water must be removed from all traps in drains. The purpose of a trap is to provide a water seal to prevent sewer gases from entering the house. Under normal use, the trap is filled with water, as shown in Fig. 3-3. To empty the trap, loosen the two large nuts with a monkey wrench or Stillson wrench, remove the trap completely, and pour out the water. Then connect the trap again and fill it with a liquid which won't freeze, such as automobile antifreeze or kerosene. However, do not use alcohol or any other liquid which will evaporate before you reopen the house. About a quart of liquid is necessary for each trap in the house. Some traps have a nut at the bottom. To empty this type, it is only necessary to remove the nut and let the water drain out.

Water must be removed from all tanks, including toilet tanks, boilers, and the like. Each toilet should be flushed, and then the last half inch or so of water in the tank removed with a sponge. Boilers usually have a drain spigot at their lowest points.

Toilet traps must also be emptied. You can drive out much of the water with your force cup, but you may have to use a syringe to remove the rest. Refill each toilet trap with about two quarts of antifreeze. Don't forget to empty the water from traps in the floor drains

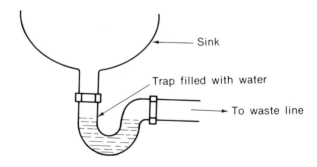

Sink

Trap filled with water

To waste line

FIGURE 3-3. Trap.

in the laundry room, cellar, or garage, if you have any, and to refill with antifreeze or kerosene.

If the house uses steam for heating, you will have to make sure that the radiators are drained. To prevent water from being held in the radiators by air pressure, you must remove an air valve from *one* of the radiators on a top floor. This will release the water in *all* the radiators so that it flows back to the boiler where it can be drained off. *Don't forget to put back the valve before starting the heating systems again in the spring.*

Draining the water from a plumbing system is not an easy task. If you can afford a summer home, you can probably afford to call a plumber to make sure that you haven't forgotten anything. If you do call a plumber, follow him around and note down everything he does. You may want to do it yourself next year.

3-2. HOW TO CLOSE A HOUSE

When you close a house for the winter, the most important problem is draining the water, as described in the preceding section. Besides the plumbing, water should not be left in old bottles around the house. Also, the pumps in washing machines and dishwashers always have some residual water in them which can be drained off by removing the covers on the pumps. In addition to freezing water, the house must also be protected from fire, gas leaks, damage caused by insects and small animals, damage from wind, snow, and rain, and from burglars or vandals.

The main electric switch should be opened, and, if the house also has gas, the main gas valve should be closed. In the spring when the gas valve is opened, all pilot lights must be relighted. It is advisable to have the gas company turn on the gas again.

There is always a danger of fire caused by spontaneous combustion of oily rags and other organic materials. The obvious solution is to remove or destroy all such materials. If any matches are left in the house, they should be kept in a closed fireproof container, such as an old coffee can.

Rodents and other animals, especially squirrels, can do considerable damage if they get into an empty house. All possible openings should be closed off, including the chimney. Besides closing the damper, you should put a box or wire netting over the chimney opening and tie it down. Squirrels have been known to gnaw through the roof. However, all these animals, as well as most destructive insects, dislike the vapors from mothballs or moth flakes or crystals, and these materials should be scattered freely throughout the house. They will evaporate but the vapor will remain as a deterrent to pests until the house is opened and aired out in the spring.

All cellar windows should be boarded, and if possible, other windows should be covered with shutters fastened from the inside. The shutter fasteners must be strong enough to withstand windstorms, since a loose shutter banging in the breeze can break a window.

As a final check, make sure all children and pets are out of the house before you lock the doors.

3-3. HOW TO KEEP PLUMBING UNCLOGGED

When you turn on a faucet, if the water trickles out instead of gushing as it usually does, it may be annoying. On the other hand, when a drain is clogged, so that water poured down the kitchen sink, for example, backs up in a bathtub, it can be traumatic. Plumbing troubles are among the worst that can happen in a home, and you should take pains to prevent them from happening.

The water lines in your home are unlikely to become clogged unless the water is hard or contains too much sediment. The minerals in hard water may be deposited on the inside of pipes, reducing their internal diameters. Eventually, they may create sufficient blockage to reduce the pressure to a point where water comes out of faucets or shower heads in trickles rather than with full force. This may take years and thus is more apt to be noticed in very old houses. A solution is to add a water softener to your input line if the water is hard. The water softener eventually pays for itself in savings on soaps and plumbing bills. If you install a water softener yourself, the dealer will be happy to explain how to connect it so that water for cooking, drinking, and washing is softened but water for your garden and toilets is untreated.

Aerators on faucets and some shower heads have small holes which can become clogged from sediment or encrusted minerals. These should be cleaned periodically. Aerators can be removed and taken apart to remove the sediment. Note carefully how the aerator comes apart, and reassemble it in the same manner. If the shower head is removable, scrape off any encrustation on the inside of the head. If you can't remove the head, try sticking a pin through every hole. If you are conscientious, you will clean aerators and shower heads two or three times a year. If you are like almost everyone else, you'll wait until you see a noticeable decrease in pressure.

Clogged drains are far more serious and you should do everything you can to prevent this trouble. The key is to know what causes clogged drains and *avoid* doing it. The most common cause of clogged kitchen drains is hot fat poured into the pipe. When the fat cools, it hardens and reduces the space through which water can flow. The restricted space now catches food particles or more fat and eventually becomes completely blocked. The solution is to make sure that no hot fat is poured down the drain. Obviously no large food particles should be allowed to enter the drain either, unless you have a garbage disposer.

Stoppages in bathroom drains are usually caused by human hair. After a shampoo, some hair inevitably gets into the drain and gets caught on the filter or drain control. When enough hair gets in, it clogs the drain. About twice a year you should pull out the drain control and clean off the hair. This should keep the drain relatively clear.

A toilet drain will rarely clog unless something falls into it that shouldn't. A common difficulty arises when a small object such as a comb or toothbrush is left lying on the toilet tank and is accidentally pushed into the bowl while the toilet is flushing. The object disappears from view but can't get through the trap in the toilet and subsequently causes a stoppage. WARNING: If you must keep small articles on top of the tank, be careful.

Drains can be kept clear by regular treatments with a caustic drain cleaner. WARNING: A caustic chemical is dangerous to touch, and its fumes are dangerous to breathe. Read the instructions carefully and follow them. About half a cup in each drain every three months should keep the drains completely free. Chemical drain cleaners will not harm a septic tank. WARNING: Do *not* use a caustic drain cleaner in a kitchen sink that is equipped with a garbage disposer, as the chemical will damage the disposer. Non-caustic drain cleaners are available; they are just less effective.

If you are lucky and careful, you may never have a clogged drain. If a stoppage does occur, you can correct it by following the instructions in Section 4-9.

3-4. SOME SOURCES OF WATER DAMAGE

Water can cause wood to warp or rot; water can cause metal to corrode; water can soften or wear away paint. In other words, water can be a very harmful agent, even though we can't get along without it. To prevent water damage, you must make frequent checks in the places where it is most likely to occur so that you can take corrective measures at the first sign of trouble.

Tubs and showers may be enclosed with tile or have other waterproof walls, but the seal where the wall meets the tub is never permanent. Check seams frequently. You may notice water leaking into a seam, but if water does leak into the floor and walls, there will be damage to wood members. A few drops won't matter, but the cumulative damage from a few drops a day can be considerable. Look all around the tub, lavatory, and shower at least once a month, and if you spot an opening, seal it with caulking compound or ceramic edging tiles, as described in Section 8-22.

Water vapor in the air will ruin paint surfaces on which it collects. This is especially true when the water vapor condenses on cool window panes and drips down on the sills. To avoid this, use as little water as possible when washing kitchen and bathroom floors. On wood floors water should not be used, since it can seep down between the joints and cause the floor to warp or crack. Steam baths and long hot showers also put a lot of water vapor in the air, which damages the finish of bathroom walls. There is no real solution for this, but you can make your baths as short as possible.

Water vapor in the air in a warm room will condense on any cold surface. Cold-water pipes, especially, start to "sweat" as water condenses on them, and the water drips off to cause damage. To prevent condensation, you can buy special insulation to cover the pipes. Fiberglas, hair, and other materials are available, and all are good. If appearances are not important, you can wrap newspapers around the pipes and tie them with cord.

If a water softener is used, your water heater should not be set at more than 140°F. The salt in your softener may corrode some metals above this temperature.

3-5. HEATING SYSTEM MAINTENANCE

When a heating system malfunctions, it can be very inconvenient, but it is not quite the emergency that stopped-up plumbing can be. It is annoying, however, and you can and should take the necessary precautions to keep the system in operation. Most of the maintenance procedures should be performed during the summer or just before the heating system is turned on for the winter.

Heating systems are classified according to the fuel used (coal, oil, or gas) and the heat-carrying medium (hot water, steam, or hot air). Each type of furnace and each type of radiator or register has its own problems. You can do most of the maintenance jobs yourself, but you should have a professional clean out and adjust the furnace every year.

An oil furnace should be cleaned and adjusted before it is turned on in the fall. However, the best time to have it cleaned is in the spring or early summer at the end of the heating season. The soot that lines the inside of the furnace can mix with moisture in the air to form harmful acids which can corrode the metal in the furnace if left all summer. A professional should be called to clean the furnace and pipes and adjust the burner. This is an important step, since if the ignition fires too soon, there will not be enough oil vapor in the furnace to burn, and if it is too late, there will be too much oil, with the danger of an explosion. Although you could probably clean the furnace yourself, it is a very dirty job, and since you will need a professional to adjust the burner, you might as well let him do the cleaning as well.

Other burners do not have quite the soot problem that an oil burner has, but they should be adjusted, too. For a gas burner, call your local gas company. For an automatic coal burner, your coal dealer can usually recommend someone.

Regardless of the type of burner, during the off-season you should shut off the main electrical switch. For a gas burner, you should also shut off the gas, including the pilot. Leave the furnace door open during the summer so that air will circulate. Don't forget to close it when it's time to start the furnace again. If you have an oil furnace, fill the oil tank at the end of the heating season so that it remains full during the summer. Otherwise, inner surfaces exposed to moisture in the air could rust.

Your professional repairman will oil the motors in your heating system as part of his job. You should add oil two or three times during the winter. Use a medium-weight oil. The motors usually have oil cups or oil holes. Add two drops at a time until these are full. In addition to the main burner motor, don't forget to oil the water pump if you have a forced hot-water system.

Your heating system must be kept clean to operate at maximum efficiency. Filters in a hot-air system, shown in Fig. 3–4, should be cleaned every month by brushing with a whisk broom and should be replaced every three months. Make sure that you have the correct size replacement filter, and install it with the arrows on the edge pointing in direction of the flow of air. Hot air registers should be vacuumed every fall just before turning on the heat. It is not necessary to do this during the heating season, as long as the filters are kept clean. Humidifiers on radiators should be cleaned every three months or so and kept full of water. Radiators should be vacuumed every two or three months, since the accumulation of dust, besides being unsightly, reduces the heat that is transmitted into a room. Also, in the fall, remove the cover of the thermostat and blow out any dust that might have collected there.

In hot-water and steam systems, water should be added to the boilers to replace what had evaporated during the heating season. Do this in the fall just before turning on the heat. Water normally contains oxygen and other gases, which can be corrosive to pipes and the boiler itself, but fortunately these gases are driven off when the water is heated. If the boilers are refilled in the spring or summer, the oxygen in the water will not be driven off and can cause damage. If water is added inadvertantly in the off-season, you should fire up the furnace to heat the water sufficiently to drive out the gases. Run it long enough to feel heat in any radiator and then shut it off. Sediment may collect in the bottom of a boiler and this should be drained off. Open the drain faucet at the bottom of the boiler, as shown in Fig. 3–5, and let the water run until it flows clear. Then refill the boiler. This should be done in the fall just before turning on the heat.

Hot-water systems collect air in the radiators during the off-season. This air must be removed before the heat is turned on. This is done by *bleeding* the radiators, as shown in Fig. 3–6. Open the small valve located near the top of the radiator, which permits air to escape. Hold a cup under the valve and as soon as water flows, close the valve, since the air is now out of the radiator. This should be done at every radiator beginning with those on the topmost floor and ending with the lowest. You should do this again in mid heating season.

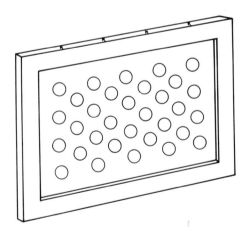

FIGURE 3–4. Air Filter.

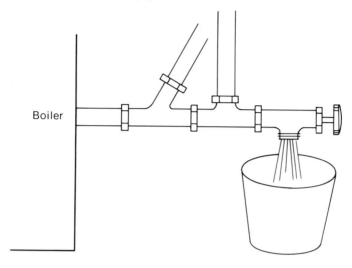

FIGURE 3-5. Draining Boiler.

The valve on a steam radiator is supposed to allow the trapped air to escape and to expand when heated so that the steam does not escape. These valves should be removed and cleaned in a strong solution of washing soda or trisodium phosphate (TSP). TSP can be purchased at hardware stores but is also available as the main ingredient of many commercial cleaning powders. Read the labels. After cleaning, replace the valves and adjust them with the radiators on so that they close when hot. The radiator should get hot quickly, but only a small amount of steam should come out before the valve closes.

Make sure that the main valves of all radiators are opened, that is, turned completely counterclockwise. Do not try to balance radiators by partially closing the main valves. These valves should always be

FIGURE 3-6. Bleeding Air From Radiator.

completely open or completely closed. The air valves can be adjusted somewhat for balancing.

An important aspect of keeping a house heated is heat leakage. Heat can escape from a house in two ways. First there are actual leaks, that is, openings through which heat truly *leaks* to the outside. Openings around radiator pipes. open joints around windows and doors, especially under doors, and cracks in floors are common examples. Each opening may be quite small, but the total area of all the openings is frequently equivalent to keeping a window wide open all the time.

A second source of heat loss is conduction. The hot air inside the house heats a window or wall, and the heat is conducted through the surface to the outside. This is especially true of windows, as you can tell by feeling how cool a window feels in comparison with a wall, but there can be considerable heat leakage through uninsulated walls.

Heat loss through unwanted openings can be minimized by closing the openings. Doors especially should be weatherproofed by installing weather stripping. Openings around window frames and door frames should be caulked or otherwise sealed. These procedures are described in Section 5–8. One frequently overlooked opening is a fireplace damper. When the fireplace is not in use, make sure that the damper is closed; otherwise, a lot of heat goes up the chimney. If a fireplace is not used for long periods, you should cover the opening with a piece of plywood or wallboard to keep in the heat. The board can be decorated to match the decor of the room.

To reduce heat loss by conduction through windowpanes, the best solution is to install storm windows. Alternatively, you can keep blinds drawn or drapes closed as much as possible, but you then lose the function of a window, which is to see outdoors. When you install storm windows, you should carefully number each sash and each house window so that you can easily fit the proper sash to each window in the fall. Numbered tabs with raised numerals are available for this purpose and are much better than penciled numbers, since they can be read even if the sash is painted. Heat loss through walls can be minimized by insulating the house, which also helps keep the house cool during hot summer days. Methods of applying insulation are described in Section 5–6.

An important part of your heating system is your fireplace; you should know how to build a wood fire. For ease in lighting the fire you should use three logs. Place the largest (in diameter) on the andirons toward the back of the fireplace, a slightly smaller log in front of it, and a third log on top over the crack between the other two. If you have no andirons, you can use ordinary bricks or pieces of large pipe. Place newspaper and kindling wood under the logs and light the paper with a match. *Make sure that the damper is open.* You may have to add more paper until the logs get hot enough to ignite, but if you use sufficient kindling wood, this should not be necessary.

Remove the ashes when a layer about three inches deep has accumulated. Subsequent fires can be built with ashes in the fireplace. However, as soon as the fire is out, close the damper, so that winds blowing down the chimney will not scatter the ashes into the room.

3-6. HOW TO PREVENT TERMITES AND DRY ROT

Subterranean *termites* are insects which eat wood. They live in damp areas underground and avoid sunlight and open space. When they find wood in contact with the ground, they eat their way into it, but never through a surface exposed to the air. The result is that they can go undetected and eat a wood member up to the paint on the surface or until the wood is no longer able to support the weight on it and crumbles.

Termites are not to be confused with flying ants, which are harmless. The difference is illustrated in Fig. 3-7. A flying ant has a body in three distinct sections, with a very thin waist between the rear two, as shown in Fig. 3-7(a). The termite, shown in Fig. 3-7(b), has a thick waist which is almost undiscernible. Termites are about ½ inch long with opaque wings; ants usually have transparent wings.

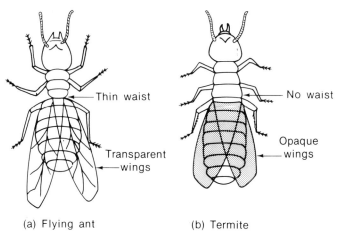

(a) Flying ant   (b) Termite

FIGURE 3-7. Insects.

Termites shed their wings when they find a new home, whereas ants keep their wings.

Dry rot is an invisible fungus which is airborne. It also eats moist wood. As the wood is eaten, it absorbs more moisture, which speeds the spread of dry rot.

Both termites and dry rot can be prevented by making sure that the timbers in your home are well ventilated, dry, and not in contact with the moist earth or a moist cement slab or foundation. Do not have wood in contact with your house and the ground. Thus, firewood, for example, should never be piled against the house outside. Also, wooden fences and frameworks should not be in contact with the house, since termites could eat their way from the ground through the fence members into the wooden members of your home. Wooden steps should not touch the ground.

Keep moisture away from the foundations of your home. Check downspouts to make sure that rainwater is carried away from the house. Any wood which is exposed to rain should be protected by paint. Blistered paint is a possible entry for dry rot.

The sills of your house, the horizontal members which are in contact with the foundation, are especially vulnerable to termites and dry rot, since they are closest to the earth. To check for damage, poke an ice pick or an awl in several places along the sill. If the pick enters too easily in any spot, it is usually a sign of damage by termites or dry rot, and further damage is likely. The damaged wood must be cut out and replaced and steps taken to eliminate the source of trouble.

Look for signs of termites *before* they reach the house. Termites prefer to remain underground but will build shelter tubes across the face of the foundation to shelter themselves from sunlight and air as they move from the earth to the wood of the house; this is shown in Fig. 3-8. Look for signs of these tubes every spring and scrape them away if you find any. Any termites remaining in the house will die because they need to return to the earth daily.

If you see swarms of flying insects near the house, check to see if they are termites. Also, in the spring, look for piles of discarded termite wings in, under, and around the house. In masonry foundations, check for cracks which would allow moisture to enter.

Poisons in the soil will usually prevent termites from getting a foothold. Chlordane, heptachlor, and dieldrin are effective and nontoxic to plants. DDT is also used but may kill plants as well. To ensure protection, you should dig a trench along the foundation, both inside and out. The depth should be 24 to 30 inches. Mix the poison as directed on the label. Chlordane and heptachlor are usually mixed with water in a 2 percent solution. Dieldrin is mixed with water in a 0.5 percent solution.   DDT is usually mixed with fuel oil or kerosene.   Pour about 1 cup per foot of length in the trench, fill with 6 inches of dirt, and add another cup per foot.   Continue, alternating 6 inches of dirt and 1 cup of poison per foot, until the trench is full.   Once properly protected, these poisons should keep termites away for at least five years.

Since proper treatment protects homes against termites and dry rot for many years, it may be better to have a professional exterminator do the job.   He will also know what to do if termites have already established themselves in the home.

On new construction, wood should be pretreated with chemicals to deter termites and dry rot.   Also, termite shields made of metal should be used on all sills to prevent moisture or termites from entering.

Mildew is another fungus which requires moisture.   Generally, it requires heat and humidity to grow, and it will not thrive in direct sunlight.   It will grow in hot, damp climates on painted surfaces which are screened from the sun by shrubbery.   On new surfaces, paint can be mixed with a mildewcide to prevent mildew.   If mildew is a problem, mildewcide should be used the next time the surface is painted.

Mildew on a painted surface looks like dirt, but it cannot be washed off easily.   A solution which has proven effective in removing it is made up of about ½ cup of trisodium phosphate (TSP) and 1 pint of bleach in about 3 quarts of water.   The exact proportions are not

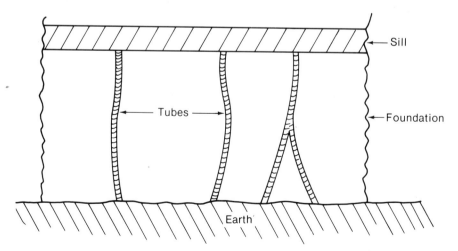

FIGURE 3–8. Termite Tubes.

critical. The mildew should be scrubbed with a stiff brush dipped in this solution. After the mildew is removed, allow the surface to dry. Then apply a mildew-resistant paint.

Mildew will also attack some textile fabrics. Clothes hanging in a dark, damp closet are particularly susceptible. A simple solution in humid climates is to keep an electric bulb lit in each closet. A 100-watt bulb will protect a moderately large closet.

3-7. ROUTINE CHECKUPS

Eventually all parts of the house wear out if not constantly renewed. You can delay and sometimes prevent an expensive repair or replacement job by checking sources of trouble and fixing or eliminating the damage before it spreads. This is the most neglected area of home maintenance. Most homeowners wait until something goes wrong and then they fix it or call in a repairman. With routine checkups they could have anticipated the damage and prevented a costly repair. Note that these repair jobs are rarely emergencies, so the homeowner is apt to be careless about them. In many cases no damage is involved, but the recommended maintenance will keep your home looking well kept and increase the resale value, when you decide to sell it. You may not feel that it is important to make all the checks described here. But you should make it a practice to look at your home with a critical eye, as if you were buying it for the first time, and fix the things that would bother you.

1. *Floors.* Constant traffic on floors causes wear and tear which can result in eventual serious damage. However, if the surface of the floor is protected, the floor should last a lifetime. The surface protection depends on the type of floor.

Hardwood floors are usually finished with varnish, shellac, or other commercial sealing coatings. They should then be covered with wax to protect the finish. Wax floors are also easier to keep clean. There are many commercial floor waxes available in paste or liquid form. Make sure that the wax you use does not have a water base, since water quickly damages a wood floor. For this reason also, never use water to wash a wood floor, and if water spills on it, mop it up as soon as possible. Water can seep into cracks and cause the wood to warp or crack. Most so-called *self-polishing liquid waxes* have a water base and should not be used on floors.

The frequency of waxing depends on the traffic. A floor which is used frequently, such as in entryways should be cleaned and waxed every three months. In less traveled areas, twice a year may be sufficient. Remember, without protection the finish will deteriorate, and the wood will crack and splinter. Wax coatings can be slippery if applied in thick coatings. Apply a *thin* layer and let dry before applying a second coating.

Tile floor coverings may be made of a number of widely different materials, such as linoleum, asphalt, rubber, plastic, and cork. These coverings should also be protected with wax to make them wear longer. Proper waxing will double the life of tile floors. Unlike wood, these materials will not be damaged by cold or warm water, but hot water may cause deterioration. You can wash tile floors with a mild soap and warm water. (If you can hold your hand in the water, it's not too hot.) Special cleaners are available for these floors, and you can get them at most hardware stores, but they are a luxury, since soap and water do an adequate job.

After it has been washed, a tile floor should be waxed. *Self-polishing* waxes, with a water base, dry quickly to a high shine. *Polishing* waxes come in both liquid and paste form and contain no water. When these dry, they leave a dull finish, which can, however, be buffed to a high luster. Polishing waxes last much longer than the self-polishing varieties. On a kitchen linoleum, for example, a self-polishing wax should be renewed every month, whereas a polishing wax can give good protection for three months.

Door thresholds take more abuse than the rest of the floor and thus should have more care. The threshold of the outside door also is subject to abuse from the elements as well as wear from traffic. Ideally, if you are conscientious, you will varnish the outside threshold every month, although most homeowners don't do this as often as once a year. As the threshold wears, a space is formed between the bottom of the door and the threshold, as shown in Fig. 3–9. This allows heat to escape and rain to come in. When this happens, the threshold must be replaced, as described in Section 8–11.

If a floor sags, it is usually a sign of impending serious trouble. Sagging may be caused by weakened beams, warped floor joints, damage to the foundation, or supporting posts sinking in to the ground. These things don't happen suddenly, and consequently the sag increases so slowly as to be almost imperceptible. Nevertheless, if sagging is allowed to progress unchecked, walls may crack, doors and windows become jammed, and floors begin to slope. Sagging floors, then, are a warning that a more serious trouble exists.

If a floor bounces or creaks as you walk on it, it is a sign that the nails holding the floor to the joist have come loose. The causes may be the same as those for sagging floors, although rusty nails may also be the reason. This condition, too, is a warning.

Part of your routine maintenance must be a check on floors to make certain that they neither sag nor bounce. If you detect no fault the first time you do this, you don't have to check again for about a year, since the process is a slow one. If you do notice a sag, look for signs of crumbling masonry, termites in sills or joists, sunken supports, or other damage in the cellar or crawl space. Sagging can also be caused by extensive remodeling that shifts the weight on the supporting members of the house. In any case, if you find no structural damage, check the sag in a floor joist with a level and check again monthly. If it gets worse, even slightly, it must be corrected by the methods described in Section 8–10. If left too long, complete rebuilding may be necessary. Repair of bouncing or creaking floors is described in Section 8–10.

Floors of all types can be damaged by furniture legs. The round metal caps on legs which are used to make the furniture more maneuverable, actually are worse for floors than the squared-off leg alone. Casters are also bad. If your furniture is not likely to be moved a great deal, put large glass or rubber coasters under the legs to avoid marring the floors.

2. *Interior walls and ceilings.* There is not much to say about maintaining walls and ceilings except *be careful!* If you are in the habit of swinging a golf club in the house, you may make a dent in a ceiling. In general, ceilings and walls will not be damaged except by abuse. When a room seems drab, you will want to paint the walls or the ceiling. Make sure, however, that you paint both, since if only the walls are painted, the ceiling then seems dingy, and vice versa. How often to paint is a matter of personal preference, but every five years

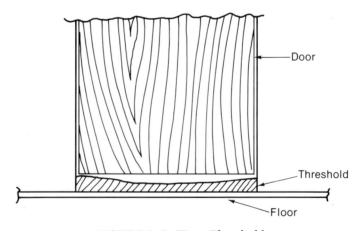

FIGURE 3–9. Worn Threshold.

is usually sufficient, unless you live in an area where the atmosphere contains an unusually large amount of soot. Some homeowners paint a different room every year, while others prefer to do the whole interior at one time.

One source of damage to walls can be a doorknob. When a door is swung wide open, the knob is the first part that hits the wall, and if it strikes too hard, a dent results. This is especially bad on plaster walls. One way of preventing this from happening is to install door bumpers to stop the door before the knob hits the wall. A typical bumper is shown in Fig. 3–10. It is simply a long metal rod with a screw thread on one end and a rubber tip on the other. The rod is screwed into the baseboard so that a spot near the edge of the door will hit the rubber tip before the knob hits the wall. To install it, make a hole in the wooden baseboard with an ice pick or an awl. If you don't have either of these tools, use a nail. Start the thread in the hole by hand and then use a wrench on the hexagonal section of the rod to screw the bumper all the way in. In tiled bathrooms where the baseboard is ceramic, you can install the bumper on the door instead of the wall. Place it a few inches above the floor and directly below the doorknob.

Walls are frequently damaged by furniture pushed against them. When a chair or sofa is near a wall, it is usually pushed against the wall every time someone sits in it. A method of preventing this is to put stops for the legs on the floor under the back of the chair. A simple stop is shown in Fig. 3–11(a), and the method of installing it is shown in Fig. 3–11(b). The stop is made of a piece of scrap lumber about ¾ inch thick and any convenient width. The length is determined by the position of the legs of the chair with respect to the wall. The hole can be any shape or may be a wide slot in the end of the board.

If a plaster wall cracks, it may be a sign that something else is wrong. You can live with a small crack, but if more cracks occur or the crack widens, check the foundation, and look for structural damage caused by termites. Cracked walls may also be a sign of weakened beams or a sagging floor. If wallpaper peels, it is usually a sign of moisture in the wall. Unexplained spots on walls and ceilings may also be caused by moisture. This may be a sign of a leak in the roof or water entering the walls from a clogged gutter. Make it a point to

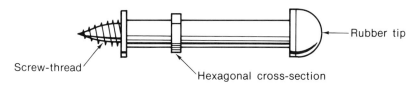

Screw-thread   Hexagonal cross-section   Rubber tip

FIGURE 3–10. Door Bumper.

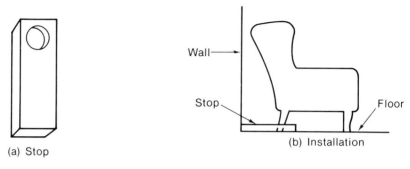

(a) Stop   (b) Installation

FIGURE 3–11. Wall Protector.

check walls and ceilings for cracks and signs of moisture in the spring and whenever else you think of it.

3. *Doors.* When doors work, you pay little attention to them, but when they don't, it can be annoying. You may tolerate a door that squeaks or rattles or one that requires extra force to close, but if the door has sagged or warped so that it can't be closed, or if rain seeps in under a door, you will have to correct the difficulty. Although these things are not entirely preventable, you can avoid some of the problems by careful maintenance.

As the house settles, door frames may get out of line, such that the latch on the door doesn't meet the hole in the striker plate. Striker plates are shown in Fig. 3–12. When the door has sagged, the latch will hit the tongue on the striker plate too low and will not go into

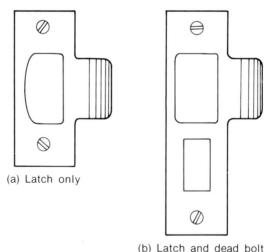

(a) Latch only

(b) Latch and dead bolt

FIGURE 3–12. Striker Plates.

the hole. Streaks or shiny marks, as indicated on the plate in Fig. 3-12(b), show where the latch is hitting the plate. In this figure, the latch is hitting the plate below the bottom of the hole. If the sag is slight, you can correct the trouble by filing the opening in the plate. However, make sure that the trouble is not caused by structural damage. Check for termites or sagging beams.

Doors can be affected by moisture and temperature. Any door which is subject to a large difference in temperatures on its two sides may tend to warp. This is especially true of outside doors, but a door between a warm kitchen and a cold garage may also warp. To prevent moisture from getting into the door and to minimize the effects of temperature changes, you should keep the door painted or varnished. Don't forget the four edges, as well as the two surfaces. The bottom edge of an outside door, including garage doors, should be painted every year. Use any color paint or varnish you have on hand, since no one will see it. On overhead garage doors, you will probably want to use the same paint as on the door surfaces.

Rain or melted snow seeping under an outside door can damage the door as well as the floors inside the house. This can be prevented by nailing a metal *drip cap* along the bottom edge of the door on the outside. Weatherproofing on the inside is also necessary to prevent drafts. The installation is shown in Fig. 3-13. On garage doors, you can nail a drip cap the full length of the door. For overhead garage doors, if appearances are not important, you can nail old bicycle inner tubes on the bottom of the door for protection from rain and drafts.

To keep doors operating properly, moving parts should be cleaned and lubricated regularly. Oil hinges yearly. On garage doors oil all moving parts every six months. Check garage doors for cracks and caulk them if necessary. Locks and latches should be lubricated

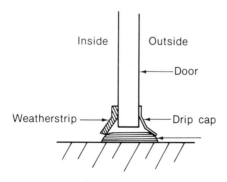

FIGURE 3-13. Drip Cap.

annually by squirting powdered graphite into them. Weatherproofing collects dirt which interferes with proper operation. When vacuuming the hall, don't forget the weatherproofing.

Sliding doors need lubrication, too. Rub tracks with paraffin, soap, or petroleum jelly. If you use jelly, wipe away any excess, since it collects dirt. Swinging doors have side plates that conceal springs and hinges. When a swinging door squeaks, remove one of the side plates and squirt powdered graphite on all moving parts.

4. *Windows.* There isn't much you can do to prevent someone from throwing a baseball through a window. However, you *can* prevent breakage from shutters flapping in the breeze. This incidentally is a common cause of broken windows around the home. Check the hooks or catches that secure the shutters once a year, usually just before your area is apt to have windstorms. Shutters should be firmly latched either in the open or closed position; they should never be free to swing with the wind. Most homeowners keep the shutters open all the time, hooking or latching them in place, and then never looking at them until something happens. Unfortunately, hooks and catches rust or pull out from the wood, and the shutter is then free to flap in the wind and break a window. See to it that the catches remain in good condition. They should be painted at least once every five years to keep them rust-free. If a hurricane or tornado is expected, it is a good idea to close the shutters and fasten them securely so that flying tree branches and other objects cannot damage the window.

Once a year you should also look at the putty in all the windows in the house. If putty shows signs of cracking or drying out, it should be replaced. How to apply putty is discussed in Section 8–1, on replacing glass. If putty is applied properly, it may never need replacing, but it will be necessary to protect it by painting over it at least once every five years. The outside of the window frames should be painted that often anyway, to protect the wood from moisture.

Metal casement windows are driven by a crank inside the house. All moving parts should be oiled once a year to keep them operating properly. At the same time you should clean dirt and debris out of the tracks, using a stiff brush, and inspect all metal frames for signs of rust. If you spot any corrosion, correct it as described in Section 9–15. Steel frames will not rust if they are covered by a good paint at least once every five years in most climates. Near salt water or in other climates where the atmosphere may be corrosive, frames should be painted every two years.

Windows sometimes stick from paint or expansion due to moisture, but with proper care windows should never get stuck. When windows are painted, you must be careful to let the paint dry on each part before sliding sashes come in contact with sills and other parts of the frame. Paint on casement windows should be allowed to dry with the windows open. Moisture may cause window sashes in double-hung windows to expand and stick in place. This can be prevented by lubricating the edges of the window and the grooves in which it slides with paraffin. You can rub an ordinary candle in the grooves and then move the windows up and down a few times so that the wax covers the edges of the windows, thus sealing the openings. You could also paint the edges of the windows with linseed oil to seal out moisture. Either protection should be applied once a year in damp climates. In dry climates, you can forget about this until windows start to get hard to move. If despite your efforts a window does get stuck, you can free it by one of the methods described in Section 8–3.

Storm windows require the same attention as regular windows. They should be inspected for cracking putty and should be painted when the other windows of the house are painted. They should be stored vertically when not in use.

The mesh in window screens may be made of galvanized iron, copper, bronze, or aluminum. Iron rusts, copper and bronze do not. However, rain water dripping from copper or bronze may cause a green discoloration on walls. To prevent rust or the green discoloration, it is desirable to paint all three of these materials every year just before installing the screens. Aluminum screens do not need painting but are more expensive.

To paint screens, mount the screen horizontally on two boxes, or sawhorses if you have them. You will need a special applicator for painting them; it is quite cheap but not always available. In a pinch, you can make an applicator by nailing a piece of old carpet to a wooden block, as shown in Fig. 3–14. The paint is placed in a shallow pan and the applicator is dipped in the paint and applied to the screen on each side. Don't have too much paint on the applicator or it will drip through the screen. The paint itself may be screen enamel or thin

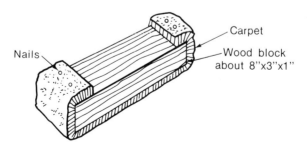

Nails

Carpet

Wood block
about 8"x3"x1"

FIGURE 3–14. Applicator for Painting Screens.

varnish. Ask your hardware dealer or paint supplier for a suitable paint.

5. *Exterior Walls.* The biggest mistake homeowners make concerning the exterior of their homes is painting too often. The outside of your home may look drab or dirty, because it is simply dirty. It probably doesn't need painting yet. A good paint job should last a minimum of five years, and some of the newer siding materials never need painting. If you paint too often, the paint film will build up on the wall until the weight of the paint itself will cause the film to crack and chip off. You should not put on a new coat of paint until the old coat is so worn that you can almost see the bare wood through it.

The newer paints are designed to become chalky as they wear. The powder coating is washed away by rain, and at the same time it tends to carry dirt with it, so that the paint job remains fresh-looking for a long time. Nevertheless, even these paints get dingy-looking, either because there has been insufficient rain to wash away all the dirt or because of an excess of soot or dirt in the air.

If the house looks drab, you can restore its fresh appearance by washing it. You can wash a house simply with a garden hose. Wash one side at a time. Since the dirt comes off more easily if the wall is cool, try to wash the shady wall of the house first, and move around the house avoiding the sun. Hosing down a house with water alone will remove most dirt and stains but will not remove oily grime or soot from oil burners. These can be removed with detergents or trisodium phosphate (TSP). You can use a siphon type of garden sprayer if you have one. A concentrated solution of the detergent or TSP is placed in a jar attached to the hose and is mixed with the water as it flows. For isolated grease and oil stains, use a long-handled brush dipped in the detergent or TSP solution.

If you see signs of chipped or peeling paint or paint worn to the base wood, then the house needs painting. If the original paint was put on correctly, it should not peel, but eventually it will wear. Before you decide to paint your home, you should consider the many different kinds of siding available to use instead.

Stucco walls and foundations and masonry should be inspected annually. Small cracks can be patched easily as described in Section 10–4. Dirt on stucco walls can be washed away with water. Oily stains need brushing with a solution of detergent or TSP.

Metal parts on the outside of a house tend to corrode when exposed to moisture. Iron and steel are usually protected by coating them with a layer of zinc. This is called *galvanizing.* Galvanized iron should not rust, but if the coating gets a small nick or hairline crack, moisture can enter and the core material will corrode. Some cut-rate materials have too thin a coating of zinc, which eventually wears off, allowing the base metal to rust. To make sure that galvanized parts are fully protected against rust, they should be painted, but paint will peel from newly galvanized metal. Allow the galvanized part to be exposed to the weather for six months to a year, and then it will take paint.

Bare iron on the exterior of your home should be painted or varnished to prevent rust. Tin plate, sometimes used for "tin" roofs, is usually steel-covered with a thin coat of tin. This should also be painted to prevent rust. For best protection, bare iron or steel and tin plate should be painted first with red lead or zinc chromate, as described in Section 9–15.

Aluminum requires almost no maintenance. It will get a weathered appearance if subjected to the elements, but it doesn't corrode. If you wish to preserve the new aluminum look, you should coat it with liquid wax when it is new.

6. *Roof.* If your roof was put on by a reliable professional roofer, you can almost forget about it. A good roof should last many years. The different kinds of roofing material and their characteristics are as follows:

(a) The most common material for roofs is asphalt shingles. This material is fire-resistant and should last at least ten years if not twice that long.

(b) Tar and gravel may be used on flat roofs or roofs with a very low pitch. Because this material is cheap and lasts only about five years, it should be avoided.

(c) Wood shingles should last about 20 years, but these roofs are flammable. Wood roofs are, however, the easiest to repair.

(d) Shingles made of asbestos and cement seem to last forever. They can be damaged by falling objects, such as tree branches, but can be replaced easily.

(e) Aluminum shingles also seem to last forever. They are available uncoated or with baked-enamel coatings which make them look just like wood. This is the lightest material to use on your roof. There is one problem with it, however: Aluminum should not make contact with other metals or electrolytic corrosion will occur. To prevent this, flashings used with this roofing must also be aluminum.

(f) Concrete tile and slate roofs never wear out but are extremely heavy. They are expensive to install and difficult to repair when damaged; they are fireproof, however.

Outside the tar and gravel roofs, the need for a roofing job occurs so seldom that you might as well have a professional do the job right. Get estimates from two or three *recommended* contractors. Once the job is done, you won't have to bother with your roof for a long time.

However, a hurricane or tornado can damage even a new roof. So can branches in contact with the roof. You can't prevent the windstorm, but you should make sure that no branches rub across the roof. If branches overhang the roof, be on the lookout for fallen limbs and remove them promptly. Check your roof every year for loosened shingles or nails that have worked up out of their holes. Shingles can be nailed down again and other nails hammered down. Cover the nail heads with roofing cement. One problem with looking for troubles on a roof, however, is that too much walking on a roof can cause damage. The best maintenance procedure is to have a good roof installed in the first place and then forget about it for 20 years or until there is a bad windstorm.

7. *Gutters.* If you inspect your gutters and downspouts once a year and make the necessary minor repairs, you can make them last at least twice as long as they do in the average home. The main problem that arises in gutters is a water stoppage caused by leaves, dirt, bird nests, or other debris. The solution is, of course, to sweep out the debris before you have a stoppage. Use an ordinary whisk broom or stiff brush to sweep out the gutters in the fall, after the trees have shed their leaves. Check them again in the spring just before the heavy rains to make sure that the water flow will not be restricted.

It is difficult to clean out downspouts, so it is best to prevent leaves from entering downspouts in the first place. This is best accomplished by installing a special wire cage, which permits water to flow into the downspout but keeps the leaves out. These cages are available at hardware stores and are very inexpensive.

It is also possible to install guards made of wire mesh on your gutters to prevent leaves from entering. These guards do keep out almost all the debris, but if some dirt does get in, it is a nuisance to clean it out. It is better to forget about the guards and just clean the gutters once a year.

When you clean out a gutter, also check it for signs of cracking or rusting. You can keep gutters in good condition by coating the insides. Linseed oil on wood gutters, applied once a year with a paint brush, will prevent the gutter from cracking. Metal gutters can be coated with varnish or liquid roof coating about once in three years. Also check the straps and hooks holding the gutters; if there is any sign of rust, clean it off and paint it.

Make certain that the water runs away from the house when it comes out of the downspout. Elbows at the bottom should be firmly in place, and troughs should be used if necessary.

8. *Safety on a Ladder.* When you check your roof or gutters, you

will probably use a ladder. You must be aware that a fall from a ladder is dangerous and take proper precautions to avoid an accident. First, check the ladder itself for weak rungs. The best place to determine this is on the ground. Place the ladder flat on the ground and step on each rung in turn. If a rung breaks while you do this, thank your stars that you discovered the problem on the ground. You can sometimes spot weak points in a wooden ladder, but not if it is painted. (If you want to give a ladder a protective coat, use transparent varnish or shellac.)

When you are putting up a ladder, make sure that there are no telephone or power lines in the way and keep your eye on picture windows that can be broken if the ladder slips. Don't put up the ladder on a windy day. Put the bottom of the ladder on solid ground about one fourth the length of the ladder away from the house. If you have the foot of the ladder too close, you may topple backward, while if it is too far away, it may skid.

Before climbing up the ladder, arrange a place to put whatever you are carrying up. Paint cans should have hooks to hang them on a rung. Tools should be held in a tool belt to keep from dropping them. Remember the safety of people below is as important as your safety aloft.

Don't reach too far when on a ladder, or it may topple over. A good rule is to keep your hips inside the rails of the ladder. Reach out with your arms, but don't bend your body. It is better to move the ladder than to risk a fall.

9. *Basement.* If your cellar is dry, it is probably in good condition. Most problems in cellars begin with moisture seeping in through cracks in the wall or a porous floor. Once a year, just before turning on the heat for the winter, check to see if your cellar seems dry. If there are signs of dampness, try to find the cause. Cracks should be patched. Porous walls or floors can sometimes be fixed with plastic paints. Repairs for damp basements are described in Section 10–5; an annual check will enable you to spot a defect and fix it before it becomes serious enough to require an expensive job.

Formerly, a warm cellar was considered a sign of wasted heat. Consequently, homeowners were advised to insulate pipes carrying hot water or hot air to keep the heat in the pipes and to put a ceiling in the cellar to keep heat on the first floor from being lost to the cellar. It is now felt that a warm cellar is desirable, since the warm air in the cellar rises to warm the floor above. The heat is thus not lost. Naturally, the cellar should be insulated from the outside as much as possible so that this heat doesn't escape. This means that frames around basement windows and doors should be well caulked. Caulking should be checked every fall. However, heat pipes need not be insulated unless the cellar gets too hot. Another advantage of a warm cellar is that it is available for storage. Tools left in a cold cellar are apt to rust, because there is always some moisture in the air, and the water vapor condenses on cold surfaces. A warm cellar can be used for storage without fear of rust or mildew.

4

Plumbing

The usual plumbing system consists of two main subsystems, one to bring clean water into the house and the other to remove wastes. The water supply subsystem consists of a pipe which brings water into the house and branch pipes running to the water heater, to the faucets, and to other fixtures throughout the house. Water is fed to these fixtures by pressure in the city water pipes. The drain subsystem consists of drains in each sink, tub, and toilet which merge into a single, large drain pipe connected to a sewer, septic tank, or cesspool. This subsystem works by gravity.

Although some plumbing jobs are too intricate or too distasteful for the average homeowner, most of the problems can be solved easily by even an inexperienced handyman. You can fix leaks, noisy plumbing, frozen pipes, faulty fixtures, and clogged drains, as well as adding a new faucet or replacing a fixture. A few minutes of your time and an expenditure of a few pennies for parts will frequently save you many dollars in plumbers' bills.

4-1. HOW TO SHUT OFF THE WATER SUPPLY

The first thing you need to know about your plumbing is how to shut off the water. The main valve is usually located near the water meter. This may be in the basement or utility room in temperate or frigid climates but may be outside the house in areas which never get frost. Turning the valve clockwise shuts off the water. To turn it back on again rotate the handle all the way counterclockwise. There are usually additional valves in the line to each fixture so that it is possible to shut off the water to a single faucet or toilet tank without shutting off all the water in the house. When a pipe breaks or a leak develops, the first thing to do is shut off the water and then decide what to do next. If in doubt as to which valve to shut off, always choose the main valve. Also, when you are about to make any repair in the water line, shut off the water to the fixture you will work on either in the line to the fixture or at the main valve. Don't forget to turn on the water when you finish the repair.

4-2. FROZEN PIPES

If you take the precautions mentioned in Section 3-1, you should never have to worry about a frozen pipe.   Nevertheless, sometimes a sudden cold spell during the night can catch you by surprise and freeze the water in a pipe leading to the outside of the house.   The danger is that you will not notice it, since you will not be using the outside faucet, and then the expanding ice will rupture the pipe.   If there is a frost and you have forgotten to shut off the water to outside faucets, do so at the first opportunity.   After closing the valve in the pipe leading to the outside tap, open the tap and allow the water in the pipe to flow out.   If no water comes out, the pipe may already be frozen.

Frozen pipes can also occur when a pipe inside the house is too close to an open window or passes through an unheated part of the basement or attic.   You will be aware that something is wrong when you open a faucet, and the water trickles out too slowly or doesn't flow at all.   Similarly, a hot-water radiator near an open window can freeze if the outside temperature is far below freezing.   Prevention is easy. Don't open windows near radiators or pipes and keep basement warmed at least slightly in any part containing water pipes.

If you do find a frozen pipe or radiator, you must take steps immediately to thaw it before the expanding ice causes a rupture.   In the case of a radiator, close the outside window and simply apply heat to the radiator.   You can use hot towels, a heating pad, an electric hair dryer, a soldering iron, or any source of heat you have available.   If the room is warm, you can just let nature take its course; the ice will melt eventually, although more slowly than if direct heat is applied.

If a water pipe is frozen, find the location of the ice by running your hand along the pipe to the coldest spot.   First, open the faucet.   Then apply heat to the frozen pipe.   You can use a small propane torch, if you have one, being careful not to burn the walls or ceiling.   If you have a soldering iron, you can strap it to the pipe with the hot tip in contact with the pipe.   Heat from the iron will be conducted along the pipe in both directions.   WARNING: When you use a torch or soldering iron, you may generate enough heat to boil the water inside the pipe.   The steam must have some means of escape, or it can burst the pipe.   Consequently, use these heating devices *only on the faucet side* of the ice block.   Then the steam can come out of the open faucet.   This is not a danger if you use a milder source of heat such as hot towels or a hair dryer.   When the ice has melted, indicated by a flow of water from the faucet, close the faucet and inspect the pipe for leaks.   If there is a leak, repair it as described in the next section.   If the temperature is not too low or if you act quickly enough, the ice will not have expanded enough to cause damage. Don't consider the job complete until you have taken steps to prevent a recurrence of the trouble.

4-3. LEAKS IN WATER PIPES

Leaks can occur in water pipes where the pipe is screwed into a threaded joint. There is no actual break in the pipe, but the sealing compound in the joint may have dried out. Leaks also occur if the pipe is broken or cracked, such as might happen from expanding ice in the pipes. In any case, you must correct the defect quickly to prevent water damage.

If the leak is easily apparent, you will know whether water is leaking from a joint or from a hole in the pipe. If the pipe is inside a wall and your first sign of trouble is water leaking on the floor or a damp wall, you will have to rip open a partition in the wall to determine the source of the leak. Don't be afraid to do this, since a plumber would have to do it anyway before he could fix the pipe. Inspect both sides of the wall to determine which can be opened with a minimum of damage. In any case, whether the leak is in the open or hidden in the wall, your first step is to turn off the water in the pipe.

If the leak is at a threaded joint, you can sometimes stop it simply by screwing the pipe farther into the joint. To do this, you will need two wrenches, one to hold the joint and the other to turn the pipe. If you use only one wrench on the pipe itself, you may twist the joint and cause a break in the pipe on the other side. Note that when you screw the pipe into the joint, you will be unscrewing it from a joint at the other end. Nevertheless, sometimes a quarter or half turn may be enough to stop the leak without causing trouble at the other end.

You can also seal the joint with an epoxy patching material, available in most hardware stores. Full directions for mixing and applying the chemicals are given on the package. The most important step is to make certain that the surface of the pipe is *clean* and *dry* before applying the patching compound. The same epoxy compound can also be used to seal small holes and cracks in pipes. The compound should be allowed to harden for about twelve hours before the water is turned on again.

Ordinary pipe-sealing compound can also be used to cure a leaking joint. Unscrew the pipe, coat the threads with the compound, and then screw the pipe back into the joint. Again, as you unscrew the pipe from one joint, you screw it into another at the other end of the pipe. To seal both joints, first unscrew the pipe at one joint and coat it with the compound.   Then screw it back far enough to unscrew the other end and coat that end also.   Finally, screw it back into the second joint so that it goes approximately the same distance into each joint. If you want to reinforce the joint, you can wrap fine cotton thread or string around the threads on the pipe after you coat it with the pipe compound.   The string swells when wet and acts as an additional seal, although, in most cases, the pipe compound alone is sufficient.

If the leak is in the pipe itself, it can be fixed with epoxy compound, as described above.   For larger leaks and cracks, patching kits are available, consisting of fiberglas cloth, which is wrapped around the pipe, and epoxy compound, which is applied first and then again on top of the fiberglas.   This type of patch is permanent and should out-last the pipe.   Again, the most important step in putting on the patch is to make sure that the pipe is clean and dry.

Unfortunately, leaks usually happen on weekends or at night when hardware stores are closed.   If you have no patching material, you can make a temporary repair, as shown in Fig. 4–1.   A piece of rubber, such as a strip from an old inner tube, is held against the leak with a C-clamp.   After the hardware store is open, you can buy a patching kit for a permanent repair.   Stores also sell pipe clamps and plugs for sealing small leaks.   These work on much the same principle as the C-clamp shown in Fig. 4–1.   The advantage of the clamp over the epoxy patching compound is that the pipe is usable immediately after putting on the clamp.   The clamp is supposed to be a temporary fix, but some have been in use for years.

If the pipe is badly corroded or has a wide split, it should be re-placed.   Use a hacksaw to cut the pipe somewhere near the middle, and then unscrew each half from its joint, using two wrenches, one on the pipe and one to hold the joint.   Measure the distance between

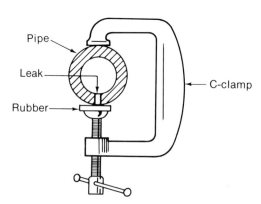

FIGURE 4–1. Temporary Repair for Leak.

the two joints. Take one of the pieces of pipe as a sample to a plumbing supply store and explain that you want that kind of pipe to cover the measured distance (you will need pipe somewhat longer to include the thread that goes into the joint). The replacement should consist of two pieces of pipe and a *union* that goes between them, as shown in Fig. 4-2. Each of the two pieces of pipe is threaded at both ends. One pipe is threaded into each joint, and half of the union is threaded on each pipe. Make certain that you slip on the coupling nut before you screw on the union. The union permits joining the pipes without twisting them. The two halves of the union are held together by tightening the coupling nut with an adjustable wrench. A packing gasket inside the nut prevents a leak at the union. Threading pipe is simple if you have the proper tools, but since you are unlikely to have them, buy pipe already threaded.

4-4. DRIPPING FAUCETS

Part of a conventional faucet is shown in Fig. 4-3. The valve stem screws into the body of the faucet. The stem washer, which is held at the bottom of the stem by a brass screw, fits into a valve seat when the stem is all the way down, and thus closes off the opening for the flow of water. When the handle is turned, the coarse thread on the stem lifts the stem and washer off the valve seat, permitting water to flow. The bonnet screws onto the main body of the faucet and prevents you from turning the handle so far that the valve stem comes clear of the faucet body. Packing in the bonnet prevents water from leaking up between the stem and bonnet.

Each time the faucet is closed, the washer is compressed against the valve seat and at the same time rotated against it. This constant rubbing slowly wears away the washer so that eventually it no longer fits tightly against the valve seat. Then the faucet will drip even when the stem is apparently all the way down. This may not be annoying

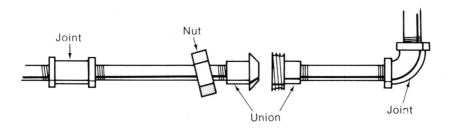

FIGURE 4-2. Pipe Replacement with Union.

but it is a waste of water that can be expensive. Furthermore, it can only get worse.

When a closed faucet drips, you can usually fix it simply by replacing the washer. First, shut off the water running to the faucet; then remove the handle. The handle is held onto the stem by a screw, but the screw may be covered with a decorative plate. The plate may be held on by a knurled collar, which must be twisted off, or by friction, in which case it can be pried off with a small screwdriver. At any rate, unscrew the screw holding the handle and lift off the handle. Now unscrew the bonnet from the body of the faucet, using an adjustable wrench, and slide it off the stem. Now you can unscrew the stem completely from the faucet. You may find it easier to put the handle back on the stem to rotate it out of the faucet. You can now get at the washer on the end of the stem.

WARNING: Many people have gouged their hands with screwdrivers while trying to remove the screw at the end of, the stem. If you hold the stem in one hand and apply a screwdriver with the other, there is a tendency to push the hands toward each other as you turn the screw. If for any reason the screwdriver slips, it moves very rapidly toward the hand holding the valve stem. To prevent this, do not use pressure as you turn this screw. Better still, put the stem in a vise instead of holding it in your hand.

After you remove the washer, replace it with a new one of the same size. You can buy an assortment of washers of different sizes very inexpensively, but most of them won't fit. It's better to find the size you need and buy some of that size only. Replace the screw holding the new washer, again being careful not to gouge your hand with the screwdriver. Before putting the stem back into the faucet, look at the valve seat and feel it with your finger. It should be smooth. If it has rough edges or if there are particles of grit on it, the new washer will

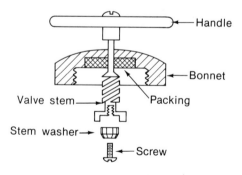

FIGURE 4–3. Parts of Faucet.

soon be chewed up. You can buy a very inexpensive seat-dressing tool to smooth a rough valve seat. Let the hardware dealer show you how to work it. It will save replacing a lot of washers.

If the faucet leaks at the top of the bonnet either when it is open or shut, the packing in the bonnet is worn. With the faucet apart, dig out the old packing from the bonnet with a screwdriver, and install new packing. Packing material looks like heavy string impregnated with graphite. Wind it around the stem until it fills the bonnet cavity. It is usually held in place with a packing nut. Some faucets use a plastic ring as the packing material, and plastic rings may be available as a replacement for the old packing on older faucets. If you need new packing, take the bonnet with you when you visit the hardware dealer and let him tell you what to use. Don't forget to turn on the water again after the faucet is repaired.

4-5. HOW TO ADD A FAUCET

If you need an extra faucet, for a washing machine for example, it is very simple to add a *saddle type* of faucet to an existing iron or copper pipe. This type of faucet is available in a kit, containing all needed parts and complete instructions. It is not necessary to disconnect any pipes to install the new faucet. First make sure that the pipe is smooth and clean. Then strap the saddle faucet to the pipe, as shown in Fig. 4-4. The two bolts in the bracket are tightened until the faucet is firmly in place. The point of contact between the faucet and the pipe is a rubber washer, which prevents leaks. After the faucet is in place, shut off the water in the pipe. Then remove the bonnet and the valve stem. Insert a drilling guide that comes with the kit and run a ¼-inch drill through the wall of the pipe, being careful not to drill into the other side. Remove the drilling guide and blow out the chips of metal, but protect your eyes as you do so. Put back the stem and screw on the bonnet, and the job is complete. Turn the water on again, and open the new faucet to flush out any metal chips remaining in the pipe. This type of faucet may be mounted in any convenient position on either a horizontal or vertical pipe.

4-6. TYPES OF PIPE

The pipe shown in Fig. 4-2 is usually made of iron or steel and is joined with threaded fittings or joints. Although it is easily cut with a hacksaw, the homeowner rarely has occasions to do anything to this type of pipe except screw in new sections or seal holes, as indicated in Section 4–3. If new pipe is needed, it can be bought cut to length and already threaded. Fittings are available in a variety of shapes, including elbows, tees, 45-degree bends, and others.

If it is necessary to add a water pipe to your plumbing to bring water to a new fixture, for example, it is not difficult to replace an existing elbow or joint with a tee and screw the new pipe in the third arm of the tee. Any new pipe must be properly supported by brackets so that there is no strain at the joints.

Copper pipe or tubing is frequently used for new water lines because it is easy to handle, can be bent around obstacles, and requires only a few tools for installation. The tubing is cut to length with a fine-toothed hacksaw or an inexpensive tubing cutter. It is soldered to fittings with a propane torch. If you are going to add extensive plumbing to your home, you should use copper tubing rather than iron water pipes. Although copper is more expensive, it will outlast iron. Also, if water in copper tubing freezes, it is not as likely to rupture the pipe, since copper is a softer metal and can be stretched slightly without damage.

Soldering copper pipe is relatively simple, even if you've never soldered anything before. A typical connection of three pipes in a tee is shown in Fig. 4–5. The ends of the pieces of tubing are polished with steel wool before inserting them in the junction. (In the figure, a tee is shown, but there are a variety of other fittings or junctions, including an adaptor to connect copper tubing to existing iron pipe.) The inside of the junction should also be cleaned with steel wool. After the parts are cleaned, the polished end of each piece of tubing is

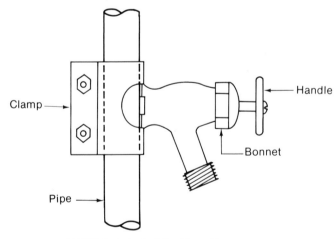

FIGURE 4–4. Saddle-Type Faucet.

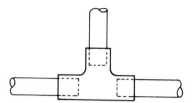

FIGURE 4–5. Junction in Copper Tubing.

coated with soldering paste, and the pipes are then inserted in the junction. Heat is applied to the fitting by directing the flame from your propane torch to the fitting itself and not to the copper pipes. As the fitting gets hot, heat is conducted to the pipes, and they soon get hot enough to melt solder. The flame is never directed at the solder or the tubing but is kept on the junction during the whole operation. The solder comes in a roll and looks like stiff wire. A convenient length, perhaps 6 or 8 inches, is unrolled from the reel, and with the reel in the hand that is not holding the torch, the end of the solder is applied at the points where the tubing enters the fitting, as indicated by the arrows in Fig. 4–5. As the solder melts, it is drawn into the junction by capillary action. Each solder joint should use about 1 inch of the wire solder. As soon as enough solder has been sucked in to surround the pipe completely, remove the torch and wipe away any excess solder on the outside of the joint with a heavy cloth while the solder is still molten.

The cost of a propane torch is not justified if you need to make only one or two connections, but for an extensive installation the cost of the torch is a very small part of the total cost of the job and can be considered part of the cost of materials. Even though you may never have another plumbing job, you will find other uses for the torch. It can be used for removing paint, defrosting frozen pipes, heating metal for bending, starting charcoal fires, and as a cookstove when camping.

The drainage system in a home is made up of pipes and traps from each fixture, which empty into a large pipe, which then carries the waste to the sewer or septic tank. The pipes from the sinks and the traps are usually made of chrome-plated brass. Coupling between sections is accomplished with large nuts, which can be loosened or tightened with a large adjustable wrench or a Stillson wrench. If you use a Stillson wrench, you should protect the chrome surfaces from the serrated jaws by padding the jaws with a few layers of cloth. The pipes themselves do not rotate, only the nuts need be turned to disassemble or assemble these pipes. The large pipe which receives the waste from sinks, tubs, showers, and other similar fixtures is called a *waste pipe*. The pipe that receives discharge from toilets is called a *soil pipe*. Both are usually made of cast iron and require special fittings. Repairing cast-iron pipe is a job for a professional plumber.

A recent development is plastic pipe, available in many different sizes, for use both for water pipes and for drains, including replacement for the large cast-iron waste pipes. Plastic pipes have not been approved by all building codes, but as of this writing, they are acceptable for use in bringing water to the house, for sprinklers, and for drainage systems in many large cities in western United States.

Plastic pipe is so simple to use with a minimum of tools that homeowners can do all their own plumbing jobs wherever it is permitted. The pipe is flexible so that it can be bent around obstructions. It is light enough for one person to handle. As a contrast, cast-iron soil pipe weighs about 10 pounds per foot of length, whereas the equivalent plastic pipe weighs less than 1½ pounds per foot.

Plastic pipe cannot be used for hot-water lines as yet, because the material may deteriorate at hot-water temperatures. Improved plastics for hot-water use are being developed, and eventually plastic will be available for all plumbing.

Sections of plastic pipe are easily joined by slipping the end of each pipe over a serrated coupling section and tightening the connection with an ordinary hose clamp. Only a screwdriver is needed to make the connection. Special tees, elbows, and other fittings are available, and the pipe can be attached to them in the same manner or cemented in place. Adaptors are also available for attaching plastic pipe to metal pipe. To cut plastic pipe, you need only a hacksaw. If the edges are burred, you can smooth them with sandpaper, a file, or even a paring knife. If you wish to cement the pipe to a fitting, an applicator comes with the special cement; so you don't need any other tools.

One big advantage of plastic pipe is that it is not damaged by freezing. It simply expands with the ice. Thus it can be used for a sprinkler system for your lawn, buried only a few inches below the surface. When it freezes in winter, you can ignore it. In the spring after it thaws, it will be as good as new.

There are many different plastic materials used for pipe, and each has its own advantages and disadvantages. A few are listed here:

Polyethylene is the cheapest and is available in rolls up to 400 feet long. It is most useful for bringing water into the house. A single length can be run from the water meter to the house inlet; it will require then only two fittings, one at each end.

Poly(vinyl chloride) (PVC) is slightly more expensive and is ideally suited for sprinkler systems and for carrying drinking water. It is available in rigid lengths up to 10 feet long.

Acrylonitrite butadiene styrene (ABS) is a lightweight, almost frictionless pipe especially adapted for waste removal to replace the common cast-iron waste or soil pipe. It is available in 10-foot lengths, with diameters ranging from about 1½ to 4 inches.

Styrene pipe has thin walls and is available in 10-foot lengths of 3 or 4 inches diameter for special drainage applications.

If plastic pipe is permitted by your building code, you can plan on using it for new or replacement applications in your home. For most cold-water pipes in the home, choose PVC. Let your hardware dealer show you the many connectors and adaptors for use with this plastic. You can even use small lengths of PVC to replace sections of broken steel or copper pipe. For large waste drains you can install ABS tubing yourself. If it is a replacement for a damaged soil pipe, the hardest part of the job will be the removal of the heavy cast-iron pipe. New installations must be approved by your local plumbing inspector, so you should submit plans to him before you start work. Dealers who sell ABS pipe can supply you with the necessary information as well as directions for installing ABS drains, pipes, and vents.

4-7. NOISY PLUMBING

Plumbing is supposed to be relatively quiet. If your plumbing system bangs or hammers when you shut off a faucet or chatters or whistles when you turn one on, it is not in normal condition and should be corrected. Although such noises do not signal a dangerous situation, they are annoying and should be eliminated, since the situation causing the noise can only get worse.

Chattering or whistling that occurs when a faucet is first opened or just before the last turn of closing may be caused by a worn washer in the faucet, worn packing, or a damaged valve seat. Check the washer first. If it is loose, tighten the screw holding it. If it is worn, replace it. If the washer is not at fault and the valve seat seems all right, replace the packing. You can check the valve seat by running your finger over it. It should feel smooth to the touch with no burrs or metal chips in it.

A banging or hammering sound in the pipes *when a faucet is closed quickly* is called *water hammer*. It is caused by the sudden stopping of the flow of water. Since water is incompressible, the energy of its forward motion bangs back and forth in the pipe until the

vibrations die down.   Sometimes this noise is accentuated by loosely
mounted pipe, which is set in motion by the water vibrations and then
bangs against the beams.   As a first step make sure that each pipe is
rigidly mounted.   Tighten supporting braces along its length and at
corners.   Iron water pipe should be supported by braces spaced no
more than 6 feet apart.   Copper pipes need somewhat less support.
It is interesting to note that water hammer rarely occurs in plastic pipe,
since the plastic can expand and absorb the shock.

   If all else fails, you should consider adding an air cushion to your
system to absorb the energy of the stopped flow of water.   Two con-
figurations are shown in Fig. 4–6.   In each configuration a tee is placed
in the line to the faucet and a sealed pipe is added to the third arm of
the tee.   The third arm contains air, but since the pipe is sealed, the
air cannot escape.   When the faucet is closed, the energy in the motion
of water pushes some water into the air chamber, where the air com-
presses and absorbs the shock.   The air chamber should be placed
close to the noisy faucet to be most effective, but it will work anywhere in the water line.

   In most new plumbing systems, air cushions are installed in the
system when the house is first built.   If your plumbing was quiet and
has now developed a noise, an existing air cushion might be full of
water because of a faulty seal at the end.   If this happens, drain the
water from the pipe and apply sealing compound to the cap on the end
of the air pipe.   In Fig. 4–6, notice that the air cushion can be below
the faucet, as at the left, or above it, as at the right.   If the air chamber
is *above* the faucet, it is easily drained by opening the faucet after the

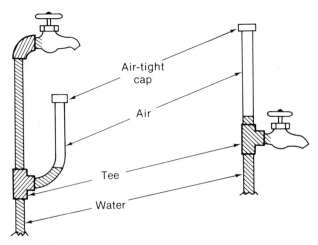

FIGURE 4–6. Air Cushion to Eliminate Water Hammer.

water is shut off. To drain the air cushion at the left, it is necessary to open a faucet at a lower level. After the pipe is drained and resealed, the water can be turned on again. If all this sounds like too much work, you can prevent water hammer by shutting off faucets *slowly.*

Pounding, creaking, and rumbling noises can occur in hot-water pipes from water that is too hot. Water should never be at a temperature above 140°F. Noises in hot-water pipes may indicate that the temperature exceeds this level, and the hot-water heater should be checked. Creaking can also be caused by hot-water pipes expanding as hot water replaces cold inside the pipes. As they expand, they may rub against the beams. If you can locate the point of rubbing, you can eliminate the noise by inserting a piece of heat-resistant material, such as asbestos, between the pipe and the beam.

A humming noise when water is flowing in pipes is usually caused by the pipes being tightly fastened to the wooden structures of the house. The hum should normally be barely discernible, but when the pipes are in close contact with the beams, the wood acts like a sounding board to magnify the noise. To loosen the pipes would only cause other noises due to vibration, but the hum can be minimized by inserting bits of foam rubber, sponge, or scraps of a soft material like felt at points where the pipe comes in contact with the wood.

4-8. TRAPS AND VENTS

The drainage system in your home empties directly into a sewer or septic tank. Drain pipes from sinks, showers, and the like (*waste pipes*) and those from toilets (*soil pipes*) are positioned so that all waste flows to the sewer by gravity. An important consideration in the design of a plumbing system is provision for preventing sewer gases from entering the house through the same pipes that carry the waste to the sewer. Sewer gases have an offensive odor and, when under pressure, are explosive. What is needed is some sort of valve which will permit water and wastes to flow unhindered toward the sewer but which will not allow gases to flow from the sewer back into the house. There is such a device, and it is extremely simple. It is called a *trap.*

A trap is simply a U-shaped section of pipe which is filled with water in normal use, as shown in Fig. 4-7. As water flows from the sink into the trap, it raises the water level above the height of the output pipe. Thus, water flows out to the waste pipe as fast as water flows into the trap, but the trap remains full of water, as shown. Any gases coming from the waste pipe are prevented from entering by this

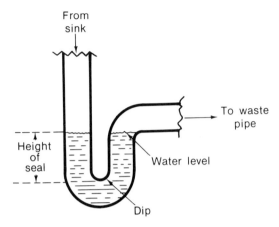

FIGURE 4–7. Trap.

water seal in the trap. The output pipe of the trap may extend horizontally through the wall to a waste pipe or may curve again and pass
straight down to a waste pipe below the floor. Note that as long as
the water level in the trap is above the *dip*—that is, the bottom of the
inside curve of the U—the trap is an effective seal, but if the water
level sinks below this point, gases can pass through the trap.

A toilet also has a water seal or trap which operates on much the
same principle. The cross section of a toilet, showing this water seal,
is illustrated in Fig. 4–8. Again, as long as the water level is above the
dip, gases are prevented from entering.

A trap is necessary in the drainage line from every sink, tub,
shower, or other water fixture. It is also needed in any drain that
empties into a waste line, such as a drain in the floor of a garage or
basement.

Although the trap solves the problem of keeping sewer gases out
of the house, any gas in the pipe between a trap and the sewer is a
potential hazard because of the danger of explosion. To solve this, the
drainage system must be *vented* so that the dangerous gases in the
pipe can be exhausted harmlessly into the atmosphere. A vented
plumbing system is shown in Fig. 4–9. The main vent pipe is usually
a large cast-iron pipe extending from the soil pipe at the lowest level
up through the roof of the house. The dangerous sewer gases are
lighter than air, and, therefore, they pass right up this pipe into the
atmosphere. They are prevented from entering the house through any
drain line by traps in every line. A separate auxiliary vent pipe is used
on each fixture, as shown in the figure. Otherwise, the seal in a lower-
level trap might be broken by siphoning when a toilet is flushed at a

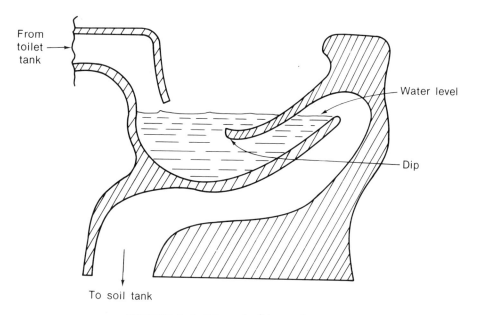

From toilet tank →

Water level

Dip

To soil tank

FIGURE 4-8. Water Seal in Toilet.

higher level. This can be explained by imagining that the toilet and sink in Fig. 4-9 both feed into the main vent pipe and that there is no auxiliary pipe. Now, when the toilet is flushed, a large amount of water rushes down this main vent past the point where the sink trap joins the pipe. The rush of water creates a suction which draws the water out of the trap in the sink. Then the sink trap ceases to be a seal and remains in this condition until more water is poured into the drain in the sink. The auxiliary vent pipe prevents the siphoning created by the large flow of water from the flushed toilet.

Your own plumbing system should have been vented properly when it was installed. However, if you are going to install extra fixtures anywhere in the house, it is important to make sure that they are vented as required by your local plumbing code. The dealer who sells you the fixture can explain what is required in the way of venting and can be helpful in planning the layout. If the new fixture is on the ground floor, the drain should empty into a waste pipe or soil pipe. On an upper floor, the drain can be attached to the large vent pipe that goes through the roof. In either case, additional venting is required and can be achieved by tapping into an auxiliary vent pipe. This means that your new fixture should be near an existing vent pipe. If not, you will have to add a vent pipe, which means a combination of plumbing work, roofing work, and carpentry. You will save yourself much work

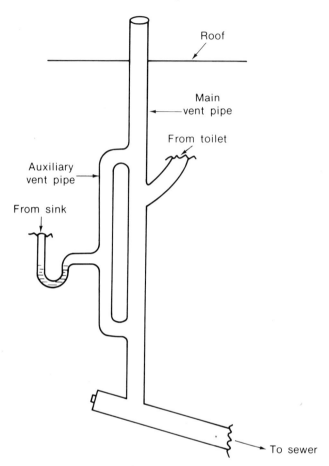

FIGURE 4–9. Vented Plumbing System.

and money if you plan your new fixture close to a vent pipe. You can determine the location of vents simply by looking at your roof and seeing where they protrude.

4–9. CLOGGED PLUMBING

All the drains in the house empty into a large waste pipe or soil pipe. The fixtures on upper floors are always close to a vertical stack pipe which runs from the large waste pipe at the lowest level up through the roof. The waste pipe is usually in the basement or under the house, and it slopes toward the sewer. When there is a stoppage in the drain system, to a certain extent your repair procedure will depend upon where the stoppage is located, and your first step is to d .termine the location of the fault.

If a single sink is blocked, and all other fixtures drain properly, the fault must be in the sink drain. On the other hand, if water empty-ing from one fixture backs up into another, the drains of both fixtures are probably all right, but the blockage must be located in a pipe into which both of these drains empty. On an upper floor of the house, because of the short runs between each fixture and the vertical stack, you will be able to locate the blockage easily. The vertical stack rarely gets clogged. If two fixtures on an upper floor empty into the same short drain to the vertical stack, and if water from one backs up in the other, the blockage is in that short length of pipe to the stack. On the first floor where fixtures empty directly into the waste pipe, a blockage in the waste pipe can affect all the drains that precede the blockage. You can determine the approximate location of the block-age by noticing which fixtures are clogged and which flow freely. The blockage in the waste pipe must be between the last fixture that is clogged and the first that is free.

Stoppages are caused by foreign matter in the drain. In bathroom sinks and tubs the most common cause of a blockage is hair in the drain. Lint and soap are also offenders. In kitchen sinks, cold grease is the most common cause of a stoppage, but food particles of all sorts are also frequent sources of trouble. In toilets, too large a wad of pa-per or other foreign matter can cause a blockage, as can soap, a comb, a toothbrush, or anything else that is dropped in accidently.

Unless something large such as a dishrag or a comb is dropped into a drain, stoppages do not occur suddenly. You will notice first that water is not flowing out of a drain as fast as it should. This is a sign that a blockage is developing. When food or other matter par-tially blocks a drain, it slows the water running out, but also other particles of food or lint catch on the partial blockage and further re-strict the flow of water, until eventually there is complete stoppage. It is easier to correct a partial blockage than a complete stoppage, so be alert to the possibility and take corrective action when you first notice a drain emptying too slowly.

When you first notice a slowdown in the drain, check for lint or hair in the path of the water. In bathroom sinks that have a stopper actuated by a metal handle near the faucets, hair frequently catches on the stopper and obstructs the flow of water. Pull out the stopper and remove hair and other dirt from it. In most sinks the stopper can be removed by rotating it counterclockwise. Just cleaning the stopper will frequently cure the trouble. Hair on the stopper also may prevent the stopper from sealing the opening completely, so that water leaks out of the sink when the stopper should be closed. Removing the hair will cure this condition, also.

If removing obvious hair or lint at the entrance to the drain does not cure the trouble, your next step should be to try to force the obstruction through the drain into the larger stack or waste pipe by using the old plumber's helper, the force cup or plunger, shown in Fig. 2–32. The cup of the plunger is placed over the drain opening, as shown in Fig. 4–10. If the sink has an overflow pipe as shown in this figure, the opening of the overflow must be stopped up by stuffing a towel or face cloth into it. This will cause the force of the plunger to be directed into the drain instead of out the overflow. The water level in the sink should be at least 1 inch above the bottom of the plunger. If there is only a partial stoppage in the sink, fill the sink nearly full so that some water will remain while you use the plunger. Now press the plunger up and down several times. The down strokes will exert pressure on the blockage to force it toward the main drain. The up strokes will tend to pull any loose dirt out of the drain up into the sink. Don't give up too soon. It may take a dozen attempts before the plunger clears the drain.

For a partial blockage, you can also try a caustic drain cleaner. This

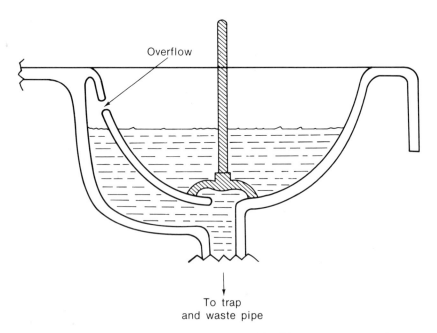

Overflow

To trap
and waste pipe

FIGURE 4–10. How to Use Plunger.

is available in most supermarkets. *Before using it, read the instructions on the can.* These drain cleaners can be dangerous if used incorrectly. WARNING: Despite manufacturer's recommendations, you should *not* use a caustic cleaner to try to clear a drain that is completely blocked. These cleaners work on hair, soap, or food particles, but if the drain is clogged from a dishrag, for example, the caustic cleaner may not work, and then you will have a pipe full of a dangerous chemical. For most partial blockages, these cleaners clear the debris. After using a caustic cleaner, run cold water through the cleared drain to clean out the chemical. WARNING: Do *not* use a caustic cleaner in a kitchen sink equipped with a garbage disposer. The chemical can injure the disposer.

If the blockage cannot be cleared with a plunger or chemical, it will be necessary to use a special tool called a pipe *auger* or *plumber's snake*. The snake is a long flexible steel cable which can be inserted into a drain or other opening and can be made to pass through curved pipe to the obstruction. A handle on one end is rotated and causes the tip inside the pipe to rotate. Various tips are used. A serrated tip will cut through a grease plug, breaking it into small particles which can be washed down the drain. A hook can be used to snare a dishrag and pull it out.

It is possible to insert the snake into the drain and push it into and through the trap until it hits the obstruction. It is easier, however, to remove the trap and insert the snake into the drain pipe leading into the wall or floor, as shown in Fig. 4–11. To remove the trap, it is only necessary to unscrew two floating nuts, one on each side of the U-shaped trap, and then to pull gently on the U until it comes off. Since the trap is full of water and the drain to the sink above it is also full of water, you should put a pail or dishpan under the trap before you remove it. When you have removed the trap, check to see that it is clear, and if necessary, clean it. It may be that a trap blocked with grease is the cause of the stoppage. If the trap is clear, insert the snake in the pipe, as shown in Fig. 4–11, and rotate the handle, pushing the snake into the pipe as you do so. When you feel the blockage, keep rotating the handle. If the blockage is caused by food particles or grease, the tip of the snake will break it up. If the obstruction is a rag, the tip will snag it. Now you can pull out the snake with the rag attached. As you withdraw the snake, continue rotating it, in the same direction as you turned it when you inserted it. If you turn it in the opposite direction, it may be unhooked from the cloth you are trying to pull out. After clearing the drain, put back the trap, making sure that the washers inside the nuts are properly replaced.

If a drain leaks at one of the nuts, it is almost certainly a defective washer. Simply replace it. You will have to specify the size of pipe in the drain when buying a new washer, or simply take the nut along with you and get a washer that fits into it.

If a toilet is clogged from too much paper or a piece of cloth, the obstruction can frequently be pushed through with a plunger. Again, don't give up too soon. After the obstruction is apparently cleared, you should check the toilet by dropping a length of toilet paper about 5 feet long into it and flushing the toilet. If the paper goes through, the obstruction is cleared, but if it blocks again, the obstruction is probably a toothbrush or comb that was dropped in accidently. You can try to pull it out with a hook on the end of a snake, but it is difficult. If you can't remove an object like a comb dropped in the toilet bowl, you will have to call a plumber. He will remove the bowl from the floor, empty it, and put it back in place. This is too complicated a job for the home repairman.

If the obstruction is in a main drain, you can clear it with a snake. Every large waste pipe in the home should have a clean-out plug, as shown in Fig. 4-12. The plug has a hexagonal head and can be removed with a Stillson wrench or an adjustable wrench. Slide the snake into the opening and along the pipe until you hit the obstruction, and operate as described above. When the pipe is clear, flush it with clean water to wash all particles of dirt out of the system. If the flow of water is slow but not stopped, you can add a chemical cleaner. Heed the precautions listed on the can.

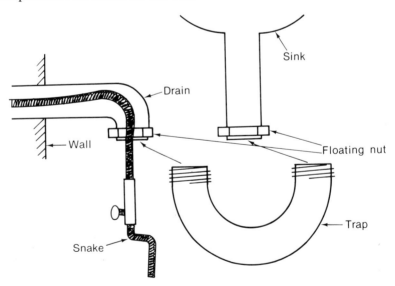

FIGURE 4-11. How to Use Snake.

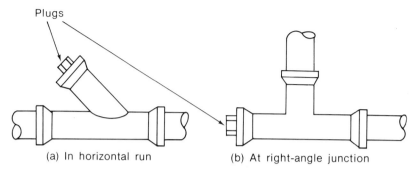

Plugs

(a) In horizontal run (b) At right-angle junction

FIGURE 4–12. Clean-Out Plugs.

For most jobs a 15-foot snake will clear the obstruction. Longer snakes up to 50 feet are available, as well as electrically operated ones. These can be rented as needed and should not be purchased, since they will be used rarely.

4-10. TOILET TANKS

There are two separate mechanisms in a flush tank, one for emptying the water and the second for filling. When the handle on the tank is turned, water rushes out of the tank into the toilet by gravity, causing the toilet to be flushed. As soon as the water starts to run out of the tank, the filling mechanism starts to operate, but the water is rushing out faster than the water coming in. When the tank is nearly empty, the opening to the outlet closes, and the tank soon fills. The valve controlling the incoming water is closed when the tank is filled.

The mechanism to empty the tank and flush the toilet is shown in Fig. 4–13. The water level in the tank is normally about 1 inch below the top of the overflow tube. When the handle is turned to flush the toilet, the right-hand end of the *trip lever* is raised and pulls up on the *linkage wire*. This in turn catches the loop at the top of the *lift rod* and thus raises the *flush ball*, which closes the opening to the toilet. With the flush ball raised, water rushes through the opening into the toilet. It is not necessary to hold the handle until all the water rushes out, because the buoyancy of the flush ball keeps it raised as long as there is water above the level of the opening. When most of the water has left the tank, the flush ball falls back into the *seat*, closing the opening to the toilet pipe. The pressure of the water in the tank holds the ball on the seat despite its buoyancy, but once the ball is lifted it stays up as long as there is water to hold it. If when the tank is refilled the water does not shut off, the water level will rise to the top of the overflow tube and any excess will flow down this tube, under the flush ball, and into the toilet.

The mechanism for refilling the tank is shown in Fig. 4–14. The water entering from the pipe below the tank is stopped by a washer on a *plunger* that blocks the pipe completely, like the washer at the end of the valve stem in a faucet. Notice that if the *float* is lowered, the plunger is raised. This is what happens when the toilet is flushed. The float rests on top of the water. As the water rushes out of the tank, the float falls, raising the plunger. Water is now permitted to flow past the valve and comes out of the *filler tube* and out of the *refill tube*. The water enters much more slowly than the water rushing out, so that the tank soon empties. When the flush ball in Fig. 4–13 closes the opening, water no longer rushes out, and the water entering through the filler tube soon fills up the tank. As the tank fills, the float rises, and the plunger moves downward to close off the water supply. When the float is high enough, the water supply is completely shut off.

The action of the water flushing the toilet is vigorous and may force too much water from the trap in the toilet, so that there is no longer a good seal against sewer gases. To prevent this, it is necessary to add more water to the toilet after the flushing is over. This is done by the refill tube, shown in Fig. 4–14, which is directed into the overflow tube

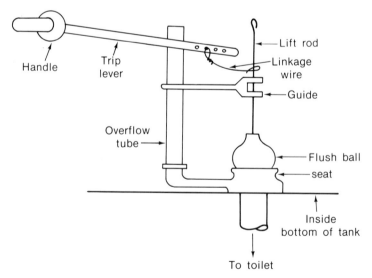

FIGURE 4–13. Flushing Mechanism.

shown in Fig. 4-13. Thus, after the flush ball has closed off the opening to the toilet, water enters the tank from the filler tube, and at the same time water enters the toilet from the refill tube, by way of the overflow tube. When the float is high enough, both are shut off.

4-11. TOILET-TANK REPAIRS

Most of the troubles in a toilet tank are easy to correct and well within the capabilities of the homeowner. Usually you can tell what the difficulty is just from looking into the tank, but if you have a clear understanding of the operation of the flushing and refill mechanisms, you can probably figure out the repair procedure just from the symptoms.

Suppose that you turn the handle and nothing happens. That is, the toilet does not flush. One possibility is that the tank is empty. Lift up the top and look into the tank. Be careful not to drop in any small objects that were placed on top of the tank. If there is no water

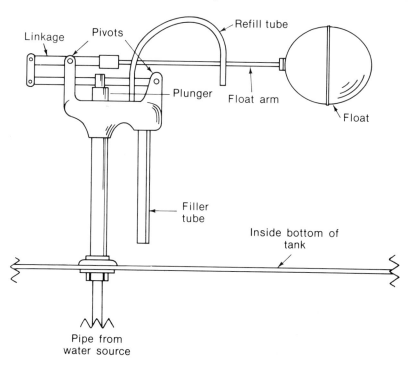

FIGURE 4-14. Refill Mechanism.

in the tank, someone probably turned off the control valve on the pipe under the tank and forgot to turn it on again. This valve should be turned all the way counterclockwise to permit water to flow. If the tank *is* full of water, the trouble is in the flushing mechanism. Refer again to Fig. 4–13. The trip lever may be broken, the linkage wire may have come loose, or the loop on top of the lift rod may have rusted off. In any of these cases, turning the handle will not lift the flush ball, and thus the toilet won't flush. All these parts are available separately at any hardware or plumbing store. As an emergency measure, if you can't get to a hardware store immediately, tie a string to the lift rod and let it hang over the edge of the tank, with the top off. To flush, simply pull up on the string. If the linkage wire is broken, you can *make* another from a piece of stiff wire.

If the toilet continues to run at the end of the flush, the flush ball may not be reseating. This will happen if the lift rod is bent so that it doesn't slide freely in the guide, or if the guide has slipped on the overflow tube so that the ball is no longer directly over the opening in the seat. The ball itself may be eroded by minerals in the water, so that even if it is seated correctly the pits and bumps on the ball prevent a good seal and allow water to continue to leak into the toilet. If the linkage wire is bent or if the ball is eroded, it is best to replace the ball with a new "flapper" type of flush ball. This takes the place of the flush ball, guide, linkage wire, and lift rod. It is very simple to install with full directions on the package and is available at most hardware stores. The guide should be loosened on the overflow tube and slipped off and discarded. The new flapper ball has a rubber ring connected to it which slides down over the overflow tube, and a chain connects the ball to the trip lever.

If the flush ball develops a leak so that it loses its buoyancy, you will have to hold the handle down to the end of the flush. To correct this, replace the ball with a flapper ball, as just described.

The toilet may continue to run because of a defect in the refill mechanism. This mechanism is called a *ballcock* (refer to Fig. 4–14). When the tank has refilled, the float should rise and push the plunger into its opening to stop the water from entering. A sketch of the plunger itself is shown in Fig. 4–15. This shows the plunger raised from its seat (the float in the tank would be lowered). The plunger has a packing and O-ring around it to keep water from emerging from the top. Water enters and flows to the refill and filler tubes. A leather or plastic washer on the bottom of the plunger seals the opening when the plunger is down. If there is a defect in this system so that water is not

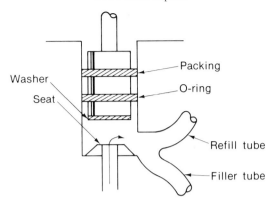

FIGURE 4–15. Plunger Detail.

shut off by the plunger, the water will rise in the tank above the overflow tube and then will flow through this tube into the toilet.

One possible defect is a worn washer on the plunger. To check this, reach into the tank and raise the float arm slightly with your fingers. If this causes the water to stop flowing, the washer is all right. If not, replace the washer. It is held in place with a brass screw which is easily removed. Take the old washer or the whole plunger with you when you buy a new one to make sure that the new washer fits correctly.

If raising the float arm stops the flow of water, the fault is in the float, the float arm, or the linkage. Check the float. It can be unscrewed from the float arm. If it has developed a leak, water will get inside it, and it won't rise enough to push down the plunger. In that case, replace the float. Newer floats are made of plastic instead of metal and last indefinitely. If the float is all right but rises to the top of the tank without shutting off the water, bend the float arm downward so that the plunger will be forced down before the float has risen to the top. Conversely, if the water shuts off too soon, filling only a small part of the tank, bend the float arm the other way to raise the water level before the plunger closes.

If a toilet has not been used for a long time, the pivots and linkage may get stiff and prevent the float arm from closing the plunger properly. You can correct this by applying one or two drops of oil on each pivot and joint, and raising and lowering the float arm a few times to work in the oil.

If a toilet tank leaks at the point where the water pipe enters the tank, the fault is usually caused by a worn gasket. With the water shut off, first flush the toilet, and then sponge out any water remaining. Grasp the ballcock (the refill mechanism) inside the tank with one hand to hold it steady, and with the other apply an adjustable wrench to the nut on the pipe under the tank. You will then be able to re-move the ballcock and replace the gasket. You can replace the whole ballcock, if you wish, in the same way. Newer ballcocks are almost completely silent in operation.

5

Climate
Control

Whether we feel cool or warm is affected by more than just the temperature of the room. *Air motion* and *humidity* are just as important as *temperature* in influencing our comfort. The heating system in your home should keep the house at the proper temperature and humidity with a minimum of air motion or drafts.

The *normal* temperature of the human body is 98.6°F (37° centigrade), and the body tries to maintain this temperature regardless of the temperature of the surroundings. When we are in motion, the body generates heat, and clothing holds this heat in, so that we feel warm even if the outside temperature is much less than 98.6°F. If it is very cold or we do not move enough voluntarily to keep our body temperature up, we start to shiver, and this involuntary motion helps generate more heat. When the surrounding temperature is too high and tends to raise our body temperature above normal, we sweat, and the evaporation of this moisture cools our bodies and helps maintain a constant temperature. If we stand in front of a fan, the flow of air increases the evaporation and thus cools us faster.

A room temperature of 70°F (21.1°C) is generally considered satisfactory, but for you to feel comfortable at this temperature, the humidity must also be correct. *Relative humidity* is the percentage of water vapor in the air compared to the amount of water vapor the air could hold if it were saturated. When the humidity is low, less than 40 percent, body moisture evaporates rapidly, and you may feel too cool even at a temperature of 80°F (26.7°C). On the other hand, when the humidity is too high, above 60 percent, body moisture cannot evaporate easily, and you feel hot and damp at temperatures below 70°F. Also, when the humidity is too high, your house itself, suffers from damp walls, and can be damaged from excess moisture in the air. With a temperature near 70°F at about 50 percent humidity, the average person would feel quite comfortable. Given sufficient money, it might be possible to design and build a climate-control system that could maintain ideal temperature and humidity conditions in every room of a house despite extremes of winter cold and summer heat. However, from a practical standpoint, we are willing to make some small sacrifices in comfort to save large amounts of money, and thus heating systems are not ideal.

Houses may be heated by coal, oil, or gas. Electricity is also used in some areas close to large hydroelectric power plants, but in most parts of the country electricity is too expensive to use for central heating. The fuel is used to heat air or water, and the heat is carried to all parts of the house by hot air, hot water, or steam. Each type of burner and heat-carrying system has its own problems.

5-1. FURNACES

Before oil burners were invented, most homes used coal furnaces. Later, in order to take advantage of the "automatic" features of oil heat, many of these coal furnaces were converted to oil by removing the grates and installing oil burners. Automatic coal-burning furnaces were also developed. In newer homes that use oil burners or gas burners, there may be no resemblance between the burner and the old-fashioned coal furnace. Nevertheless, all these burners are referred to as furnaces whether they burn oil, coal, or gas.

An automatic furnace of any type is controlled by a *thermostat* which is a temperature-controlled switch, usually located in or near the living room in your home. It has a small lever to set the desired temperature. When the temperature in the room drops slightly below this temperature, the thermostat closes, turning on the furnace. When the room temperature is slightly higher than the setting, the thermostat opens, shutting off the burner. If the thermostat is dirty or worn, it will not operate correctly.

To check a thermostat, remove the cover. If there is dirt inside, use a vacuum cleaner to clean it out. Dirt can get in between the contacts and prevent the thermostat from turning on the furnace. When the thermostat is clean, check its operation by moving the control lever over a wide range. You should hear a click as the thermostat makes and breaks contact. Make sure that the wires running to the furnace are firmly attached to their mounting screws. If the thermostat seems defective, unscrew these wires and bring them together. If the furnace starts when the wires are brought together but will not operate otherwise, you need a new thermostat. Remove the old one and ask your hardware dealer for a replacement.

Too much dirt in a thermostat can also cause the contacts to stick together when they should separate. In this case, the furnace continues to run after the room has reached its proper temperature, and soon the house gets too hot. The thermostat should be cleaned with a vacuum cleaner at least once a year to prevent this. Sticky contacts can be cleaned by pulling a piece of fine sandpaper between them. Do not use emery paper.

Before you assume something is wrong with your furnace, make sure that the main switch is turned on. Too often a homeowner has called a repairman for his furnace only to discover that the only "trouble" was failure to turn on the main switch after turning if off for maintenance.

If the room in which the thermostat is located reaches its preset temperature before other rooms are sufficiently warm, the thermostat will open, shutting off the furnace. Outer rooms will be too cool for comfort. A possible solution is to locate the thermostat in an outer room, but if you do this, it will not solve the problem of different temperatures in different rooms. The outer rooms will reach the desired temperature, but the room where the thermostat was will be much warmer. You can accomplish the same thing by simply moving the lever on the thermostat to a higher setting. It is almost impossible to *balance* radiators so that all rooms reach the same temperature at the same time. Some hot-water systems have special valves on radiators which can be adjusted to control the heat, and air ducts in hot-air systems can be partially closed, but any adjustment in one room affects the heat in all others. Some trial-and-error experimenting will be necessary, but *moving the thermostat will not solve the problem.*

Gas as a fuel has many advantages over coal or oil. Gas requires no storage tank, whereas with the other fuels you will need a coal bin or an oil tank, either of which takes up space which can be used for other purposes. A gas flame produces much less soot and smoke than either oil or coal and thus is "cleaner." However, in most locations gas is more expensive than either of the other two fuels and may be prohibitively high in extremely cold climates.

Gas burners require almost no attention. When the burner is operating properly, air mixes with gas in a predetermined ratio and the mixture burns with a blue flame which has a bit of yellow at the tip. If there is no yellow, there is not enough air mixing with the gas, whereas too much yellow indicates that too much air is getting in. If the flame is not correct, look for the air-intake shutter and adjust it until a small tip of yellow appears in the blue flame.

As long as the gas burner shows a proper flame, you can forget about it. However, breakdowns usually occur on the coldest day of winter, and it is better to anticipate and prevent trouble rather than to repair a fault later. Thus, you should have your gas burner checked periodically by your local gas company or a reliable gas-burner repairman. If this is done every three years, your burner should give you many years of service. Your repairman will clean the burner, adjust the flame, and look for defective parts. Watch him do it the first time, and you may decide that you can do it yourself later, since it is not a difficult job.

If a gas burner will not work at all, first check to see if the pilot is lit. *Do not smoke while working on a gas burner.* If the pilot is out, it may have been blown out by a strong gust of wind or the gas may have been shut off because of some civil emergency. Before trying to relight the pilot, make sure there is no odor of gas. It is dangerous to light a match if there is gas in the room. The proper procedure is to shut off the gas in the line to the pilot. You will find a valve in the line with a straight handle on it. When this handle is parallel to the gas pipe, the line is open. Close it by turning this handle so that it is perpendicular to the pipe. Now wait about half an hour so that any gas which may have leaked into the room can dissipate. Open the valve again and allow about 15 or 20 seconds for the gas to get to the pilot. Light a match, and, holding it with a pair of pliers, apply it to the tip of the pilot. On some burners there is a red safety button which must be pushed, and there should be a tag indicating the proper procedure to relight the pilot. Look for this tag and follow the instructions. Relighting the pilot should solve the immediate problem, but you should also look for the cause of the shutdown. If the pilot is located in a drafty place, you should shield if from drafts. If the pilot light is too small, you can increase the amount of gas reaching it by adjusting a small screw in the line. The flame should be about 1 inch long at the tip of the opening.

If the pilot light is lit and the thermostat is in working order, and the furnace still won't operate, the trouble is probably due to a defective *thermocouple.* This is a device which generates a voltage when it is heated, and this voltage is applied to open an electrically operated valve which allows gas to get to the main burner. With a little care you can replace a thermocouple yourself. The two wires to the valve are attached to screws. Loosen these screws and disconnect the wires. The thermocouple attached to these wires is usually screwed in place with a hexagonal screw or nut. Use an adjustable wrench to loosen it. Replace the unit with a duplicate thermocouple, obtainable in many plumbing shops or service outlets.

Not much can happen to a coal furnace to keep it from operating, but soot can reduce its efficiency. When the furnace is shut down for the summer, it should be throughly cleaned. Besides wasting heat, soot combines with water vapor in the air to form corrosive acids, which can damage the metal parts of the furnace. To clean the furnace, first close all dampers and drafts so that wind blowing down the chimney will not blow loose soot out of the furnace. Use a stiff wire brush to scrape soot off of all surfaces exposed to the fire. Then remove the loose soot with a vacuum cleaner with a long hose attachment.

Soot and ashes must be removed from smoke pipes, ash pit, and ash cleanout chambers. The pipe may be taken apart and each section cleaned separately. Water and soap or detergent can be used to make the job easier. Before dismantling the smoke pipe, label each section so that you will be able to reassemble the sections in the correct order. When the pipe is reassembled, make sure there are no leaks. Leaks in smoke pipe can be sealed with ordinary asbestos cement applied with a putty knife, trowel, or an old kitchen spatula.

Grates in a coal-burning furnace can be coated with ordinary motor oil during the off-season to keep them from rusting. Door hinges should also be oiled. When you refire the furnace in the fall, this oil will burn off harmlessly.

Oil burners should also be cleaned every year in the off-season. Soot should be removed in the same manner as described above for coal furnaces. All surfaces which may rust should be coated with motor oil or household lubricating oil. This oil will burn off when the burner is put back in service in the fall. Shut off the main switch to the burner during the summer, but don't forget to turn it on again when you start the furnace in the fall.

The fuel tank for your oil burner should be filled for the summer to prevent water vapor from causing rust. If the tank is left empty or partially full, water vapor in the air trapped in the tank may condense and cause leaks due to rusting. If a tank develops a leak, you can make a temporary repair, as shown in Fig. 5–1, using a toggle bolt assembly obtainable in most hardware stores. The unit contains a toggle bolt, rubber gasket brass washer, and nut, mounted on a threaded rod, shown in Fig. 5–1(a). The toggle bolt is pushed into the

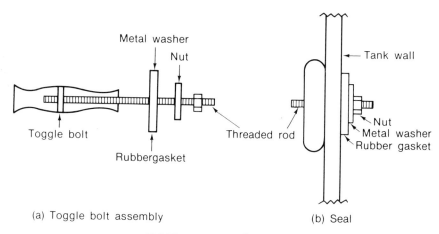

(a) Toggle bolt assembly   (b) Seal

FIGURE 5–1. Tank Repair.

tank through the hole in the wall. You may have to enlarge the hole
to do this. Then the nut is tightened on the outside, squeezing the
rubber gasket against the side of the tank, as shown in Fig. 5–1(b).
This makes a good seal. However, any seal of a leak in a tank should
be considered *temporary*, since if a leak occurs in one place, there are
probably other weak spots which will develop into leaks later. In
an emergency, you can close a pinhole leak with ordinary chewing
gum.

    If the oil burner fails to operate, first, make sure there is fuel in the
tank. Don't rely on the gauge on the tank, but remove the cover and
push a long stick inside to see if there is really fuel there. Gauges
frequently become defective. Your next check should be your thermostat, discussed earlier in this section. If you have fuel and your
thermostat is in working order, your best bet is to call a service man.
You may be able to fix the trouble yourself, but if you make a mistake
so that too much oil gets into the furnace before it fires, there could
be an explosion. Since this is a dangerous area, it is better to let a
professional handle it. In general, it is wise to call in a professional
repairman every year when the burner is shut down for the summer.
He will clean the furnace (a messy job, anyway) and reset all controls,
as well as checking the operation of motors, pumps, and filters. A
good annual checkup can keep your oil burner operating efficiently
and save you a lot of trouble. It is worth the expense.

5–2. HOT-AIR SYSTEMS

The first central heating plants were hot-air systems similar to that
shown in Fig. 5–2. The furnace itself burned coal or wood, which
was fed into the fire chamber through the firing door. Ashes were
removed through a door at the bottom of the furnace. Cold air from
outside the house entered the furnace through the cold-air inlet. This
fresh air surrounded the fire chamber but never came in contact
with the flames. As the air became heated, it expanded and became
lighter than the air in the house. Consequently it rose in the hot-
air ducts and entered each room through a register set in the floor.
As more hot air entered a room, the cooler air already there tended
to leak out through cracks in window frames and other minute openings in the building.

    As the hot air flows through the hot-air ducts, it loses some of
its heat. As a result, rooms farthest from the furnace receive air
which is not as warm as the air reaching the nearer rooms. To equalize
the heat, dampers are provided in the ducts, and these can be set

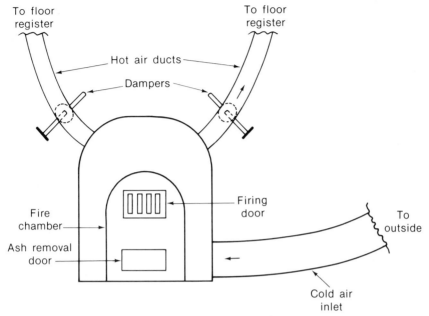

FIGURE 5-2. Gravity Hot-Air System.

to block the flow of air to the nearer rooms partially, or, if desired, completely. The flow of hot air in the ducts is also affected by wind outside the house, so that the rooms on the windy side may be cooler than those on the sheltered side. Again, the dampers can be adjusted to compensate for this.

The major disadvantage of this system is that on a very cold day, the outside air is many degrees below a comfortable temperature, and this air must be heated above normal room temperature so that it will rise in the hot-air ducts. This requires a hot fire in the furnace and high rate of fuel consumption. In practice, the fire burns continuously in a coal furnace, since starting a new fire when the furnace is dead is an undesirable chore.

A modern forced hot-air system is shown in Fig. 5-3. The hot-air ducts, leading from the furnace to the rooms to be heated, feed registers which are located at high points on the walls rather than at floor level. In each room or area a register near the floor feeds to a cold-air return. A blower near the burner draws the cold air in the room back into the heating chamber to be reheated. A filter in the line removes dirt which might damage the blower motor. The filter also cleans the recirculated air. The cold air which returns to the furnace may be only a few degrees below room temperature, so that the amount of heat required to bring it up to a suitable temperature is much less than in the gravity system. Although the same air is apparently circulating continuously, some fresh air leaks in from outside through the usual cracks in window and door frames and other openings in the house. This supplies the necessary change of air in the system.

The forced hot-air system is frequently used with a gas burner in moderate climates. The blower motor and burner are both turned on automatically by the thermostat when the room temperature falls below the temperature setting on the control, and both are shut off when the desired temperature is reached. If the burner were to operate without the blower being on, the concentration of heat could be dangerous. To prevent this, control circuits do not allow the burner to ignite until the motor is operating.

There isn't much that can go wrong with the gravity hot-air system of Fig. 5-2. In practice, the furnace usually supplies more heat than is needed, so that if leaks develop in air ducts, the loss of heat would not be noticed. The ducts must slope up from the furnace so that hot air will rise to the registers above. If a duct sags so that part of it has a downward slope, hot air may not pass beyond the peak, with the result that the room fed by the duct will be cold. If then a room is cold, check the slope of the duct leading to it, and if necessary,

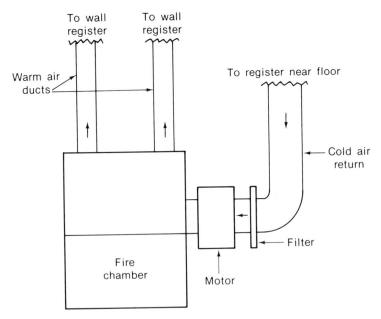

FIGURE 5-3. Forced Hot-Air System.

prop it up correctly. A duct can also be blocked by rags and other foreign objects dropped into a register accidentally. When this happens, the duct will be warm up to the blockage and cold above it. Dismantle the duct at the point of trouble and remove the impediment. Reassemble the duct as it was originally. If dirt rises from the registers, it is a sign that you forgot to clean the ducts. This should be done routinely once a year, as described in Section 3–5.

In both systems, if the ducts are made of lightweight metal, they will expand as they are heated by the warm air passing through. This expansion can cause creaking noises, which may be objectionable but are not otherwise harmful. The noise can be deadened by placing sponge rubber or felt pads at points where the duct comes in contact with the wooden members of the building. Vibrations in the ducts can also cause noise, and this can be cured by making sure the ducts are firmly anchored in place.

Noisy operation can be caused by trouble other than faults in the ducts. If noise comes from the furnace itself, it is usually caused by vibrations of loose parts. Shut off the burner, and look for loose bolts and nuts. Tighten everything inside and out. If noise comes from the blower, the blades of the fan may be rubbing against the frame, or loose cables may be interfering with the blades. Bend the blades, if necessary, or tie any loose cables out of the way. Dirt on the blades can also cause vibrations in the blower. Look for dirt, and remove it with a vacuum cleaner.

Dirt streaks on walls and ceilings near hot-air registers are signs that air ducts need cleaning. If the air filter is kept clean and changed periodically, as discussed in Section 3–5, this problem should not arise. The cold-air return is a prime source of dust, and this should be cleaned annually by removing the covers on the registers near the floor (in forced-air systems) and vacuuming out all visible dust.

If fuel bills suddenly get high, the trouble may be due to a loose belt on the blower motor, clogged filters, or blocked air ducts. If the blower belt is loose or slipping, look for an adjustable pulley to take up the slack. You should be able to move the belt about 1 inch with your finger when it has the correct tension. If it is too tight, it will cause the motor to cut out because of too great a load. If too loose, it slips so that the fan doesn't turn as fast as it should to keep the air circulating. If a pulley is loose on a shaft, it produces the same effect as a loose belt. That is, the blower doesn't rotate as fast as it should. If you see a shaft turning inside its pulley, look for a set screw on the pulley, and tighten it until the pulley is firmly fixed on the shaft. Always check the filter for dirt and clean if necessary. Filters are cheap, and the cost of replacing the filter every month during the heating season is negligible. You may prefer to do this rather than try to brush out the accumulated dust.

If too much heat is supplied, check your thermostat. It is possible that someone pushed it to a higher setting. If not, the thermostat may be stuck in the *on* position. Check your thermostat as explained in Section 5–1, and if it is defective, replace it. Too little heat is usually a sign of a blockage in the system, but it can also be caused by a loose belt or pulley or a loose connection at the thermostat.

5–3. HOT-WATER SYSTEMS

There are two kinds of hot-water heating systems, gravity and forced. A gravity hot-water system is illustrated in Fig. 5–4. The fire in the furnace heats water in a boiler to about 170 or 180°F. The hot water, being lighter than the cooler water in the pipes, rises into the radiators above the boiler. From the radiators, heat is given off into the several rooms, and the water becomes about 20°F cooler. The cooler water returns to the boiler by way of the return pipes. Since the water expands when it is heated, an expansion tank, located at the top of the system (usually in the attic), is provided to accommodate the excess water. This tank is usually open to the air and may have an overflow pipe connected to a drain, although with proper operation, the tank should not overflow.

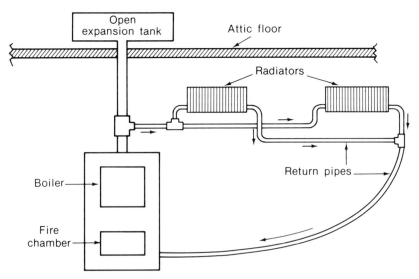

FIGURE 5–4. Gravity Hot-Water System.

In the forced hot-water system, shown in Fig. 5–5, a pump is added to keep the water circulating. The system is completely sealed, including the expansion tank, so that the water is under pressure. This permits heating the water above the normal boiling point, and water temperatures may be as high as 250°F. When the system is cold, the expansion tank has some air in it, and this air is compressed as the water expands, thereby increasing the pressure.

Since the water is *pumped* through the system, water leaves the radiators when the pump is operating, even if it has not yet given up its heat to the radiators. This happens when the ambient temperature is only slightly below the thermostat setting. Thus, the water returning to the boiler would still be hot, and little fuel would be used to bring it up to a hot temperature again. Notice that in the forced system it is not necessary to have the expansion tank above the level of the radiators.

In the gravity system, the main pipes are comparatively large, about 3 inches in diameter. In the forced hot-water system, more heat is carried because of the higher temperature and pressure, and thus smaller pipes may be used. The main pipe may be only 1½ inches in diameter, and the risers to the radiators may have a diameter as small as ½ inch.

If you keep water in the system and vent the radiators periodically, you should have no trouble with your hot-water system. When you have a serviceman make his annual maintenance checkup, ask him

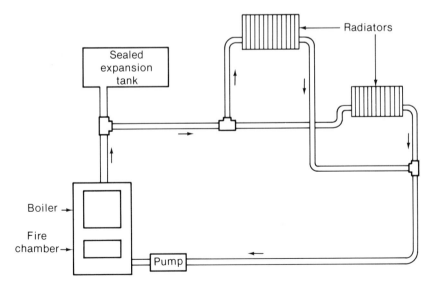

FIGURE 5–5. Forced Hot-Water System.

to show you how to add water to the boiler. This is done simply by opening a valve. The proper water level is indicated by a fixed red mark or arrow on a water gauge on the boiler. The actual water level is shown by a movable black arrow on the same gauge. When the black arrow falls below the red mark, you must add water until the two coincide. From five to ten days after you add water, you should vent the radiators, using the technique described in Section 3–5. Some systems are equipped with a control which adds water automatically when the level is too low.

The pump and the pump motor both need oiling periodically. If there is an oil cup, add one or two drops of oil once a month, but do not add oil if the cup is full.

Leaks in pipes or fittings in the hot-water heating system are repaired in the same way as leaks in water pipes, described in Section 4–3. Make sure that any patches or compounds used to seal the leaks will stand the higher temperature of the heating system. Most sealing compounds are safe even at the high temperatures of a forced hot-water system, but as a check ask your hardware- or plumbing-supply dealer when you buy the material. When applying a sealing compound or plastic patch, make certain that all surfaces are dry and clean. It is usually necessary to drain the water out of the system above the damaged pipe before tackling the job of fixing a leak. Don't forget to refill the pipes after the leak is repaired.

5–4. STEAM HEAT

In a steam heating system, water in the boiler is heated to boiling so that it is converted to steam. The steam rises in the pipes faster than hot water or hot air, so that steam heats a cold house more quickly than any other method. A steam system is shown in Fig. 5–6. Notice that there is only one pipe connected to each radiator. Steam rises from the boiler and enters the radiators through these pipes. When the radiator is cold, the steam valve on the end opposite to the pipe is open, and air in the radiator is pushed out through the valve as steam comes in at the other end. When all the air is out of the radiator and steam has reached the valve, heat from the steam expands the valve, sealing it. As a result, very little steam escapes.

As the radiators give off heat to warm the house, the steam inside cools and condenses to water. The water flows back to the boiler through the same pipe that brought the steam. Since the water flows back in a trickle, it is possible to have steam rising and water returning in one pipe at the same time. Note, however, that the pipe must slope toward the furnace. If there is a dip in a pipe, water could collect there and block off the pipe to the passage of steam.

A steam boiler has a few attachments which are quite different from anything on a boiler in a hot-water system. Three of these are shown in Fig. 5-7. The water gauge in Fig. 5-7(a) is on the side of the furnace and shows the water level in the boiler. The top of the water in the glass tube is at the same level as the top of the water in the boiler, so that the water level is easily discernible. The proper level is about midway in the glass tube. Usually, you should fill the boiler so that the glass is about three quarters full, as shown in Fig. 5-7(a). As steam is lost from the system, the level will drop, and when the glass is only one quarter full, fill it again to the three-quarter level. There is a cold-water pipe with a valve on it leading to the boiler. Turn the valve counterclockwise to let water enter the boiler, and shut it off when the water is at the correct level.

The steam gauge in Fig. 5-7(b) is mounted on top of the boiler and indicates the steam pressure inside the boiler. If everything else is working, this can be ignored. In general, the pressure should not exceed 15 pounds per square inch. Since you cannot be expected to watch the pressure gauge 24 hours a day, a safety valve is also mounted on top of the boiler, illstrated in Fig. 5-7(c). This valve pops open automatically when the pressure exceeds the safe limit and permits steam to escape until a safe pressure is reached, at which time it

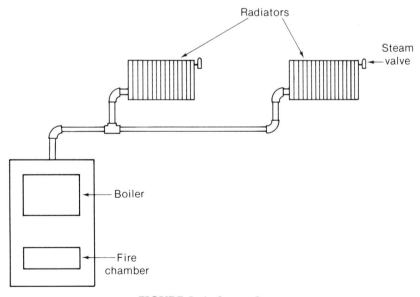

FIGURE 5-6. Steam System.

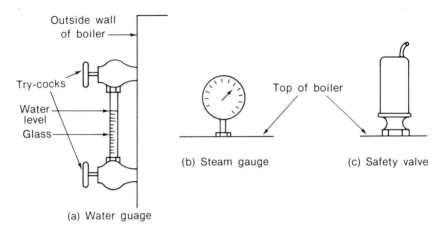

FIGURE 5–7. Parts of Steam Boiler.

closes. Since the valve may not open for several months or even years as long as everything is working properly, you may have a nasty suspicion that it may not operate when required. Thus, for most valves a test lever is provided so that its operation can be checked. Make it a point to test the operation of the valve a few times during the heating season. If the valve is defective, replace the whole unit. With the furnace off and the boiler cool, unscrew the valve, using a pipe wrench or adjustable wrench on the hexagonal section. The valve is threaded so that it comes off easily, and a new one can be screwed into the opening.

Leaks in steam pipes or at joints can be fixed in the same manner as leaks in water pipes, as described in Section 4–3. Make sure that all surfaces are clean and dry. Most sealing materials will withstand the temperatures of steam pipes, but, to make sure, check with your hardware dealer when you buy the material.

If one radiator remains cool when the rest heat up, steam is not reaching that radiator. Check to see that the valve at the input end (where the pipe enters) is open. Someone may have closed it accidentally. The valve should be turned completely counterclockwise to open it. If the steam valve on the radiator is defective, it may not permit air to escape, so that the steam cannot get in. To check this, remove the steam valve completely. If the radiator now fills with steam (when the furnace is going), the steam valve is at fault. Close the input valve before too much steam enters the room. The steam valve can be cleaned in kerosene or a strong solution of trisodium phosphate (TSP) and water, or, if too badly dirty, can be replaced with a new valve, which is quite inexpensive.

If the radiator still won't get hot, there may be a water block in the line or in the radiator itself. The radiator should slope toward the input pipe so that water condensing inside flows back to the boiler. If water remains in the radiator, the system will be noisy, and if enough water remains, it may block the entrance of steam. Radiators may tilt in the wrong direction because of sagging floors. To correct this, put small blocks of wood under the feet of the radiator farthest from the input pipe, as shown in Fig. 5–8. If the floor or structure has sagged so that the main pipe slopes in the wrong direction, put blocks under all four feet of the radiator to pull up the pipe and make it slope toward the boiler.

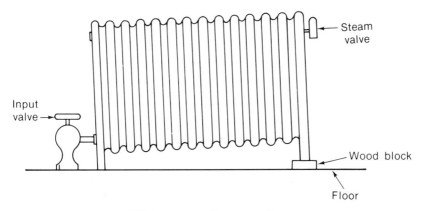

FIGURE 5–8. Tilting a Radiator.

If water leaks at the input valve, it is usually because of worn packing. A typical valve is shown in Fig. 5–9. Water or steam is prevented from coming out of the tip of the valve by packing held tightly against the shaft. If this packing material gets worn, it no longer makes an effective seal. Sometimes you can compress it sufficiently by tightening the packing nut with an adjustable wrench, but if this doesn't work, you will have to put in new packing. To remove and replace it, first make sure the radiator is cool and then remove the valve handle by unscrewing a screw in the center. Remove the packing nut with an adjustable wrench and slide it up and off the shaft. The old packing will come with it. Remove the old packing with an ice pick or screwdriver, and wind new packing material into the packing nut around the shaft. Packing looks like graphite-impregnated string and is obtainable at any hardware store. When you put in new packing, wind it in a clockwise direction so that it will compress when the packing nut is tightened.

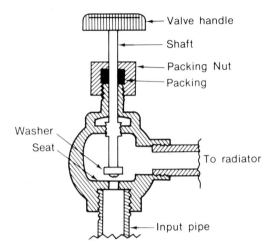

FIGURE 5–9. Radiator Valve.

Valves in hot-water radiators may leak in the same manner and for the same cause. The solution is the same, except that the radiator must be drained first. This means that the whole system must be drained until the water is below the level of the radiator valve that needs new packing. After replacing the packing, refill the water system before firing the boiler.

Valves on steam radiators should be either all the way open or all the way closed. In water radiators, however, valves can be left partially open as a means of regulating the amount of hot water coming in. In this way, you can cut down the heat in radiators that are too hot.

5–5. RADIANT HEAT

Instead of radiators or hot-air registers, heating units can be placed in floors, walls, or ceilings. In such a system, the heating unit warms the person by radiation so that you feel as comfortable and warm with air temperatures of 65°F as you would in a room heated to 70°F by other methods. In a typical radiant heating system, copper tubing is placed just below the floor. In ranch-type houses on a concrete slab, the copper tubing is embedded in the concrete. A standard hot-water furnace heats water to somewhere between 100 and 120°F (about 38 to 50°C), and this warm water is circulated through the copper tubing. This system of heating is very economical after the initial installation, because the water has to be only moderately warm. It is amazingly comfortable, because floors are warm to the touch, and there are no cold spots in the room. In areas where electricity is not too expensive, electrical cables may be used instead of copper tubing and water.

In the hot-water radiant system, the furnace requires the same attention as the furnace in a conventional hot-water system, but no other maintenance is required. The electric system requires no maintenance whatsoever and will work without attention as long as electricity is available. A disadvantage of radiant heating is that carpets do lower the efficiency, and for best results floors should be bare.

5-6. INSULATION

The purpose of insulation is to keep heat where it is supposed to be. Insulation holds heat in your house in the winter and prevents heat from getting in during the summer. In addition to making your home more comfortable all year round, insulation helps you save on fuel bills. In areas that experience subzero temperatures during much of the winter, the savings on fuel bills will pay for the cost of insulation in less than two heating seasons. In areas that have winters with frequent temperatures between 0 and 30°F, it may take three years to save enough on fuel to pay for insulating. Even in the warmest parts of the United States, fuel savings will pay for insulation, although it may take more than five years to amortize the cost.

If your home is already completely insulated, you need do nothing further about this problem. Insulation does not age, and although it may lose some of its effectiveness in time, you could not improve the situation enough, either in comfort or in fuel savings, to justify replacing it or adding to it. If your home is not insulated or only partially insulated, you should consider adding insulation, especially in cold climates. You can do much of the work yourself, although you might want to call in professionals to do a thorough job on exterior walls, where special equipment is required.

Insulating material is available in a variety of forms and materials. Most work on the principle that air is trapped in the spaces between particles or layers of the material, and this "dead" air is a poor conductor of heat. Other types use aluminum foil as a reflector in combination with other materials. The aluminum foil keeps heat out of the house in summer by reflecting it back outside. In general, aluminum alone is not good enough to retain heat inside the house in winter, although it is useful in tropical climates to keep houses cool. When aluminum is attached to other insulating material, the combination can be very effective, but it is also very expensive. In general, the handyman should not use reflective materials for insulation.

An important consideration in selecting an insulating material is the effect of moisture in the air. As warm air in the house comes in contact with cool outside walls or windows, water vapor in the air condenses on the cool surface. This is especially noticed as a mist on cold windowpanes, but this condensation is also present on the inside surface of cold outside walls. When an insulating material is inside the outside wall, moisture condenses on the inside surface of the insulation, which is inside the wall, because this surface is cooler than the room temperature. If the moisture works its way into the insulation, the wet material then acts as a heat conductor rather than an insulator, since water conducts heat better than air. In other words, *wet* insulation is worthless. To prevent moisture from seeping into the insulation, a *vapor barrier* should be provided. This is simply a layer of nonporous paper, plastic, or aluminum foil on the inside surface of the insulating material. Good insulating materials have a vapor barrier attached. When mounting the material, it is important to have the vapor barrier toward the inside of the house, as shown in Fig. 5–10. If moisture condenses on the vapor barrier, it cannot get through and eventually evaporates back into the room. The insulation remains dry.

One type of insulating material is in the form of *loose fill*. This is the only material that can be used to insulate a wall of a house that is already built, without ripping off panels or plaster. The material consists of small particles of mineral wool, wood fiber, or

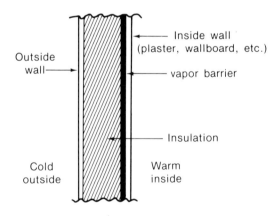

FIGURE 5–10. Vapor Barrier.

vermiculite (a form of mica). In unfinished attics it can be poured out of bags between the joists in the floor. In walls of existing houses, special equipment is required to blow the insulation into the crevices. Mineral wool is relatively inexpensive, but can irritate the skin if it is handled too much. Since no vapor barrier is provided with loose fills, you must first place a layer of building paper between the joints in the attic floor, and then the loose fill can be simply poured over the paper. Make sure the sheets of paper overlap so that there are no gaps where moisture can get through to the insulation. The depth of insulation should be at least 2 inches. The thicker the insulation, the less heat loss there will be, and thus the greater will be the fuel savings, but beyond 3 inches the savings in fuel will not pay for the extra material.

Insulating panels are wallboards with built-in insulation. Although they are not effective for cold climates, they are sometimes used on walls and ceilings of an extra room added in the cellar or to wall off a garage to make it into a spare room. These panels are available with decorative designs on them, so that they simplify construction of the new room, because no paint or papering is required. However, this material should be used only in moderate climates and only for the "extra" room.

Flexible insulation is available in *blankets*, which are long rolls, and *batts*, which are usually 4 or 8 feet long. These may be of mineral wool, wood fibers, or fiberglas, and come in thicknesses of 1 to 6 inches. The standard width just fits between studs spaced 16 inches apart, and extra-wide batts are also available. If you use batts or blankets, buy material with a vapor barrier already attached. Flame-proof blankets are more expensive but may be worth the investment.

Blankets are probably the most efficient of the insulating materials. Use a thickness of 2 to 4 inches. Above 4 inches the additional fuel savings is negligible, and below 2 inches the material is not effective. You will need a special tool to install blankets or batts—a *stapling gun*. You could use a hammer to nail the material in place, but a stapler is much faster and easier to use. A stapling gun is not very expensive, and you will probably find many uses for it, as, for example, to install seat covers in your car. If you don't want to buy one, many stores that sell insulation, including the large mail-order houses, will let you borrow a stapling gun if you buy insulation and staples. You have to leave a deposit on the stapler, but you get your money back when you return it. Installing flexible insulation is very easy. Place the material between the studs and drive staples into the studs through the double layer of paper. Staples should be put in every 10 to 12 inches in vertical studs but can be spaced about 18 inches when the batt is placed between joints in an attic floor. Be sure the vapor barrier is toward the *inside* of the house, and also make certain that the vapor barrier is continuous by having the edges of one blanket overlap the next.

It would be nice to insulate your whole house, but you can effect a noticeable saving in fuel just by insulating your attic. The proper places for attic insulation are shown in Fig. 5–11. In Fig. 5–11(a), the attic is unfinished, and thus there is no need for heating it. The insulation is placed on the floor of the attic (over the ceiling of the room below) with the vapor barrier *toward* the heated room. In this figure, a crawl space is also shown, and if you can get under the house, you can staple batts or a blanket under the first floor also, again making sure the vapor barrier is toward the heated room. In Fig. 5–11(b), the attic has a finished room, and the insulation must be carried around this room as shown. Again, the vapor barrier is toward the inside of the house.

5-7. STORM WINDOWS AND DOORS

In cold weather, the wall of a room next to the outside of your house is usually colder than an inside wall. This wall cools the air next to it, and since cold air is heavier than warm, the cool air moves down toward the floor and warmer air moves across the room to fill the void. If your house is insulated, the dead air space in the outside wall will keep this wall of the room warmer and the air motion will not be as great. That is, it would not be as great except that the cold windowpanes create the same effect. Air is cooled by the cold pane and sinks toward the floor. Warmer air moves toward the window

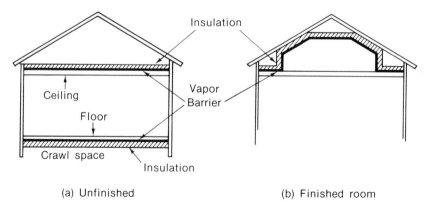

(a) Unfinished   (b) Finished room

FIGURE 5–11. Attic Insulation.

and in turn is cooled. It, too, moves toward the floor, pushing the air there away from the window. The result is that the air is in constant motion, away from the window at floor level, and toward the window in the upper half of the room. Therefore, you feel a draft coming from the window, and if you are like most homeowners, you attribute the cause of the draft to air blowing in through a crack in the frame or between the sashes. The truth is this draft occurs from the normal air motion, even if every opening is tightly sealed.

If there were a dead-air space in the window as there is in an insulated wall, the inside pane would not be as cold, and the air motion, and thus the draft, would be greatly reduced. The answer is storm sashes, or storm windows. A storm window is simply an extra sash containing windowpanes, which is placed over the window, usually outside, so that a dead-air space exists between the storm sash and the window. Anything that creates the dead-air space will work to reduce drafts and incidentally save fuel by preventing heat from leaking out through the windows. You could, for example, simply place a sheet of plywood over the window, but then you would not be able to see through. Storm windows should be transparent.

The cheapest method of creating the desired dead-air space is to tack or tape a sheet of transparent plastic over the window frame *inside the house.* This may not be elegant, but it is effective, with only a little reduction in transparency. Materials for this purpose are sold by mail-order houses and most building-supply stores.

If you live in a cold climate, you should have storm windows, both for added comfort and fuel savings. If your home has none, you will have to make them yourself or have them made, since it is unlikely that your local building-supply house carries storm windows. It would be impossible to stock the wide variety of sizes needed. Making the storm sashes is not difficult, and materials are available in kit form for wooden and aluminum sashes. Measure your window frames carefully on the outside where the storm window will fit. The simplest arrangement is to have the storm sash held by two hangers at the top of the frame and hooked inside at the bottom. In this way the dimensions are not critical and you may even find some second-hand storm sashes that can be used. For a neater appearance, you might want to tailor the sash to the window opening, but this is more difficult. In any case, once you've determined the dimensions, follow the directions in the kit. No special tools are required. Aluminum frames are cut with a hacksaw or any fine-toothed saw. Remove all burrs after sawing by filing smooth.

If possible, storm windows should be designed so that they can be installed from inside the house. It is difficult and dangerous to have to carry sashes up a ladder to mount them. The sash must be small enough and light enough so that you can maneuver it through an open window and mount it on its hangers from inside the house. This is not as important a consideration in one-story bungalows.

It is possible to buy combination windows which contain both screens and storm sashes. These are mounted permanently and are self-storing. That is, both the screen and storm sash are always contained in the window, but each is moved to the proper position as required. The storm sash is in place during the winter, and the screen in the summer. These combination windows have a higher initial cost than separate screens and storm sashes, but they require less maintenance and last longer because of less handling. If combinations are installed, the homeowner is freed from the tasks of installing and removing storm sashes and screens.

When you buy glass for your storm windows, ask to have it cut to size. It should be 1/16 to ⅛ inch smaller than the opening in each direction. Usually there is no extra charge for cutting the glass, but even a small nominal charge is worth paying to save yourself the trouble. The installation of glass in doors and windows is described in Section 8–1.

If your storm sash fits snugly in an opening in the window frame, it is more difficult to install if the frame is distorted because of settling of the house. The type that fits against the window frame is not subject to this difficulty. In either case, the storm sash should fit tightly so that air cannot circulate freely from outside into space between the storm sash and the regular house window. If spaces or cracks are visible, close them with weather stripping, as described in the next section.

Wooden sashes should be painted to prevent the wood from absorbing moisture which can distort the sash. However, too much paint may affect the fit of the sash in the frame and should be avoided. In general, paint only when the bare wood can be seen or the paint is so thin that you think it won't last the season. Aluminum sashes do not require paint, but you may want to clean off oxides occasionally. Special cleaning compounds for aluminum sashes are available in most hardware stores.

A storm door creates a dead-air space for a door just as a storm sash does for a window. If you have storm doors, use them, but the fuel savings may be small, because not much heat is lost through a door that is well weather-stripped. If the outside door opens on an entryway which has another door leading into the house, with both doors closed the entryway acts as a dead-air space and reduces drafts.

If there is no entryway, a storm door can be effective in reducing drafts.

If the outside door of the house has a window in it, then the storm door should have a window located at the same level; but if the outside door is solid, the storm door should also be solid. The window in a storm door is usually made of glass, but plastic sheeting can also be used. An excellent material is plastic reenforced with wire mesh. It is much lighter than glass and is shatterproof.

5-8. WEATHER STRIPPING

Windows and doors must fit loosely enough so that they can be opened and closed without too much effort. Thus, there is always a crack around each window and door through which heat can escape or cold air can blow in. Even if your home is insulated and furnished with storm windows, the cracks and openings add up to a large source of heat loss. Sealing these cracks will result in additional fuel savings, as well as increased comfort. Weather stripping around windows and doors to seal the crack can result in savings of as much as 20 percent in fuel costs.

There are many types of weather stripping, and they all work well. Years ago, before special weather-stripping materials were manufactured, homeowners frequently rolled up newspaper and fastened the rolls over the openings around windows and at the bottom of doors. This worked, too, and was probably just as effective as the special materials sold for the purpose today. Materials come in rolls or rigid strips and include felt, foam rubber, plastic, wood, and metal, as well as such combinations as felt with a metal backing or plastic tubing with a sponge-rubber core. In new buildings, metal weather stripping is usually included in all double-hung windows and is concealed between the edge of the sash and the frame. If your home does not have weather stripping, you can buy kits of the metal material and install it yourself according to directions, and the result will be an effective and unobtrusive weather stripping. However, it is more expensive than other materials and it requires much more work to install.

If you are concerned with costs and not too concerned about having the weather stripping show, you should shop for the flexible materials such as felt, plastic, or foam rubber. Some of these are available with adhesive backing, so that they can be installed with very little effort and no tools, except a pair of scissors or a knife to cut the material to the right length. If you buy material without the adhesive backing, you will have to tack it in place. Tacks should be spaced about 4 inches apart.

When you apply weather stripping to a double-hung window, you must seal all the cracks. Attach the material to the frame so that it presses against the window sash, at the sides and bottom of the bottom sash, and at the sides and top of the top sash. Also attach a strip to the top of the bottom sash so that it overlaps the crack between the two sashes. Alternatively, the material could be fastened to the sashes, pressing against the frame, but usually the material is fastened to the fixed portion of the window and presses against the movable part. If the material is mounted correctly, it will be slightly compressed, but it will not be so tight that the window cannot be opened. For metal windows you must use material with an adhesive backing, but for wooden sashes, you can fasten the material either with tacks or adhesive.

For metal casement windows, you can use any of the adhesive-backed weather-stripping materials. There are also special plastic or metal materials, specifically for casement windows, made with a channel which is held on the window only by friction. These are the easiest to install.

Weather stripping for doors utilizes much the same principles. The material can be attached to the door or the frame but must close the cracks when the door is closed. Since a door is opened more often than a window in winter, the weather stripping on doors takes more punishment than that on windows, so a long-lasting material should be used. Check with your building supplier or hardware dealer on the qualities of the materials available.

Rain and snow blowing in around cracks in the door, especially at the bottom, can damage the door, even if it is weather-stripped. The edges of the door should be painted often, as mentioned in Section 3–7, and a drip cap should be installed, as shown in Fig. 3–13.

As a house settles, cracks may appear which permit heat to escape or cold breezes to blow in. Look for these openings and seal them before cold weather arrives. Some of the more common faults occur around door and window frames, at junctions of floors and walls, around pipes entering through floors or walls, and between floorboards in old-fashioned floors. Openings around door or window frames should be caulked as should all openings between two different materials, such as between wood and masonry, metal and masonry, or wood and metal.

When your house was built, caulking was probably installed at every point where two different materials met, such as between the masonry and the rest of the house and between metal flashings and other roofing material. The caulking compounds harden and crack in time and have to be renewed. Caulking compound is a putty-like material which sticks to wood, stone, metal, and other building materials and is available in a wide variety of colors. When it sets, it remains elastic so that it can correct for different rates of expansion of the surrounding building materials. It can be purchased in tubes and is squeezed out like toothpaste or in long rolls like spaghetti. It is also available in bulk and in disposable cartridges which are used with a caulking gun. Most caulking compounds can be painted. For small openings you can use the roll type and apply it with your fingers or squeeze the compound from a tube. For large openings you should use a caulking gun, which you can usually borrow from the store that sells you the caulking compound. Make sure the surfaces are clean and dry and that all old, dry, caulking material is scraped out. If a hole is very deep, stuff it with a fiber filler such as oakum to about 1 inch from the top before adding the caulking compound.

When a house is built, there are gaps because its dimensions are not held to the precision of fine machine work. Thus, floors and walls do not meet exactly. To cover cracks between floor and walls, a piece of molding, called a *shoe mold*, is nailed to the wall all around the room at floor level. If moldings and similar decorative trim were not used, houses would be prohibitively expensive because of the necessity of maintaining dimensions accurately. As a house settles, molding may loosen, opening cracks to heat loss. If you see a shoe molding raised slightly from the floor, you should nail it down again. Hold the molding flush against the floor and nail it to the wall with finishing nails. If it is a small molding, you may drive the nails into the floor. If the molding is distorted, pry it loose with a chisel and replace it, or renail it flush with the floor.

When a pipe passes through a hole in the wall or floor, there is usually space around the pipe which permits cold air or heat to pass through. This space is usually covered with a decorative flange to conceal the hole, but the flange does not prevent heat loss. You can seal the hole with putty, caulking compound, or any sealing material. If the pipe gets hot from hot water or steam, use a sealer that will withstand the temperature.

In old-fashioned houses, flooring was a single layer of boards butting against each other. These boards shrink with age and leave cracks in the floor. Again, you can use any sealer to fill the cracks. One inexpensive, but effective method is to sweep sawdust into the cracks and then pour shellac over the sawdust. As the shellac hardens, it makes a good seal.

5-9. ATTIC FANS

Your attic gets very hot in the summertime, and rooms just below the attic receive some of this heat. Typically, on a hot sunny day the temperature in the attic can be 125 or 130°F and in the rooms just below the attic 100°F. When a fan is installed to suck the hot air out of the attic, the attic temperature can be brought down quite close to the outside temperature, and the rooms below do not get nearly so hot.

For a simple installation, place the fan in an attic window pointing outward so that it sucks the hot air out and pushes it outside. Doors to the attic from the rest of the house should be kept open so that hot air throughout the house is pulled up to the attic and forced outside. The fan should fit snugly in the window frame or into a board mounted in the frame. In choosing a fan, first determine the volume of air in the house approximately by adding the volumes of the rooms. Then select a fan that can move that much air in about one minute. If you want to cool only a few rooms, add the volumes of only these rooms, and keep the rest of the house shut off from these rooms simply by closing doors. Of course, the rooms to be cooled must be connected to the attic by open passageways. If your house has insulation and an unfinished attic, a fan is unnecessary. However, the attic will still get hot, and to prevent a build-up of heat, the attic should be ventilated by having openings to the outside at opposite ends. The openings can be open windows or louvers. In either case, the openings should be screened to prevent insects and birds from entering and nesting in the house.

6

Electricity

There is nothing very difficult about electrical work around the house, but you may not be allowed to do some of the jobs, even though you are perfectly capable of doing adequate work. Local electrical codes will restrict you in many repair jobs, and for a good reason. It seems so easy to string up wires to carry electricity that many people simply do it themselves without bothering about local restrictions. Unfortunately, too often a do-it-yourself electrician uses wire which is too small for the load or strings the wire improperly, and the result is a fire of electrical origin. To minimize the likelihood of fire, almost all cities require that all new electrical work be inspected and approved by a city inspector. Some cities are even stricter and insist that all new installations be done by a licensed electrician. It is unwise to try to install new electrical work without having an inspection, because if you then have a fire in your house, even though caused by something else, your insurance policy may not cover the damage if the illegal wiring is discovered.

You can and should make simple electrical repairs which involve no changes in wiring. Thus, you can replace a defective switch or outlet, you can fix or replace a broken doorbell, or you can replace an old light fixture with one of modern design. In general, if the repair job entails no changes in the house wiring, don't be afraid to tackle it yourself.

Repairs that require changes in the house wiring are best left to a licensed electrican. This occurs usually when an extra room is added but can also arise if you wish to add a wall switch for a light fixture which has a pull chain. If you wish to make any changes yourself, first consult the city inspector to find out the requirements of the local electrical codes, then comply with these requirements, and, finally, have the work inspected and approved.

If you are not familiar with electricity, it can seem quite mysterious. You don't have to be an engineer to make repairs. In fact, you can replace defective items without knowing anything about how they work; but if you know how things work, repairing is easier and may even be enjoyable. You should learn at least the basic principles explained in Section 6-1.

6-1. FUNDAMENTALS*

To get a better understanding of electricity, it is useful to compare it to the water system in a household. Water reaches the home through large pipes or mains and is under pressure so that it will be forced out of an open faucet, which may be many feet higher than the water main. When a tap is opened, a current of water flows in the pipe from the main to the tap. The velocity of the current depends on the diameter of the pipe and also on its smoothness. In general, the larger the diameter and the smoother the pipe, the faster will be the flow of current. However, there is a limit determined by the pressure in the main. Electricity is quite analogous. The water main is replaced by the electric power lines which lead to the house. The electricity is under "pressure." This pressure is called *electromotive force (e.m.f.)* and is measured in *volts*. When a suitable connection is made to an electrical appliance, current flows, and the speed of this current depends on factors akin to the smoothness and diameter of the water pipe. In general, the larger the diameter of the wire, the faster will be the electric current. The conductivity of the metal used to make the wire is similar to the smoothness of the water pipe. Some metals, such as copper and silver, are excellent conductors. These are said to have low *resistance*, and current flows through copper, for example, much faster than through iron. Nickel and tungsten are typically poorer conductors which tend to slow down the current. The velocity of electrical current is measured in *amperes*.

Assume that a long garden hose is connected to a water faucet. The pressure may be 80 pounds per square inch. If the hose has an inside diameter of about 1 inch and is quite smooth on the inside, water will flow through it rapidly when the faucet is opened wide. However, if the hose is only ¼ inch in diameter and is not smooth, the flow will be restricted. If a larger hose is connected to the open end of the ¼-inch hose, the water will not move faster through this added hose, since the velocity of flow is limited by the smaller hose. In the same way, if electric current flows through several conductors sequentially, the velocity of the current is limited by the total resistance in the circuit.

In one sense, the analogy between electricity and water breaks down completely. If a water faucet is opened, water pours out. But electricity does not pour out of a wall outlet or an empty lamp socket

*G. J. Wheeler, "How to Repair Electrical Appliances", Reston Publishing Co., 1972.

even when the switch is turned on. Thus, electricity or electric current flows only in a *complete circuit*. This is illustrated in Figs. 6–1
and 6–2. At a power station a difference in *electrical potential,* or
e.m.f., or voltage is generated. Two wires run from the power station
to every house receiving electricity, as shown in Fig. 6–1. These wires
go through a distribution center in each home and then to the various
electrical outlets in the home, such as wall receptacles. In effect, then,
each wall receptacle has two terminations which are connected all
the way back to the power station or voltage source, as shown in Fig.

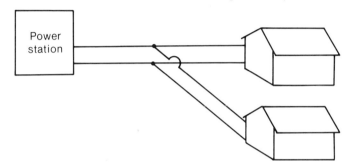

FIGURE 6–1. Power Distribution.

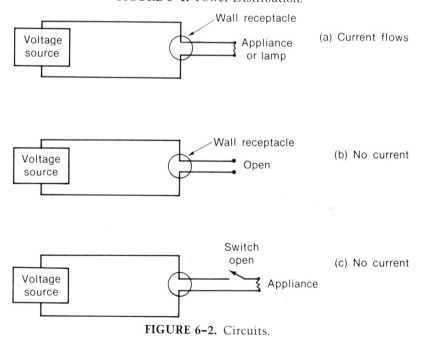

FIGURE 6–2. Circuits.

6-2.   When an appliance or lamp is plugged into the receptacle, the circuit is completed and current flows. This is illustrated in Fig. 6–2(a). The wiggly line labeled "appliance or lamp" is the standard electrical symbol for a resistance and is used here to represent the electrical resistance of the appliance.   In Fig. 6–2(b), the receptacle has nothing plugged into it, and thus no current flows, since the circuit is incomplete.   Similarly, in Fig. 6–2(c), an appliance is plugged into the receptacle, but its switch is in the *off* position. Again, the circuit is incomplete, and no current flows.

The difference in potential, that is, the voltage, between the two terminals in a receptacle is what pushes electricity through a circuit. The two wires or terminals together form a *line*, and each wire by itself is referred to as a *side of the line*.   In practice, for safety reasons (explained in the next section) and for simplicity and economy of installation, one side of the line is grounded.   That is, it is physically attached to the earth.   This side is then called the *grounded* side of the line, and the other side is the *hot* side.   This means that a voltage exists between the hot side and anything else that is physically attached to the earth.   In a home, the cold-water pipes are also *grounded*, that is, attached to earth, and thus a voltage exists between the hot side of the line and the cold-water pipes. This is illustrated in Fig. 6–3. The plug is removed from the line cord leading to a socket containing a bulb, such as in a table lamp.   One wire is attached to the hot

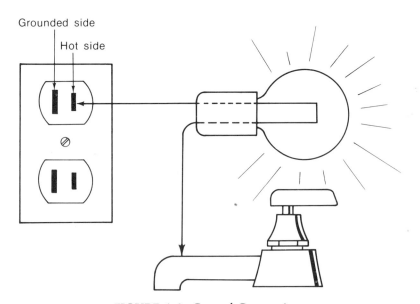

FIGURE 6–3. Ground Connection.

side of a receptacle and the other to a faucet or water pipe. The bulb lights. If the wire at the receptacle is moved from the hot side to the ground side, the bulb will not light. Thus, the arrangement shown in Fig. 6-3 can also be used to determine which side of the line or receptacle is hot and which is grounded. Similarly, if you touch the hot side of a line and a ground, such as a water pipe, you will get a shock; but you will not get a shock from touching the ground side of the line and another grounded object. You will *not* get a shock even if you touch the hot side, as long as you do not complete the circuit by touching anything else that is grounded. This means you must not be standing on ground or on a damp floor. This explains why birds are able to alight on high voltage wires without adverse effects. They do not complete the electric circuit with any part of their bodies.

If you look carefully at a wall receptacle, you will notice that one of the two slots for a plug is longer than the other. This is shown in Fig. 6-4. It is common practice to connect the longer slot to the grounded side of the line, as indicated in the figure. The screw in the center, holding the mounting plate to the wall, is also grounded in most installations. Although the slots are of different lengths, the plugs on most lamps and appliances have prongs which are the same width. Thus, a plug can be inserted to connect either side of the appliance line to either side of the house line.

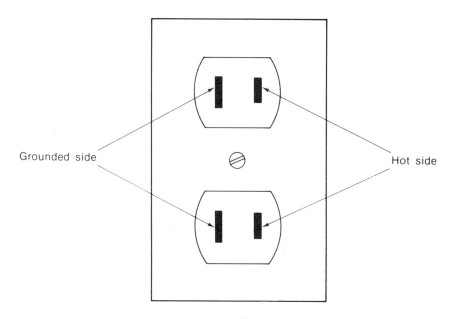

FIGURE 6-4. Wall Receptacle.

In industrial appliances, for safety reasons it is desirable to attach the case of the apparatus firmly to ground. This is usually done by using a three-pronged plug and a special receptacle. The receptacle has a third hole which is round and connected directly to ground, as shown in Fig. 6–5. A wire from the case of the appliance is connected to the round prong on the plug so that the case is grounded when the appliance is plugged into the receptacle.

When electrical current flows through a resistance, it is converted to some other form of energy. This may be heat, light, or mechanical motion, or some combination of these. Thus, when current flows through the filament in an electric bulb, it is converted to light, and when current flows through the heating element in a toaster, it is converted to heat. However, the bulb also gets hot, and the heating element glows. That is, in both of these examples, and in every electrical apparatus, some of the electrical energy is converted to unwanted heat or light.

The unit of electrical current is the ampere. This is a unit of velocity indicating flow of electrical charges per second, just as water current is measured in feet per second. The amount of electrical *power* consumed by an appliance is measured in *watts*. For appliances which produce light or heat, the power consumed in watts is equal to the *product* of the *current* times the *voltage*. For example,

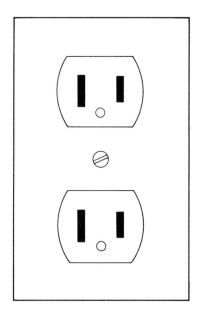

FIGURE 6–5. Wall Receptacle with Ground Connection.

one model of electric toaster is rated at 115 volts, 1320 watts. This means that in operation the toaster will draw 1320/115 = 11.5 amperes. Appliances which have motors that produce motion usually use less power than the product of current times voltage. For example, one model of juicer draws 1.75 amperes at 115 volts. The product is 201.25, but the juicer actually uses only 125 watts.

You pay for electrical energy on the basis of the amount of power used and the time it is used. The unit is a *kilowatt-hour (KWH)*. A kilowatt is 1000 watts and kilowatt-hours are the product of kilowatts and hours. Thus, if you used the 1320-watt toaster for ¼ hour and the 125-watt juicer for 1/5 hour, you would use ¼ × 1320 plus 1/5 × 125, or 330 + 25 = 355 watt-hours = 0.355 KWH. Note that if a 50-watt bulb is left on for 10 hours, it uses only ½ KWH.

When electric current flows through copper wire, there is some power dissipated, even though the wire is an excellent conductor with very low resistance. The greater the current for a fixed diameter of wire, the greater will be the power absorbed by the wire. This power loss becomes evident as heat. When too great a current flows through a wire, the heat generated may burn the insulation and cause a fire. The safe current-handling capacity of a copper wire depends on the diameter of the wire. Thus, the choice of wire size, not only for house wiring but also for line cords for individual appliances, is affected by the expected current.

The electrical system in a home consists of a service line from the main power lines to the house, a distribution box where the service line divides into many branch lines going to separate rooms, and finally the receptacles and sockets to which the electric appliances are connected. The usual voltage for most electrical appliances is nominally 115 volts, although they will work well at any value between 110 and 120 volts. However, some modern high-power appliances, such as electric ranges and electric clothes dryers, require twice this value to furnish enough power to supply sufficient heat. (Recall that the power is the product of volts times amperes.) To supply both 115 volts and 230 volts, a three-wire service line connects the main power line to the house. This line, shown in Fig. 6–6, has one wire grounded, and each of the other wires is at a potential of 115 volts. Alternating current is used, and the voltages on the two hot lines are out-of-phase. This means that when one is 115 volts above ground, the other is 115 volts below, and the difference between them is 230 volts. This last voltage is used to operate ranges, clothes dryers, and other high-voltage appliances, while small appliances are operated between either hot wire and ground.

Before considering the current requirements of house wiring, it is

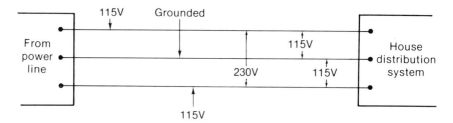

FIGURE 6–6. Three-Wire Service Line.

necessary to know what current is drawn by each appliance. Typical values of current for various appliances are shown in Table 6–1. Individual appliances may have slightly different requirements, but, in general, those appliances which supply much heat or do heavy work draw greater currents. A typical household may have 20 or 30 appliances, but fortunately only a few are used at any one time. The exact value of current drawn by an appliance or information from which this value can be determined is supplied on a name tag affixed to the appliance, or this information may be engraved on the appliance itself.

Table 6–1. Typical Current Requirements

Appliances	Current Drawn (amperes)
100-watt bulb	0.9 amp
Phonograph	0.5
Television set	1.6
Refrigerator	2.0
Small fan	0.5
Blender	2.5
Juicer	2
Vacuum cleaner	6.0
Freezer	5.0
Garbage disposer	7.5
Dishwasher	12
Clothes dryer	20
Toaster	12
Iron	10
Space heater	14
Waffle iron	12

From the information in Table 6–1, it is possible to "design" the house wiring for a typical home. One possible arrangement is shown in Fig. 6–7. Each line in this figure represents a two- or three-wire electrical line. A three-wire service line connects the distribution box to the main power line. The service line is rated for 100 amperes and has a 100-ampere fuse or circuit breaker in series with it. The service line also passes through the electric meter before entering the box so that the amount of energy used may be determined. Several branch circuits emerge from the distribution box, and these are rated and fused according to their use. The *lighting* circuits are rated at 15 amperes each. These are wired throughout the house for lamps, small fans, electric razors and toothbrushes, radios, and television sets. One branch line may service two or three rooms. A better arrangement is to have one branch for overhead lights and one or more for wall outlets in living room and bedrooms. Since heavier loads are required in the kitchen, the *appliance* circuits leading there are rated at 20 amperes each. The overhead lights in the kitchen should be on one of the 15-ampere circuits. The 230-volt branches are used for high-power equipment, and a separate branch should be used for each 230-volt appliance, such as the clothes dryer, air conditioner, and range.

If too many appliances are in operation on a single circuit simultaneously, the total current drawn can exceed the safe rating of the wire. To prevent overheating and possible fires from excessive current, each branch has a fuse or circuit breaker, which is designed to open the circuit when the rated current is exceeded. If an appliance has a short circuit, it will draw excessive current, since the short presents a lower resistance path across the line than the regular circuit. This will blow a fuse or open a circuit breaker. However, an open circuit breaker or blown fuse may also result when too many appliances are connected on one circuit, so that the total current drawn

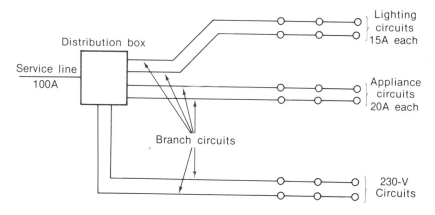

FIGURE 6–7. Typical Wiring Arrangement.

exceeds the rating of the circuit. Overloading is not usually dangerous, but it can be a nuisance.

6-2. SAFETY

WARNING: ELECTRICITY CAN BE LETHAL! This is something you
must keep in mind whenever you do electrical work. If you pay attention to what you are doing, there is not the least danger, but if you
allow yourself to be distracted or are careless, you may be in trouble.
As long as you understand the danger, it is easy to avoid it.

One side of the house line is grounded, that is, firmly attached to
the physical earth. The cold-water pipe in your home is also grounded,
and, if the hot-water pipe is connected to the cold, as through a common faucet, the hot-water pipe is also at ground potential. This is
done for safety reasons, since if the electrical line were allowed to
"float," there could be a very large voltage between the line and ground,
even though the two wires in the line were only 115 volts apart. Large
appliances should be physically grounded, especially if they are near
water pipes. To do this, a wire is attached to a bare spot on the appliance, such as under the head of a screw, and the other end is attached
to a water pipe by means of a grounding clamp. If you disconnect this
ground connection to repair or move the appliance, make sure to connect it again before plugging in the appliance again. Probably nothing
will happen if you fail to do this, but there is always a remote possibility that the insulation on the line cord could be worn enough to permit
the hot side of the line to contact the case of the appliance. If that
happened and you touched the case and a water pipe, you would get an
electrical shock. When the case is grounded, this cannot happen. A
contact between the hot side of the line and the grounded case would
blow a fuse, but there would be no danger of shock.

As mentioned in the preceding section, every electrical line in
your home is protected by a fuse or circuit breaker to prevent too much
current from flowing. Too much current can cause wires to get hot
enough to start a fire. When a fuse blows or a circuit breaker opens,
it is usually a sign of either an overload or a defective appliance. If the
fuse blows as soon as an appliance or lamp is switched on, it is usually
a sign of a short circuit in the device. You can replace the fuse (or
reset the circuit breaker), but the circuit will be broken again if
you try to turn on the defective appliance. If the circuit opens because of an overload, there will be a few seconds or even minutes
delay between the time the last appliance was turned on and the cir-

cuit was broken. The solution is to move one or more appliances to another circuit.

If a circuit breaker is used to protect a circuit and it shuts off, it is simple to flick the switch back to reset it. If a fuse is used, however, when it blows it must be replaced. Do not try to bypass a fuse by placing metal foil or a penny under it. This is dangerous, since the line is then not protected against too much current.

When you are working on a circuit, you should shut off the electricity to that circuit. You can do this by unscrewing one of the fuses controlling that circuit, without affecting the operation of electrical appliances on other circuits. This is preferable to shutting off the main switch, but if you are not sure which fuses control the circuit you want to work on, play it safe by pulling the main switch.

To eliminate the necessity of shutting off all the electricity to make a repair, take the trouble to learn what fuses control which circuits. To do this, simply turn on lights and plug lamps in receptacles and then remove fuses (or open circuit breakers) one at a time. Each time you remove a fuse, some lights will go out, identifying the circuits controlled by that fuse. Record the information on a card or piece of paper, and put the record in the fuse box so it will be there when you need it.

6-3. HOW TO REPLACE A WALL SWITCH

When you flip on a wall switch and nothing happens, the bulb may be burned out, the fuse may be burned out, or the switch itself may be defective. Before rushing out to buy a new switch, make sure that the bulb and fuse are both all right. If your house has circuit breakers instead of fuses, check to see that the circuit breaker for the troublesome switch is in the *on* position. If everything else is in working order, you can suspect the switch.

The visible part of a switch is a wall plate with a rectangular hole through which a plastic lever protrudes. Fig. 6–8 shows what is under the wall plate. The plate is held on by two screws which are screwed into two corresponding holes in the switch itself, as shown by the dotted lines. The switch is also held in the junction box by two screws. Two wires are connected to the switch terminals, which are screws with large heads. To get at the switch, first disconnect the electricity by pulling the proper fuse or shutting off the proper circuit breaker. If you are not sure which fuse controls the circuit, shut off the main switch. Now remove the screws holding the wall plate, and take off

the wall plate. If the plate is stuck because of paint, you can pry it off
with a knife or screwdriver. Remove the two screws holding the
switch in the junction box and pull the switch out of the box. The
wires attached to the switch are usually quite stiff, but don't be afraid
to pull the switch out, since the wires will give. If either of these wires
is loose, that could be the source of the trouble. Tighten the terminal
screws, push the switch lever to the *on* position, and turn on the
electricity again (put back the fuse or turn the circuit breaker on).
If the light controlled by the switch goes on, the trouble was a loose
connection. Shut off the electricity again, push the switch back into
the junction box, and put all the screws and the wall plate back as they
were. Turn the electricity on, and you are finished.

If there is no loose connection, the switch itself is probably bad.
When the switch is in the *on* position, it is supposed to make an electrical connection between the two wires attached to its terminals.
Thus, you should be able to turn on the lights simply by bringing the
two wires together. This is, in fact, how you check the switch. With
the electricity disconnected, remove one wire from the switch and
hook it over the other wire at a bare spot. Better still, fasten both
wires under a single screw so that they make a good electrical connection. Now turn on the electricity by putting back the fuse, and the
lights should go on. This shows there is nothing wrong with the rest
of the circuit, so the switch must be at fault.

To replace a switch, simply buy a new one and install it in the

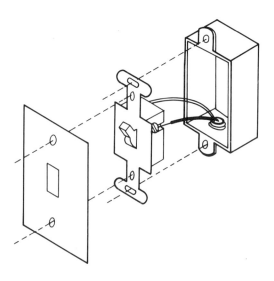

FIGURE 6–8. Wall Switch.

same manner. These switches are available with the switch lever in a variety of colors, so that you can pick one to match the decor in the room. Instead of the common snap-action switch, you may decide to put in one of the new special switches. Mercury switches look just like the common snap-action switches but are silent. In a bedroom or bathroom you may want a noiseless switch, and the mercury switch is the answer. Another type of switch has a push button instead of a lever. A dimmer switch has a knob which can be turned to make the lights dim or bright. The best part of working with any of these switches is that they all fit in the same junction box, and changing from a snap-action switch to any other type is simply a matter of unscrewing a few screws and then putting them back.

Where two or more switches are close together, it is common practice to place them in one large junction box and cover them with a larger wall plate with the proper openings. Wall plates are usually made of thin metal, but you can also buy them made of wood or plastic and in a wide variety of shapes and designs.

In a large room or long hallway, it is usually desirable to be able to turn on the lights from two locations at opposite ends of the room. To do this, it is necessary to use special switches called *three-way* switches. These look exactly like the simple *on-off* switch shown in Fig. 6–8, except that they have three screw terminals, and three wires come out of the junction box. The electrical circuit is shown in Fig. 6–9. The ground wire from the fuse box runs to the light controlled by the switches. A wire runs from the light to the first switch, and two wires run between the two switches. The second switch is connected to the hot side of the fuse box. When the switches are connected to the same wire, as shown in the figures, the circuit is closed, and current flows, lighting the lamp. If either switch is thrown

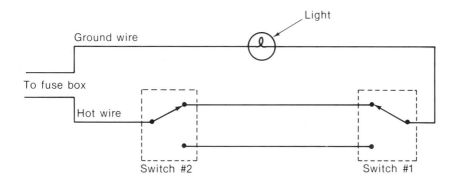

FIGURE 6–9. Three-Way Switches.

to the other wire, the circuit is interrupted and the light goes out. If one of the switches goes bad, you must replace it with another three-way switch.

6-4. HOW TO REPLACE A RECEPTACLE

In your home you probably have wall receptacles in every room of the house for plugging in lamps and appliances. The common type of receptacle is shown in Fig. 6-4. Receptacles rarely become defective, but when internal springs or contacts wear, appliance cords may fall out, and you may want to replace the receptacle. Also, if you have small babies in the home, you may want to install *safety receptacles*. These are receptacles which have slots that close when an appliance cord is removed, so that it is impossible for a child to stick a piece of metal into an empty receptacle. Changing a receptacle is as easy as changing a switch. First, shut off the electricity. Remove the one screw holding the wall plate in place. The receptacle is held in the junction box in exactly the same way as the switch. Remove the two screws holding it to the junction box, as shown in Fig. 6-8 for the switch. Then remove the two wires from the terminals of the old receptacle and fasten them to the terminals of the new receptacle. Reassemble and turn on the electricity again.

There are occasions when you would like to plug three or more appliances into one receptacle and are faced with the problem of three cords to plug in and only two jacks to plug them into. First of all, this is a bad practice, and you shouldn't do it, but if you *must*, you can use a three-way plug, illustrated in Fig. 6-10. This is plugged into a receptacle and in effect changes one jack to three. When you do this, make sure that the sum of all the current drawn by the various appliances does not exceed the rating of the circuit. Thus, in a 15-ampere circuit, for example, it is safe to have a phonograph, a television set, and a lamp. (Current ratings are shown in Table 6-1.) However, if you had a space heater on the circuit, it might not be safe to add any other appliance.

6-5. CORDS AND CONNECTORS

An extension cord enables you to bring electricity to a point where there is no electrical outlet. It consists of a two-wire cord with a plug on one end and one or more jacks on the other. For home use, extension cords are available from 6 to 25 feet in length, and longer

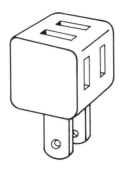

FIGURE 6–10. Three-Way Plug.

cords are available for industrial applications. Most extension cords will handle 10 amperes and can be used with a vacuum cleaner, for example. However, if you want to use a toaster or a waffle iron in your dining room and need an extension cord to reach an outlet, make sure the cord is heavy enough to take the current. To be safe, read the power on the appliance and divide by 100 to get a current rating with about a 10 per cent margin of safety. Thus, a 1500-watt toaster would be rated 15 amperes. The extension cord used with it should be capable of handling this current. To satisfy most home applications, it is a good idea to have one 20-ampere extension cord and a few 10-ampere cords.

The cord on an appliance is called a *line cord*. Since line cords and extension cords must be flexible to go around objects or to permit movement (with vacuum cleaners and electric irons, for example), they are always made of stranded wire. If a single solid wire were used for each conductor, it would have to be large enough to carry the current required by the appliance. For most appliances, the wire size required could be achieved only in a stiff wire. Thinner wire is flexible but will not carry sufficient current without overheating. However, if several thin wires (or strands) are grouped together in a single conductor, they share the current equally and thus can carry heavier currents without overheating. All line cords use stranded conductors. Cross sections of individual conductors are shown in Fig. 6–11. Each conductor consists of a bundle of strands of thin wire. This bundle is tightly enclosed with a wrapping of fiber, called a *lay*, and then covered with rubber insulation. There are several different types of line cords, but all those used with home appliances have the conductors wrapped in fiber and rubber, as shown in Fig. 6–11. The more popular line cords have conductors with seven or ten strands, but for heavy-duty installations, wires with as many as 65 strands in each conductor are used.

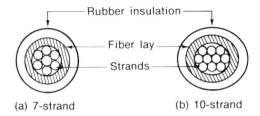

(a) 7-strand   (b) 10-strand

FIGURE 6–11. Stranded Conductor with Wrapping.

When you strip insulation from a conductor in a line cord, it is important that you do not cut into any of the strands. If you break a few strands, the appliance will operate properly, but each of the remaining strands will carry more current than it should. For example, suppose that a toaster which draws 10 amperes has a line cord with ten-strand conductors, as shown in Fig. 6–11. Each strand then carries only 1 ampere, and these strands can be relatively thin wires. However, if six strands break because of too much flexing or poor installation, the remaining four will have to carry the 10-ampere load, and each will carry 2.5 amperes. This will cause the line cord to get hot in the vicinity of the break. You can use a jackknife to strip insulation, but you should not use too much force. Cut into the insulation *lightly* by rotating the knife around the wire about 1 inch from the end, as shown in Fig. 6–12. When the insulation is cut all the way around, the severed portion can be pulled off like a sleeve. The fiber lay between the strands and the rubber insulation protects the strands from the knife, and there should be little risk of cutting the wire strands as long as the job is done carefully. After pulling off the sleeve, the fiber lay can be unwrapped, as shown on the conductor at the left in Fig. 6–12, and can be cut off with a pair of scissors or a knife.

For most low-power appliances, such as clocks, juicers, and lamps, which draw less than 2 or 3 amperes, the most common type of line cord is the popular *zipcord*, shown in Fig. 6–13. This consists of two conductors, like those shown in Fig. 6–11, joined together by a thin rubber bond. It is called "zipcord," because the two conductors are easily separated by tearing the thin rubber membrane joining them.

For heavier work, such as mixers and vacuum cleaners, *jacketed cable* is used. The wrapped conductors are separated by additional fibers which increase the insulation between them, both electrical and thermal. The two conductors and extra fibers are encased in a rubber or plastic jacket. This type is called SV cord, and its construction is shown in Fig. 6–14. In general, jacketed cable will take more abuse than zipcord.

For appliances which draw more than 5 amperes, special *heater cord* is preferred. This is used on toasters, waffle irons, irons, and other appliances that furnish heat rather than motion. In heater cord, each wrapped conductor shown in Fig. 6–11 is also wrapped with asbestos fibers. Then the two conductors are brought together and a layer of asbestos is wrapped around both. Finally, the package is encased in a braided jacket of cotton or nylon. Heater cord is illustrated in Fig. 6–15.

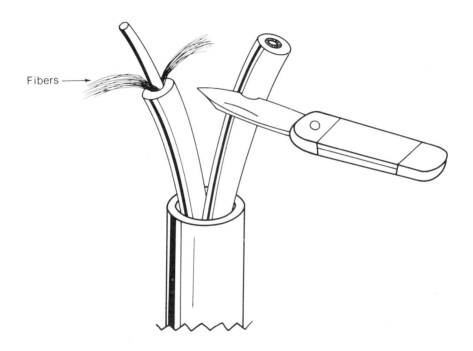

Fibers

FIGURE 6–12. Stripping Insulation.

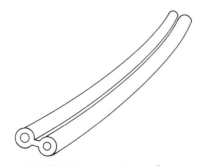

FIGURE 6–13. Zipcord.

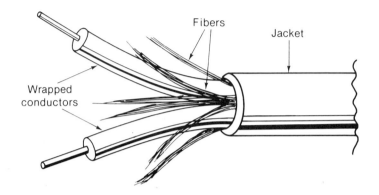

FIGURE 6–14. SV Cord.

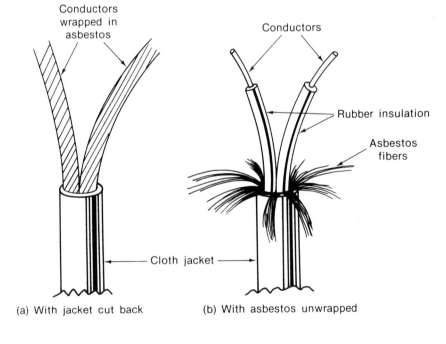

(a) With jacket cut back   (b) With asbestos unwrapped

FIGURE 6–15. Heater Cord.

The current-carrying capacity of the line cord depends on the wire diameter and not on the insulation. Thus, a zipcord line with #10 wire can carry 25 amperes, whereas an asbestos heater cord with #18 may be limited to 5 or 6 amperes. Nevertheless, in general, heater cords are used for appliances that draw more current; jacketed cable is used where the cord itself is subject to abuse; and zipcord is by far the most common because of its simplicity and is used wherever there are no special demands on the line cord.

When a cord is shortened or replaced, it is necessary to attach a plug to it. It is important to connect a cord to a plug so that the connection will not be subject to strain when the cord is pulled. When attaching a cord to a plug, you can remove strain from the connections by tying a knot in the line cord after passing it through the connector. The typical "Underwriters' knot" is shown in Fig. 6–16. First, you slip the plug over the line cord, as shown in Fig. 6–16(a). The first

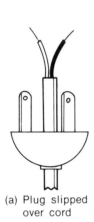

(a) Plug slipped over cord

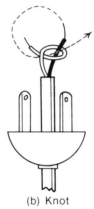

(b) Knot

(c) Connected

FIGURE 6–16. Strain-Relieving Knot.

loop of the knot is shown in Fig. 6–16(b), with the rest of the knot indicated by a dotted line. The knot is slid down to the end of the insulation. Any kind of knot will do as long as it prevents the cord from being pulled out of the plug. The two wires are now stripped, passed around the blades of the plug, and the stripped portion tightened under the mounting screws, as shown in Fig. 6–16(c). The wire should not be crossed over itself under a screw, as tightening may cause it to break.

If the appliance draws less than 2 amperes and has a zipcord line cord, you can use a gripper plug. Here there is no strain-relieving knot, no stripping of wire, and no contact screws. Although the connection can be damaged by jerking the line cord, with reasonable care it can give adequate service indefinitely. There are many varieties of gripper plugs on the market, and all come with simple instructions for installing. WARNING: *Do not use on anything but zipcord and in low-current applications.*

Extension cords and line cords should last indefinitely if they are not abused. Some of the more common mistreatments which you should avoid are listed here. You should never pull a plug out of an outlet by yanking on the cord. There may be no apparent damage, but continued yanking can break some of the strands of wire. Never run extension cords where they can be stepped on, such as under a rug, or squashed, such as under a door. The unusual pressure can damage the insulation, causing a hazardous situation. Never run cords next to metal surfaces, especially near hot radiators. Heat can dry out the insulation, causing it to crack, and the cord may then short-circuit to the metal surface. Never use tacks or staples to hold cords along moldings or door frames, since insulation can be damaged. However, it is all right to hang a cord on hooks along a molding. A better way is to buy a special outlet strip which attaches to a molding and provides receptacles at any point on the molding.

6–6. DOORBELLS

The basic circuits for a doorbell are shown in Fig. 6–17. A bell transformer is connected permanently to the 115-volt house line. This transforms the voltage to a safe low value, usually about 12 volts for a bell or buzzer and up to 24 volts for a set of chimes. The push buttons, then, are located in low-voltage lines, reducing the danger of electric shock. Because these wires have a low-voltage difference, they can be run in walls and under floors without the precautions required for the 115-volt line.

In Fig. 6–17(a), a circuit for a single push button is shown. When the button is pushed, the circuit is closed, and the bell rings. In Fig. 6–17(b), a circuit using chimes and two push buttons is shown. There are two separate circuits, each controlled by a different push button. Two different chimes are used to differentiate between front and back doors. The letters R, C, and F stand for "rear," "common," and "front," respectively.

If you have bells or buzzers in your home and wish to install chimes instead, you may have to change the transformer. The voltage output of the transformer is marked on the nameplate, but you must find the transformer. This is usually located near the fuse box. When you buy a set of chimes that suits you, notice what voltage is required, and if your present transformer is inadequate, you will have to buy a new

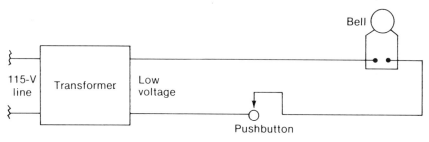

(a) Front door only

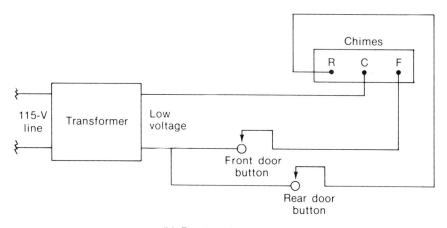

(b) Front and rear doors

FIGURE 6–17. Doorbell Circuits.

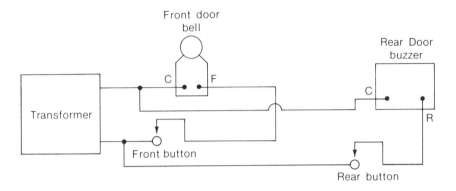

FIGURE 6-18. Separate Front and Rear Bells.

transformer to go with the chime set. If the front and rear bells are close together, it is easy to remove them and transfer the wires to a chime set. You will have to trace the wires back to the transformer to find which are the common ones. In Fig. 6-18, the common wire at each bell is labeled C, and the other wires are labeled F and R (for front and rear). Simply attach one of the C wires to the center terminal of the chime set. You can cut off the other common wire. Connect the F and R wires to the indicated terminals on the chime set (these are usually labeled). The job is done.

If the front bell and rear buzzer are widely separated, you will have to run a wire from one push button to the location of the chime set. For example, you place the chime set at the location of the front doorbell. Now you must run a wire from the rear button to the chime. If you wish, you can pull the old rear buzzer wire out of the wall and use it, or you can leave it, but disconnect it from the push button. To run a wire up to the chime set, tie a long piece of string to a wire which is already there. Then go into the cellar and pull that wire out of the wall so that the string is inside the wall instead. Make sure that an end of the string still protrudes from the wall near the chime. Now attach a second wire to the end of string in the cellar, and pull both wires back up into the wall by pulling the upper end of the string. Make connections as indicated in Fig. 6-17(b).

If a bell does not ring when the button is pushed (assuming that it worked before), the trouble may be in the fuse box, the transformer, the wires, the push button, or the bell itself. The most common source of trouble is the push button. Remove the cover from the button either by unscrewing two screws or by prying with a small screwdriver if no screws are visible. You will see two wires, which should be firmly attached to terminals on the push button. Remove these two wires and touch them together. If the bell rings, the trouble is definitely the push button. Cleaning the contacts with sandpaper is usually all that is required. However, a new pushbutton is very inexpensive and is easily installed in place of a defective one.

If touching the wires together does not cause the bell to ring, check the *output* of the bell transformer. WARNING: Be careful not to touch the input or primary side of the transformer, since that side has 115 volts across it. The input side has two heavy wires connected to it, whereas the output side has two thin wires. Touch a screwdriver blade across the two transformer output terminals momentarily. There should be a spark if the transformer is in good condition. Alternatively, if you have a voltmeter, you can measure the output voltage of the transformer. It should be close to its rated voltage but does not have to be exact. If there is no voltage at the output, replace the transformer. Shut off the electricity when you do this, and connect the four wires on the new transformer to the same points that the four old wires were connected. For best results, solder the connections, and put insulating tape over each soldered joint. You can also use solderless connectors, which look like black thimbles. These are threaded onto a pair of wires twisted together and serve to hold the wires firmly and to insulate them at the same time.

If the transformer and push button are all right, check the wires. If insulation wears on a pair of wires, they may rub together and cause a short circuit. If you find bare spots on wires, cover them with insulating tape.

Finally, if all else seems operative, the trouble may be the bell itself. If you have a voltmeter, check the voltage at the bell with someone holding in the push button. If no one else is around, remove the wires from the button and twist them together when you make this voltage test. If you do not have a voltmeter, remove the two wires from the bell and touch them together momentarily while the push button is held in or the wires there are twisted together. There should be a spark indicating voltage at the bell terminals. If there is voltage and the bell does not work, try cleaning the contacts with sandpaper. If this doesn't cure the trouble, the coils may be burned out, and the easiest solution is to replace the bell.

Since bell systems are usually on low-voltage circuits, it is not necessary to take precautions against electric shock, except when working at the bell transformer. Nevertheless, it is dangerous to be too complacent, and you should approach all wiring cautiously, and ask yourself what voltage is on the line you will be touching.

Some bell systems operate off a battery instead of a transformer and are thus completely separate from the house electric circuit. Such a system cannot have a burned out transformer, but it can have a dead battery. You can check a battery by placing a bulb of the proper voltage rating across its terminals. If the bulb lights, the battery is working. Note that an ordinary 115-volt bulb will not light when placed across a 6-volt battery, so it is necessary to use the proper bulb.

7

Materials
And Joints

The most common building material in your house is probably wood, and wood is used for many of the repair jobs that you will do. In addition, you will also use wallboard, tiles, adhesives, and an assortment of other materials. In many cases you will have a choice of material, and you should know the pros and cons in order to make a wise choice.

7-1. LUMBER

You can save money on lumber if you buy the right wood for the job. Typically, you can use inferior finishes where wood doesn't show, as inside walls or under floors. Even where finish is important, you may be able to economize by buying boards with knot holes and cutting the wood you need from the length between imperfections. You must decide what wood you want as well as what grade.

Wood from broadleaf trees is generally harder than woods from trees with needles. Pine, fir, redwood, cedar, and the like are called *softwoods;* ash, oak, mahogany, walnut, and other broadleaf trees are *hardwoods.* Hardwoods are usually stronger than softwoods but are also more difficult to work with. There are some exceptions, however. Thus, gumwood and poplar, both classed as hardwoods, are easy to work and not very strong. Table 7-1 lists some of the more common woods and their characteristics. For structural applications, you

TABLE 7-1. Characteristics of Woods

Wood	Hard or Soft	Moisture Resistance	Decay Resistance	Workability	Strength
Ash	H	Fair	Excellent	Difficult	Excellent
Birch	H	Fair	Fair	Difficult	Excellent
Cedar	S	Good	Excellent	Good	Fair
Cypress	S	Good	Excellent	Good	Fair
Douglas fir	S	Poor	Poor	Easy	Good
Mahogany	H	Excellent	Excellent	Difficult	Excellent
Maple	H	Excellent	Good	Difficult	Good
Oak	H	Excellent	Good	Difficult	Excellent
Pine	S	Good	Poor	Easy	Good
Poplar	H	Fair	Poor	Easy	Fair
Redwood	S	Good	Excellent	Easy	Fair
Spruce	S	Good	Poor	Easy	Fair
Walnut	H	Excellent	Good	Difficult	Good

would want woods resistant to moisture and decay. Workability is always a consideration. If you will be driving many nails or screws into a board, you will want a wood that is easy to work with. For general building construction, softwoods are usually used, whereas hardwoods are used for furniture and decorative trim. Moldings are usually made of pine, and dowels of birch.

Lumber is graded according to quality by a series of numbers or letters. The highest quality is #1, if numbers are used, or grade A, if letters are used. Grade designations are indicated in Table 7-2.

TABLE 7-2. Grades of Lumber

Grade	Description
#1 and #2 Clear ⎱ A and B ⎰	Almost entirely free of imperfections; best quality
C Select	Small imperfections which can take a fine paint job
D Select	Lowest grade suitable for painting
#1 Common	Some small knots; can be used without waste
#2 Common	Slightly larger knots than #1 Common; no waste
#3	Larger knots, pitch; some waste
#4	Big knots, pitch; not durable
#5	Knotholes; loose knots

You should not use grade #5, and use #4 only for temporary structures, such as concrete forms or props.

Another consideration in selection of lumber is the direction of the grain in structural pieces. The grain is specified as *flat* if it is parallel to the wide dimensions of the cross section of a board and vertical if it is perpendicular to the wide dimensions. Flat-grained lumber, as shown in Fig. 7-1(a), is stronger than the vertically grained lumber shown in Fig. 7-1(b), but may be selected on the basis of appearance.

Lumber sizes are usually specified as the size before drying and milling the boards. Thus, a board which is said to be 1 inch thick may in fact be only ¾ inch thick. If you want specific dimensions, make sure that you specify *actual* rather than *nominal* dimensions. Lumber is usually sold by the board foot. Board feet is the product of the thickness in inches times the width in feet times the length in feet. These are nominal dimensions. For example, a board nominally ¾ inch thick, 10 inches wide, and 4 feet long would have $\frac{3}{4} \times \frac{10}{12} \times 4 =$ 2½ board feet. Occasionally, lumberyards have sales of specific sizes or

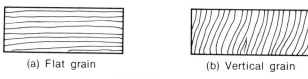

(a) Flat grain   (b) Vertical grain

FIGURE 7-1. Grain.

grades of lumber, and if you can use them, you may save money buying the sale material instead of the exact wood you need.

In addition to flat boards and structural pieces such as 2 × 4's or 4 × 10's, lumberyards carry lumber for special purposes. Three of these are shown in Fig. 7-2. Tongue-and-groove flooring, shown in Fig. 7-2(a), is used for finished floors. Note the slight bevel at the joint so that a good contact can be ensured at the surface of the floor. Beveled siding, in Fig. 7-2(b), is used for sides of houses. Other similar sidings are also available. The lapped boards, in Fig. 7-2(c), have a number of applications where a tight joint is required. Special shapes available for decorative purposes are shown in Fig. 7-3. A few of the almost unlimited variety of shapes for moldings are shown in Fig. 7-3(a). Decorative strips for valances and other uses are shown in Fig. 7-3(b). Again, there is a large variety, which is constantly growing. Table legs and balusters, shown in Fig. 7-3(c), are a few of the turned shapes. The uses for the many varieties of shapes supplied by your lumber dealer are limited only by your imagination. For example, you might want to use pieces of molding or lengths of a closet rod as shelf props in a bookcase.

If you use poorer-grade lumber, don't throw away sections of boards that have loose knots. Frequently you can tighten the knots with glue and save some material. Invariably you will have some extra lengths of wood or scraps when you have a carpentry project, and you will wonder whether to save them or throw them away. Scraps of decorative trim and moldings should be saved. Scraps of ordinary boards should

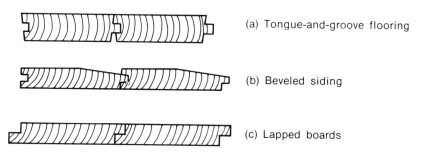

(a) Tongue-and-groove flooring

(b) Beveled siding

(c) Lapped boards

FIGURE 7-2. Boards for Special Applications.

be saved up to a point: These pieces make good sanding blocks, but how many do you need? Use a cardboard carton for these scraps, and when it gets too full, use some of the scraps for a fire in your fireplace. Larger pieces should always be saved, since you can cut needed small pieces from a good larger one. Pieces of structural lumber, 2 × 4's and larger, and pieces of plywood should be saved, because these are stronger materials that can be used for braces.

7-2. PLYWOOD

Plywood consists of several layers, or *plies*, of wood bonded together with glue and having the grains in adjacent plies perpendicular to each other. A given thickness of plywood is much stronger than the same thickness of a solid board of the same wood. Douglas fir is the most common material for plywood, but plywood with hardwood faces is available for cabinet work and other decorative applications. Fir plywood comes in *exterior* type, which is waterproof, and *interior* type, which would deteriorate if subjected to the elements for too long a period.

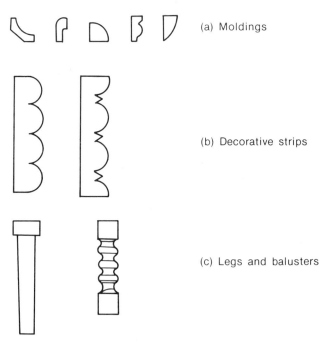

(a) Moldings

(b) Decorative strips

(c) Legs and balusters

FIGURE 7-3. Special Shapes.

The grade of wood in plywood is designated by letters, as follows:

A   Fine appearance
B   Smooth, can be painted
C   Contains knotholes or splits
D   Large knotholes

The inner plies are usually grade C in exterior plywood and may be grade D in the interior type. The designated grade indicates the surface plies, which can be A, B, or C in exterior and even D in interior. The surface plies do not have to be the same. Thus, A-B interior plywood has grade A on the front, grade B on the back, and grade D for all inner plies. When buying plywood, don't buy A-A if one side will not be seen. For structural uses, you can buy the lowest available grade, C-D.

When cutting plywood with a saw, it is almost impossible to prevent a ragged edge on one side. The raggedness is caused when the sawtooth emerges from the wood. Therefore, always have the sawteeth enter the plywood on the better side. If both sides will be exposed, use a fine saw to minimize the roughness.

The edge of a plywood board is not very pretty, and you may want to finish it. You can use decorative moldings sold specifically for the purpose or cover the edge with a special filler, which is applied like putty. The best solution is plywood *edging tape*, which is a thin, flexible tape made of wood. It is available in fir, mahogany, walnut, and many other woods, and has an adhesive backing. To apply it, simply stick the tape to the edge of the plywood, and apply heat by holding a warm iron against the tape. Full instructions come with the tape. If the tape protrudes beyond the surface of the plywood, simply sand it off, using fine sandpaper around a small block of wood.

7-3. WOOD JOINTS

The most common wood joint is a *butt* joint, where two pieces of wood are simply butted against one another, as shown in Fig. 7-4. The joint can be held by nails or screws. Screws are stronger than nails in a butt joint, but for additional strength, one of the joints shown in Fig. 7-5 should be used. The *rabbeted joint,* shown in Fig. 7-5(a), is stronger than a butt joint, since the horizontal board is supported by the rabbet. The *dado,* or slot, in the vertical member in Fig. 7-5(b) gives additional support and is excellent for shelves. Both the rabbet and dadoed joints should be secured with nails or screws *and* a strong glue. The miter joint, shown in Fig. 7-6(a), is used for appearances and is basically not very strong, although it can be strengthened by the addi-

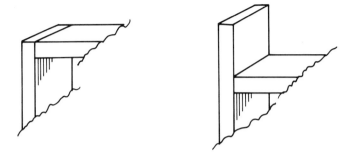

FIGURE 7–4. Butt Joints.

tion of a block in contact with both boards, as shown. Nails and glue must be used in a mitered joint. Dowels, as shown in Fig. 7–6(b) are stronger than screws when properly applied. They can be used with butts, rabbets, or dadoes.

 A rabbet can be cut with a hand saw, power saw, or sabre saw. A dado is best made with a power saw but can be made with a chisel. For doweling, use a drill the same size as the dowels, about half the thickness of the boards being joined. Drill through both pieces simultaneously, holding them together and making sure that the hole is at least 1 inch into the inner piece. Cut the dowel to length so that when its end is flush with the outside surface, it will protrude 1 inch into the inner piece. Coat the contacting surfaces of the boards with glue, and also cover the dowel with glue. Drive the dowel into the hole, using a scrap block of wood on the end so that your hammer will not mar the surface of the board. It will be easier to drive in the dowel if you round the tip slightly with a file or sandpaper.

 The *mortise-and-tenon* joint is a strong joint used in window screens and furniture. The parts of the joint are shown in Fig. 7–7. The *tenon*, shown in Fig. 7–7(a), is simply a tongue extension cut on

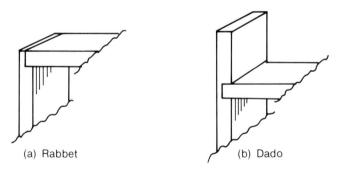

(a) Rabbet   (b) Dado

FIGURE 7–5. Stronger Joints.

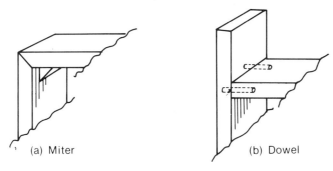

(a) Miter   (b) Dowel

FIGURE 7-6. Special Joints.

the end of one piece to be joined. The *mortise,* shown in Fig. 7-7(b), is a rectangular opening cut in the second piece to receive the tenon. The two parts must fit closely and are held together with glue. When it is desired to conceal the joint, a *blind mortise* is used, as shown in Fig. 7-7(c). The rectangular mortise goes only part way through the second piece, and the tenon is cut shorter.

The tenon can be cut easily with an all-purpose saw or any small hand saw. First, mark the outline of the tenon on all the surfaces of the piece to be cut, as shown in Fig. 7-8(a). Then, cut on all lines with

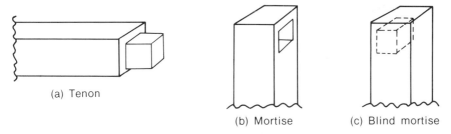

(a) Tenon

(b) Mortise   (c) Blind mortise

FIGURE 7-7. Mortise and Tenon.

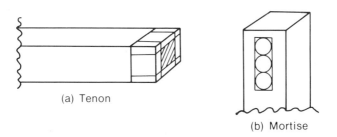

(a) Tenon

(b) Mortise

FIGURE 7-8. Cutting Mortise and Tenon.

the saw, leaving the tenon on the end. To make a mortise, first mark the outline, as shown in Fig. 7–8(b), and then drill out as much material as possible. Finish both parts with a chisel and sandpaper, making frequent trials to ensure a good fit.

7–4. ADHESIVES

Old-fashioned animal glues are rarely used today, because better adhesives have been developed. However, with the wide variety of adhesives available, it is sometimes hard to tell which is the best for a particular job.

The most popular glue is white poly(vinyl acetate). This is a milky liquid, usually packaged in squeeze bottles, and it dries clear. This adhesive can be used for bonding wood and most porous materials, such as paper, cloth, leather, or cork. It should not be used for metal or plastics. The glue sets in half an hour and reaches full strength in 24 hours. It is *not* waterproof. When applying this adhesive, the materials and the room in which you work should be at a temperature of at least 70°F.

For stronger joints or in applications requiring a waterproof bond, plastic resin glue should be used. It too must be worked in temperatures above 70°F. These glues set in about six hours, so the bond must be well clamped.

The strongest adhesives are epoxy cements. These are expensive and more difficult to apply. You must mix two materials together and apply immediately. Parts must be clamped for about ten hours. This glue requires a working temperature above 70°F.

If you must do your gluing in a cold cellar or garage, you will have to use casein glue. It comes in powdered form and is mixed with water as needed. It forms a strong bond on wood but is not waterproof.

When you are gluing, make sure that the contact surfaces are clean and dry. Scrape or sand off any layer of old glue or paint which would prevent the new glue from reaching the porous surface. Follow the instructions on the label on mixing and applying the new glue. Especially important are temperature restrictions. After gluing, clamp the joint so that parts stay in contact. If clamps cannot be used because of odd shapes, use your ingenuity to devise ways of holding the bond together with rope or strips of cloth.

For special jobs, such as installing tiles or linoleum, use the adhesive recommended by the supplier. These adhesives may not be so effective on wood, but they are specifically designed for the materials specified.

7-5. PANELING

In addition to solid wood and plywood, you can get large panels for use in your home made of hardboard, gypsum wallboard or plastic laminate. They are all easy to apply and have excellent durability.

Hardboard is made of pulverized wood fibers processed into a dense, rigid material. The outside surfaces can be covered in a wide variety of finishes, including simulated wood, leather, plastic, or any color of paint or enamel. Hardwood panels are available in sheets up to 4 by 8 feet in thicknesses of 1/4 or 1/8 inch. It can be used for wall panels, counter tops, bench tops, and even floors and doors. When it is nailed, edges must be supported. Nails should be at least 1 inch long, spaced 4 inches apart. Hardboard can be cut with a saw, drilled, planed, and sanded.

Gypsum wallboard consists of plaster between two layers of cardboard. It is available in sizes up to 4 by 12 feet and thicknesses up to 1/2 inch. It can be used for walls and ceilings. It can be cut easily by scoring with a knife and just breaking it along the mark. It can be nailed, but care must be taken not to break the paper. In normal application, wallboards are nailed to studs, and the seams between adjacent boards are filled with joint cement. The joint is then covered with tape, and a second thin layer of cement is applied. The joint is then sanded and is ready for painting. Although wallboard is cheap, more care is required in installation.

Plastic laminate is more expensive than other paneling, but it makes a surface which is good-looking and easy to clean. Further, it needs no finishing. It comes in 1/16-inch sheets for most applications, but for small jobs 1/32-inch material is also available. It can be scored with a knife and broken to size. It is cemented in place with a special adhesive supplied with the laminate. Just follow the instructions.

7-6. ALUMINUM

Aluminum is not thought of as a building material, but it is now available in so many sizes and shapes that it can be used in many odd jobs around the home. It is found in sheets, rods, bars, tubing, and angles, as well as in many decorative designs. Some alloys are soft enough to be worked with ordinary woodworking tools. You can use aluminum angles for structural pieces, such as in frames for tables or supports for shelves. Round or rectangular tubing can be used for table legs and awning supports. Aluminum channels can be used as window guides. Special parts for the home include aluminum gutters and aluminum siding. Aluminum sheets can be cut with scissors or metal shears. Soft aluminum bars and tubing can be cut with a hand saw, harder alloys with a hacksaw or all-purpose saw. Aluminum can be drilled, nailed, planed, and painted.

7-7. WALL FASTENERS

There are many different types of fastenings for attaching to a wall anything from a light picture to a heavy cabinet, and new types are continually being developed. For a specific job, ask the advice of your building-materials supplier. Some of the more common fasteners are described below.

You can use ordinary nails or screws if you can fasten the material to be hung to a wall stud or part of the framework of the house. For a large cabinet this is the first choice. Remember that studs are 16 inches apart between centers. You can sometimes locate studs by tapping on the wall. There is a hollow sound between studs and a solid feel right at the stud. If you have difficulty, buy an inexpensive stud locator, available in most hardware stores, and follow the instructions.

If you have to locate something heavy between studs, you may be able to use a "bridge" for reinforcement, as shown in Fig. 7-9. Locate the studs and fasten a flat board to the studs by screws. The board

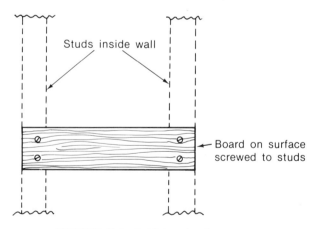

FIGURE 7-9. Bridging Studs.

should be about 18 inches long and at least 1 × 4. Heavy objects can then be supported from any part of the board. For very heavy objects, use a longer board attached to three or more studs.

For lightweight objects, such as toothbrush holders, towel racks, small pictures, and the like, there are many hangers available. Some are simply pushed into plaster walls with the fingers or held in place with a thin brad. Some are glued in place. Towel racks and other bathroom appurtenances usually come with their own fasteners and instructions for installing.

For heavier pictures and mirrors up to about 40 pounds in weight, you can use a simple picture hook. This is fastened to the wall by a nail which is held in the hook at an angle to the wall. The nail is driven into the wall by tapping with a hammer. On plaster walls, put a piece of transparent tape on the wall at the spot where the nail is to enter, to keep the plaster from cracking. These hooks come in a variety of sizes, graded according to the weight they will support.

When it is necessary to fasten a heavy weight to a hollow wall, simple screws or nails do not furnish enough support, since the portion in the wall is a small part of the total length of the screw. There are three types of fasteners especially adapted for hollow walls; these are illustrated in Fig. 7-10. The *toggle bolt*, shown in Fig. 7-10(a) and (b), has wings which are normally held open by springs. A hole must be drilled in the wall large enough to insert the bolt with wings folded. The fixture to be hung must be placed on the bolt first and then the wings. The wings are pushed through the hole in the wall, as in Fig. 7-10(a), and the wings are opened by the springs when they are inside the wall. The wings are pressed firmly against the inside of the wall when the bolt is tightened, as shown in Fig. 7-10(b). One disadvantage of this type of fastener is that if the bolt is removed, as to remove the fixture, the wings fall inside the wall and cannot be retrieved.

The *expansion screw anchor*, usually called a *molly* anchor, is shown in Fig. 7-10(c) and (d). It consists of a thin metal sleeve and a machine screw. The hole required in the wall can be smaller than that for a toggle bolt. The molly anchor is inserted as shown in Fig. 7-10(c), and when the screw is tightened, the sleeve deforms, as shown in Fig. 7-10(d). Now the screw can be removed, and the sleeve remains in place. The screw can be reinserted with a fixture mounted on it.

The *plug*, shown in Fig. 7-10(e), may be made of plastic, lead, or fibrous material and is simply a hollow sleeve, inserted in a close-fitting hole in the wall, which accepts an ordinary wood screw. The hole through the center is tapered with the narrow end inside the wall. When a screw is driven into the plug, the plug expands, tightening its

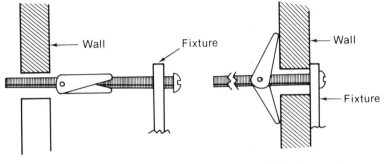

(a) Toggle bolt with wings folded   (b) Toggle bolt fastened

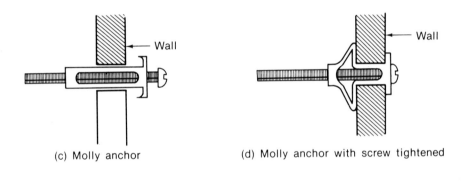

(c) Molly anchor   (d) Molly anchor with screw tightened

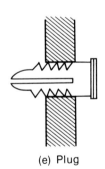

(e) Plug

FIGURE 7-10. Fasteners for Hollow Walls.

hold on the wall. In addition, the inner end expands against the inside of the wall to increase the holding power.

Permanent fasteners for masonry walls and floors use the expansion principle of the plug shown in Fig. 7–10(e). These anchors for masonry are made of plastic or lead for smaller bolts and of steel to accept heavy lag screws. Unlike the plug, they are entirely contained in the hole in the masonry and, when expanded, grip firmly. To install an expansion anchor, first a hole must be drilled in the masonry. You can use a *star drill*, which is essentially a cold chisel with two cutting edges at right angles to each other. It is held in place with one hand and struck with a heavy hammer. A simpler method is to use a special masonry bit in an electric drill. These are available in sizes up to ½ inch, but with ¼-inch shanks so that they can be used in ¼-inch electric drills. When drilling, press firmly so that the masonry bit does not slip. Slipping tends to dull the bit.

8

Inside
The House

Ordinary wear and tear in your home produces a slow deterioration which is hardly noticed. Then one day you look up from your newspaper and discover that crack in the wall, the worn spot on the floor, or a dingy ceiling. Even such obvious things as a sagging door or a stuck window are not emergencies, but at some point you do decide to attend to these matters, and most of them you can fix by yourself. For the most part, interior repairs can be done at your leisure, although some tasks, such as repairing a broken window, may require your immediate attention. This chapter covers the repairs that might be required on windows, doors, walls, ceilings, floors, and stairs.

8-1. HOW TO REPLACE GLASS

Replacing a broken pane in a window or door is a simple job that you can do yourself with no prior experience. You will need putty or glazier's compound and a package of glazier's points, as well as a piece of glass to fit the opening. All supplies are available in most hardware stores or in glass-supply outlets.

The first problem is to remove all pieces of the broken glass and the old putty from the frame. When you are removing the glass, wear heavy gloves of the sort sold for gardening to protect your hands from slivers. If the putty is very old and dry, it can be scraped out easily with a screwdriver or chisel. Otherwise, it may be necessary to hammer on the head of the chisel, but if you do, you must keep the chisel at a low angle to the wood and be careful not to gouge the frame. If the old putty is extremely hard, it can be softened by heating it with a soldering iron or torch, and then it should be easy to remove it. Old glazier's points should come out with the old putty. Use a pair of pliers to pull out any points that remain.

When the frame is *clean*, a thin ribbon of putty must be placed all around the opening as a "bed" for the glass. This bed of putty prevents leakage and also protects the glass from shock and vibration. However, if the putty is placed on the bare wood, the wood will tend to absorb the oil in the putty, causing the putty to dry out quickly and become brittle. To prevent this, the wood should first be coated with linseed oil or thinned oil-based paint. Then the bed of putty can be applied. The coating of oil saturates the wood so that it doesn't draw oil from the putty. A small wad of putty is rolled between the hands until it takes the form of a thin rope. This rope is applied in a thin ribbon all around the frame and pressed firmly in place with the fingertips.

You can buy glass cut to size from your dealer, so it is never necessary to cut the glass yourself. Most hardware dealers will cut the glass free of charge. Measure the opening accurately and order the glass about ⅛ inch smaller in each dimension to allow about 1/16-inch clearance on each side. If the opening is not rectangular, cut a piece of cardboard to the proper shape, and bring it to the dealer as a pattern. Press the glass carefully but firmly in place against the bed of putty, and secure it with two glazier's points on each of the four sides. *Glazier's points* are thin triangular pieces of metal. They are placed against the glass with one point of the triangle stuck firmly in the wood of the frame, as shown in Fig. 8–1. A special tool called a *point set* is used to help drive in the points. This is simply a piece of metal which is placed over each point as it is installed, as shown in Fig. 8–1(b), so that the points can be driven in easily by hitting the top of the point set with a hammer. A point set usually comes free in each package of points, but if you don't have one, you can use a screwdriver instead. While you are hitting the tool with a hammer, the head of the hammer remains in contact with the glass at all times.

Add a few more glazier's points about every 4 or 5 inches all around the edges of the glass to hold the glass in place before applying the final layer of putty. This final seal is also applied with the fingertips,

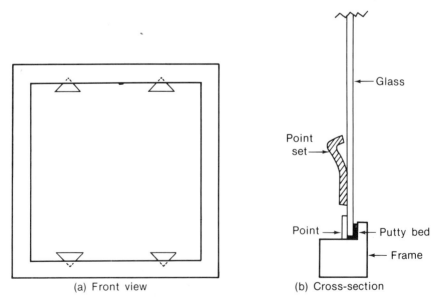

(a) Front view　　　(b) Cross-section

FIGURE 8–1. Installing Glazier's Joints.

but it is then smoothed with a putty knife at an angle, as shown in Fig. 8-2, which illustrates the cross section of a complete putty seal. Any excess putty is removed with the putty knife. Note that the *points* hold the glass in place; the putty merely prevents leaks. After the putty is smoothed, you can apply an oil-based paint over it immediately. This paint layer harmonizes with the window trim, but more importantly, it keeps the putty from drying out.

Panes for metal windows are installed in the same manner, except that special spring clips are used to hold the glass instead of glazier's points. These clips fit into holes in the metal frames. Remove the old putty, being careful to save the clips. Clean the frame and lay a bed of putty. Press in the glass and hold it, with the clips inserted in the same holes as before. Put on a final layer of putty and seal it with paint. For metal windows you should use double-strength glass.

8-2. SASH CORDS

A window sash is balanced by weights attached to sash cords. When a sash cord breaks or a weight slips off the end of a cord, the window is no longer counterbalanced and tends to fall when raised. You can keep the window open, if necessary, by propping it up with a piece of wood, but sooner or later you will want to replace the cord. This is a simple job, once you have solved the mystery of how to get at the cord. Figure

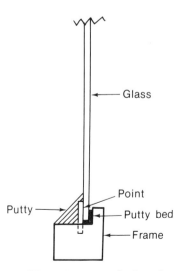

FIGURE 8-2. Finished Seal.

8-3 shows the window tracks in a common double-hung window, as well as the stops and other parts of the window frame. The upper sash moves in the outside track, and the lower in the inside. The two tracks are separated by a *parting strip*, which is held in a slot between the tracks by friction. Pulleys at the top of each track support the sash cords. Counterweights attached to the cords move up and down in a deep well behind the tracks as the windows are lowered or raised.

Figure 8-4 shows how a sash cord is attached to a window. A knot on the end of the cord fits into a socket or large indentation in the side of the sash. The rope above the knot lies in a groove along the side of the window, but the groove is too narrow for the knot to slip through. The sash cord passes over its pulley at the top of the track and is attached to a weight. Each window sash has two weights supporting it, and ideally the sum of the weights of the two counterweights should equal the weight of the sash, although friction between the tracks and the sash permits some deviation from this ideal. When a sash is all

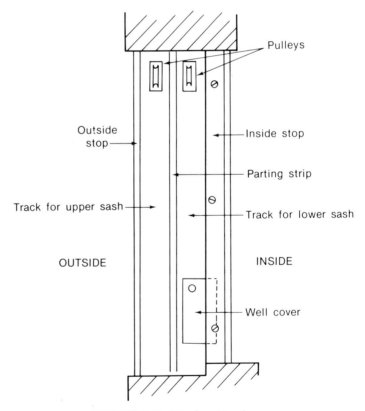

FIGURE 8-3. Window Tracks.

the way down, its counterweights should be near the top of the well.
When the sash is fully raised, the weights should not touch the bottom of the well.

To replace a broken sash cord, it is necessary to remove the sash.
For an upper sash, it is necessary to remove the lower sash as well.
The first step is to remove the inside stop. Remove the screws holding
it to the frame (refer to Fig. 8–3), and pry the stop loose with a screwdriver or an old chisel. The first time this is done, you will break the
paint seals between the stop and the frame. After that, it will be easy
to remove the stop. With one stop removed, you can lift out the lower
sash. It is not necessary to remove the stop on the other side unless
you are going to replace both sash cords attached to the one sash.
With the sash removed, you can get at the well cover. One or two
screws must be removed, and then the well cover can be pried off,
revealing the weights inside the well. Pass a new rope over the pulley
and attach the inside end to its proper weight. Tie a knot in the outside end, as shown in Fig. 8–4, and push the knot into the socket on
the side of the sash. Put the window back in its tracks and replace the

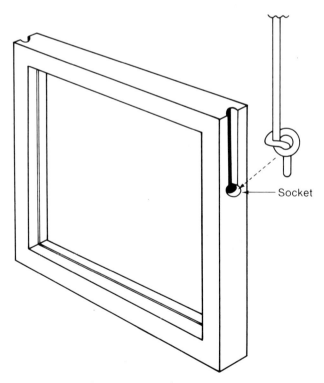

FIGURE 8–4. Sash and Cord.

inside stop. When the knot is placed in the socket and the sash is near its bottom position, the rope should be cut to the proper length so that the weight is near the pulley. Buy *soft* rope specifically designated for sash cords.

For a top sash, you must remove the bottom sash as described above and also pull out one parting strip. Then the top sash can be removed, and the cord replaced as described above. When the bottom sash is removed to get at the top sash, it is necessary to remove the cords from the bottom sash. Just pull the knots out of their sockets, but be careful not to let go of the ropes suddenly. Holding the knot, let the weight pull the rope until the knot is next to the pulley. Then it is safe to release the knot, since it won't slip past the pulley.

8-3. STUCK WINDOWS

When a double-hung window is stuck and cannot be opened, the trouble is due either to dampness which caused the sash to swell or to paint that has been applied improperly and has sealed the window to its stop. Freeing a stuck window is not a difficult task, but the methods used depend to some extent on the cause.

If a sash is stuck because paint has hardened, joining the sash to a stop or to the sill, it is necessary to break the paint seal. Use a putty knife, if you have one, or any other thin blade, and insert it between the sash and the stop. Tap the blade lightly with a hammer, and simply cut the paint. Alternatively, you can force an old chisel or a hatchet blade between the bottom of the window and the frame from outside. As you tap on the back of the hatchet or the handle of the chisel, the taper forces the window open, breaking the paint seal. Once the window has moved, it usually can be opened easily. Scrape away the extra paint so that the window will not jam again when it is closed. If you wish, you can sand the edge to make it smooth. If none of these methods is effective, you must remove the inside stop and free the window in the same manner described in Section 8-2 for replacing a sash cord. Pry off the stop carefully, since you will be breaking the paint seal as you do.

When a sash sticks because of dampness, you can sometimes loosen the window by hammering the stop away from the sash. Use a small block of wood between the hammerhead and the stop so that you do not mar the stop. Again, if this method is ineffective, you can free the window by removing the inside stops and the sash. If the sash moves stiffly without the stop in place, it indicates that the sash itself is swollen. Remove the sash, and plane or sand the edge so that it moves freely. Before putting it back, rub the edge with paraffin or wax. This lubricates the sash so that it slides better and also forms a seal against moisture.

When steel casement windows are difficult to move, the trouble may be due to excessive paint but is most often caused by inadequate lubrication. Oil all moving parts at the first sign of sticking. Sand off any rust spots, and touch up with a rust-resistant primer. Break paint seals by moving the window back and forth a few times, and scrape away any accumulated layers of paint.

8-4. THE PARTS OF A DOOR

To understand instructions for fixing door troubles, you must be familiar with the terms used by carpenters to describe the various parts of a door and door frame. These terms are used frequently in how-to-do-it books, but unless they are defined, the home repairman may find the instructions difficult to follow.

The parts of a door are illustrated in Fig. 8-5. Horizontal bars are called *rails*. In the figure there are three rails. Vertical bars are *stiles*.

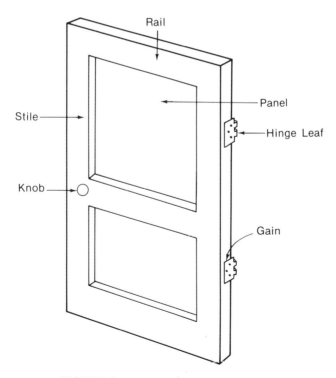

FIGURE 8-5. Parts of a Door.

The thin portions of the door between stiles and rails are called *panels*. If a door is solid, it has no rails and stiles, and the door may be thought of as one large panel. A hollow door has a framework of stiles and rails which is completely covered with thin veneer sheets on both sides to give the appearance of a solid door.

The doorknob and latch are on one edge of the door, and the hinges are on the opposite edge. The door frame is usually mortised or cut out to accommodate the hinge so that the surface of the hinge is flush with the surface of the edge of the door. The mortised recess for the hinge is called a *gain*, as indicated in Fig. 8–5. A typical hinge is shown in Fig. 8–6. One leaf is attached to a gain in the door and the other to a gain in the door frame. A removable pin joins the two leaves of the hinge. There is usually an ornamental knob attached to the hinge similar to the knob at the top of the pin, but since the ornamental knob has no functional purpose, it is sometimes omitted. A hole through the knob permits access to the bottom of the pin. Most doors have two hinges, but heavy outside doors in your home may require three.

Part of a door frame is shown in Fig. 8–7. The parts of the frame next to the sides and top of the door are called *jambs*. Fastened to the jambs are *stops*, which are simply strips of wood to limit the movement of the door. The door is in contact with the stops when it is closed. The jamb on the latch side of the door has a gain cut into it

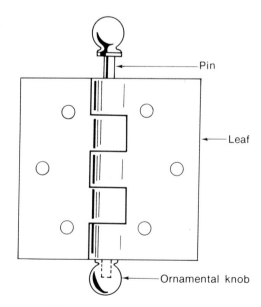

FIGURE 8–6. Door Hinge.

to accommodate the *striker plate*, which engages the latch. This plate is mounted with its surface flush with the surface of the jamb.

The bottom of the doorway is called the *threshold*. For outside doors the threshold is usually a board under the door, but inside the house, floors may be continuous from one room to another without a raised threshold.

8-5. HOW TO FIX A BROKEN DOOR

Doors take a lot of abuse, but with a little imagination, damage to doors can be covered up, and broken doors can be repaired at a minimum of cost. The repaired door may not be as good as new, but it will function as it is supposed to, and only a critical eye could detect the repair work.

When the veneer of a hollow door is broken, for example, from bumping into a piece of furniture or from being bumped by a tricycle, you can glue a new layer on top of the old veneer and hide the

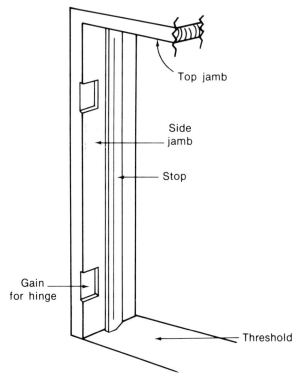

FIGURE 8-7. Door Frame.

hole completely. If the damage is on the side of the door which contacts the stops, the extra thickness would not permit the door to close.
Simply cut the new veneer to leave a margin of about 2 to 6 inches
all around it. The new veneer will then look like a decorative panel on
the door. You might like it so much that you will want to glue a
similar "panel" to the other side of the door. If only a small part of
the door is damaged, use a patch of decorative veneer to cover it.
Veneers are available in many colors and with a variety of designs.
Follow the manufacturer's instructions to install the veneer, since
some come with an adhesive backing.

A more serious problem is a broken stile on the hinge side of the
door. This can happen to any door that is banged too hard, but storm
doors are especially susceptible. If the door is only cracked, you can
glue the parts together again. Pry open the crack, as shown in Fig. 8–8.
Place a chisel or screwdriver near the bottom of the crack to hold the
two surfaces apart. Coat the surfaces with adhesive. If the door is a
storm door or other outside door, use waterproof glue or any of the new
adhesives that can withstand the elements. Remove the chisel, and
squeeze the two parts of the crack together. Tie strips of an old sheet
around the door to hold the crack closed until the glue dries.

When a more durable repair job is required, such as when a piece
of the door is broken off completely, you can use dowels (wooden
rods) to hold the two pieces together solidly; this is shown in Fig. 8–9.
First, glue the two parts together by coating the surfaces of the breaks
with glue. Now drill holes for dowels along the edge of the door.
These holes should be spaced about 5 or 6 inches apart and should be
deep enough to penetrate the larger section about 2 inches. The diameter of the dowels depends on the thickness of the door. For thick
doors use ½-inch dowels and drill ½-inch holes for them. For doors

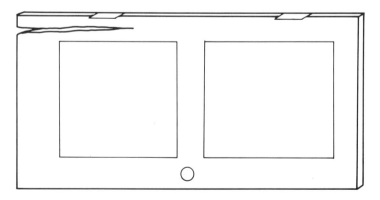

FIGURE 8–8. Crack in Door.

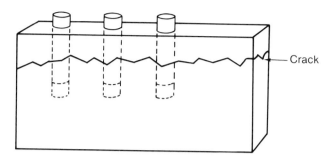

FIGURE 8-9. Mending Door with Dowels.

less than 1 inch thick, thinner dowels can be used. Cut the dowels to length so that they will extend at least 1½ inches beyond the crack. Coat the dowels with glue, and then tap them in with a hammer so that the ends are flush with the edge of the door. When the glue on the dowels dries, the repaired door will be as sturdy as a new one. The only difficult part of this job is drilling the holes for the dowels straight without coming out the side of the door. If you stand astride the door as you drill, it is fairly simple to hold the drill parallel to the faces of the door.

If the split is under a hinge, you may want to move the hinge. Cut a new gain, as described in the next section, a few inches above or below the old mortise, and install the hinge there. The old gain can be covered with a scrap of wood which is cut to fit. Fasten the block with glue or brads, or both. Drive the head of each brad below the surface with a nail set and fill the hole with putty or wood filler. Also use filler in the cracks around the block if it is not an exact fit. When the block and jamb are repainted, they will look like one solid piece.

8-6. HOW TO HANG A DOOR

The cost of labor for installing a new door is frequently more than the cost of the door itself, and it therefore pays to hang a door yourself. With a little care you can do a professional job.

First, the door must be fitted to the opening. If you are lucky, you may be able to buy a door which is just the right size, but more likely you will have to settle for one that is larger than the doorway and trim it down. You should allow about 1/16 inch at the top and two sides. For an outside door, allow about ¼- to ½-inch clearance above the threshold. The space is not critical, since you will cover it with a drip cap and weather stripping, as in Fig. 3-13. For an inside door without a raised threshold, allow at least ⅜ inch at the bottom, and more if the door has to clear linoleum, a rug, or an irregular floor. A space of up to 1 inch at the bottom of an inside door is no problem.

If you have to trim off only a small amount to make a door fit, use a plane. Plane the bottom first, and then along one side. When planing across the grain, usually at the bottom of the door, do not run the blade of the plane off the side, since it may splinter the edge. Plane from both edges toward the middle. This is not a problem when planing with the grain. If you have to take off more than about ¼ inch of wood, you can saw off the excess and then touch up the surface with a plane or sandpaper to smooth it.

If you are replacing a door, you can use the same hinges that were used on the old door and in the same locations on the jamb. You will have to cut new mortises or gains for the hinges only on the door itself. If you are hanging a new door, you will have to cut mortises in both the jamb and the door, and you will have to buy hinges. When buying hinges, tell your hardware dealer the size and thickness of the door, and let him show you a selection of appropriate hinges. The next problem is locating the hinges. Place the door in the opening and prop it up with pieces of wood, cardboard, or anything handy, so that it is correctly positioned in the opening. Now wedge some thin pieces of wood on the latch side so that the door is shoved tightly against the hinge jamb, as shown in Fig. 8–10. If there are hinges already on the jamb, mark their positions accurately with a sharp pencil on the door. If this is a new installation, jab the point of a sharp knife held horizontally in the crack between the door and the jamb so that it marks both simultaneously. The top hinge can be anywhere from 6 to 9 inches from the top of the door, and the bottom hinge can be 6 inches to 1 foot from the floor. After you have marked the location of the hinges, take down the door.

Place a leaf of a hinge on the edge of the door, as shown in Fig. 8–11, and using it as a pattern, mark around it with a sharp knife. The inside edge of the hinge should be ¼ to ⅜ inch from the edge of the door, as shown in Figures 8–10 and 8–11. The exact dimension is not critical, but it should be noted carefully, and the corresponding dimension on the jamb (from the hinge to the stop) should be the same or a hair larger. The positions of the mortises are then located on the door, as shown in Fig. 8–12. Similar outlines are drawn on the jamb. Support the door solidly with its hinge edge up. Do not try to cut out the mortise in one piece. Drive a chisel along the edges of the large face of the mortised piece with the bevel pointing inward. Make several additional cuts with your chisel across the face of the mortise, as shown by the dotted lines in Fig. 8–12. Finally, drive your chisel into the side *with the*

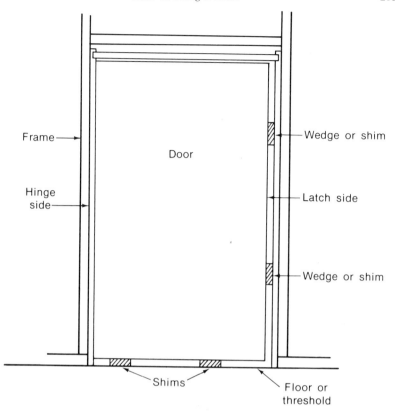

FIGURE 8–10. Positioning Door for Locating Hinges.

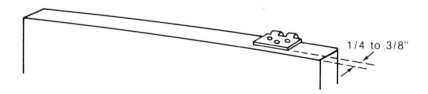

FIGURE 8–11. Marking Hinge Position.

bevel up, cutting out the mortise in small chunks. If you happen to cut the mortise too deep, place a piece of cardboard under the hinge when you mount it. Cut the gains in the jamb in the same manner. Screw the hinge leaves in their proper positions. Now lift the door so that the leaves intermesh and drop in the hinge pins. Installing a latch and striker plate is discussed in Section 8-7.

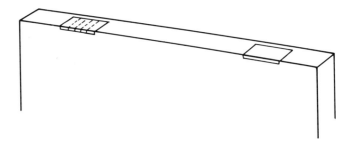

FIGURE 8-12. Cutting Mortises.

As soon as you can, after hanging a new door, make sure that you coat all surfaces with a primer to prevent moisture absorption which could warp the door or cause it to swell. A final paint or varnish coating can be done more leisurely, as long as the surface is protected.

8-7. LOCKS AND LATCHES

After a new door is hung, a latch or lock must be added. Many old-fashioned locks require large mortises to be cut out of the edge of the door, but modern locks can be installed in round holes. To install a modern lock you need only a brace and assorted bits. When you buy a lock, you will also receive a template, which will enable you to locate the position of the holes to be drilled accurately. Drill sizes are also indicated in the instructions with the lock set. When you drill through the door, drill from one side only until the point of the bit just emerges from the opposite side. Then pull out the drill, and finish the job by drilling into the door from the opposite side. If you were to drill all the way through from one side, the emerging drill could split the wood.

If you want to use a lock that requires a large mortise, drill out as much material as possible, as shown in Fig. 8-13, and then finish the job with a chisel. The body of the lock goes into the opening, and an additional gain must be cut around the opening to accommodate the plate of the lock. The surface of the lock should be flush with the edge of the door.

The striker plate is mounted on the jamb. In addition to the gain cut for the striker, you must cut out extra material for the bolt or latch to enter. Again, the job is simplified if you follow the instructions and use the templates furnished with the lock set. If you happen to cut

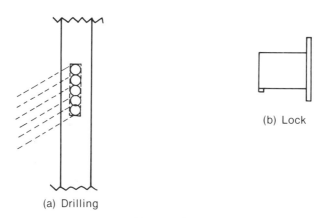

(b) Lock

(a) Drilling

FIGURE 8–13. Drilling a Mortise for Lock.

too deep a mortise for the striker plate, use cardboard to shim it up flush with the surface of the jamb.

Some doors are never locked, and some need no inside handle to close them. For example, a door in a hall closet does not need a lock and can do without an inside knob. In such cases, you can use a spring latch, which requires neither mortising or drilling. A hook is attached near the top of the door, and the spring latch is fastened to the upper jamb to mate with the hook when the door is closed. A knob is fastened to the outside of the door to pull it open. The latch holds the door closed, but a slight pull disengages the latch. Such a latch is very easy to install.

8–8. HOW TO CURE DOOR TROUBLES

When a door sticks, the trouble may be caused by settling of the house and a resultant distortion of the frame around the door, by swelling of the wood due to moisture, or by one or more loose hinges. At any rate, don't be in a hurry to use a plane to try to make the door fit. Planing a door that has swelled from too much moisture may make the door easy to open again, but when the moisture dries out, the door may then shrink and be too small for the opening. This is especially noticeable in areas that have well-defined rainy seasons. In such climates, it is important that all surfaces of the door, including edges, be protected from moisture by painting them regularly. Coating the edges with paraffin also helps.

The first thing to do when a door sticks is to check the hinges. A loose hinge will allow the door to tilt in the frame. Tighten all screws. If screws turn too freely because the thread in the wood is stripped, you should fill the screw hole with wood filler. If you have no wood filler handy, try putting small strips of wood or wooden toothpicks in the hole and then driving the screw back into them. The screw forces the scraps of wood to take on a thread, and if the hole was not completely stripped, the scraps will blend into the sides of the hole and make a good bond.

If the hinges are tight, try to determine where the door is sticking. Some possible misalignments are shown in Fig. 8–14, greatly exaggerated. In Fig. 8–14(a) there is a gap near the top hinge, and the opposite edge of the door contacts the frame. If there is sufficient clearance around the door except at this point of contact, the door can be realigned by pushing it away from the frame at the bottom hinge. Remove the screws holding the bottom hinge to the frame, and insert a piece of cardboard as a shim between the hinge and the frame. This will tend to move the door slightly counterclockwise and should straighten it in the frame. In Fig. 8–14(b), the gap is near the bottom hinge. This can be corrected by putting a cardboard shim under the top hinge. In Fig. 8–14(c), contact is at the striker plate. Check for loose screws in both the striker and the latch. This difficulty can usually be solved by cutting deeper mortises for either the latch or striker or both.

If shimming the hinges doesn't cure the trouble, the fault may be caused by a distorted frame. If the top of the door on the latch side is rubbing against the frame, as in Fig. 8–14(a), you can pull the frame

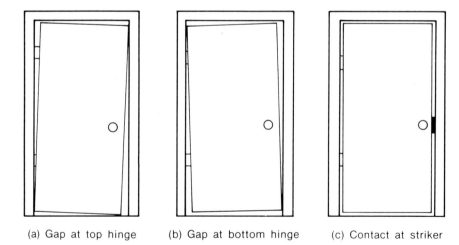

(a) Gap at top hinge   (b) Gap at bottom hinge   (c) Contact at striker

FIGURE 8–14. Door Misalignments.

back into line by driving a long nail into the opposite jamb just under the top hinge. Use a finishing nail 3 or 4 inches long, and use a nail set to drive the head below the surface. If you wish, you can cover the nailhead with putty and paint over it so it won't show, but since the nail cannot be seen when the door is closed, you don't have to be that meticulous.

If shimming a hinge causes the door to rub all along the latch edge, take out the shim and mortise the other hinge a little deeper. That is, in Fig. 8–14(a), the top hinge should be mortised deeper to pull the top edge of the latch side away from its jamb.

If a door rattles when it is closed, there is too much play at the latch. This happens when the striker plate is too far from the stop on the jamb, as shown in Fig. 8–15(a). When the latch is engaged in the striker, there is a gap between the door (shown by dotted lines) and the stop. Any slight breeze can move the door against the stop and away again, causing it to rattle. The cure is to move the striker closer to the stop. With the door closed, note the size of the gap, and then cut the mortise for the striker to move the plate about the same amount. It will be necessary to fill the old screw holes with a wood filler, and after it hardens, drill starting holes for the new positions of the screws. Otherwise, the screws would slip back into their old positions and pull the striker away from the stop again.

If the striker plate is too close to the stop, as in Fig. 8–15(b), the latch will not be engaged, since it doesn't quite reach the hole. The door then will not stay closed. If only a slight shift of the plate is needed, loosen the screws slightly, pull the plate in a direction away from the stop, and insert a strip of cardboard between the edge of the striker and the edge of the mortise. Now tighten the screws, and the plate will be shifted away from the stop by the thickness of the card-

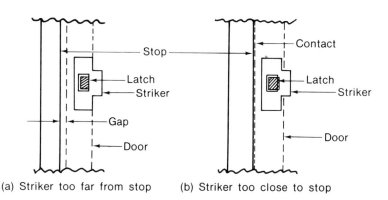

(a) Striker too far from stop   (b) Striker too close to stop

FIGURE 8–15. Improper Striker Positions.

board. If a larger shift is needed, file out the opening in the striker, using a fine file, or move the striker away from the stop by filling the old screw holes with wood filler and drilling new screw holes.

If a door won't stay closed, the trouble may be caused by a vertical misalignment of the striker and latch. This happens when either the door or the frame settles. Look for marks on the striker plate which show where the latch is hitting it. If these marks are lower than the opening (the usual case), it is necessary to lower the opening in the plate. This can be done by moving the whole plate lower on the jamb, or simply by filing the opening so that the latch is engaged.

If a door warps because of excessive moisture on one side, it can sometimes be straightened simply by drying it thoroughly. If this doesn't work, support the door with its curved side up and place heavy weights on it to force it into line. Let it stand this way for a day or two, and the door should then be usable.

8–9. STAIRS

If a flight of stairs is rickety and needs strengthening, call a professional carpenter. However, there are some minor stair repairs you can do yourself, and if you take care of your stairs, you will never need a major repair job.

A cross-sectional view of part of a flight of stairs is shown in Fig. 8–16. The steps are supported on two long beams called stringers, one on either side of the flight. On very wide steps, a third stringer

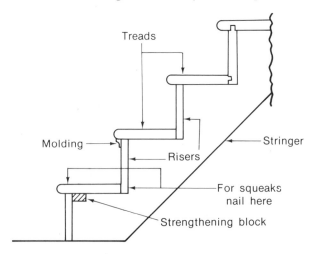

FIGURE 8–16. Stairs.

may be used in the middle. The stringers have cut out spaces for the treads and risers. The treads and risers are nailed to the stringers and also nailed to each other. In the figure, the top riser is shown with a tongue-and-groove joint to the two treads it joins. The other joints shown are simple butt joints. In practice, a flight of stairs will have all the joints of one variety, but both are shown in the figure for illustrative purposes. The tongue-and-groove joint is usually glued and nailed and is thus somewhat stronger than the butt joint, which is only nailed. A decorative molding, as shown under the nose of one tread, is sometimes added.

When stairs squeak as you walk on them, the noise is caused by a loosened tread rubbing against a riser or against one of the stringers. You can stop the squeak by squirting a lubricating powder into the crack between the tread and riser, but this is only a temporary solution. Solve the problem completely by nailing the tread firmly to the risers. If you can get to the underside of the stairs, also nail the risers to the treads (refer to the bottom tread in Fig. 8–16). Use finishing nails, 2 or 3 inches long, and space them about 3 inches apart. For best results do *not* drive the nails perpendicular to the surface. Instead, drive them at an angle and have alternate nails slope in alternate directions so that the nails are not holding in the same direction. For an additional bond, nail and glue a small block of wood under the stairs at the junction of a tread and riser, as shown under the bottom tread in the figure. Countersink any nailheads on the surface of the stairs, and fill the hole with putty colored to match the coating on the stairs.

Constant use wears the treads, and eventually you will decide that new treads are needed. If the treads and risers are connected with butt joints, it is a simple matter to pry up the treads and turn them over. Of course, if someone has already done this, the bottom side will be too worn also, and then you must get new treads. If the nails holding the treads are set at angles, as they should be, you may find it difficult to pull the tread up off the riser. Use a small all-purpose saw between the tread and riser to cut all the nails. Then when the tread is off, you can drive out the nails if you intend to reverse the tread and use it again. If the treads have decorative moldings, pry off the moldings before trying to remove the treads.

For treads joined to risers by a tongue-and-groove joint, you can saw off the tongue as you saw the nails. When you reverse the tread, fill the groove on the bottom side with wood filler, and paint over it. Don't worry about not having tongue-and-groove joints. Most stairs do not have them.

If looks are not too important, on cellar stairs for example, you can simply cover worn treads with sheets of ½-inch plywood cut to the size of the tread. Just nail the plywood to the top of the tread. A similar approach, but more decorative, is to use tiles or linoleum as a cover. To do this, first fill in depressions on the tread with floor filler, and then cement the linoleum or tiles on top of that. An ornamental molding or metal strip can be placed along the nose (front) of each tread to hide the seam between the linoleum and the wood.

8-10. WOOD FLOORS

The common wood floor used in most houses consists of two layers. The subfloor, or bottom layer, is a layer of flat boards nailed directly on the large supporting joists. These boards usually are laid at an angle of 45 degrees to the joists, although in some cases they are laid at right angles. The floor itself is made of tongue-and-groove flooring, as shown in Fig. 7-2(a), and repeated here in Fig. 8-17. Each board has a tongue along one edge and a groove on the opposite edge. In addition, the opposite ends of the boards may also have a tongue and a groove, respectively. Where the subfloor is laid at an angle of 45 degrees to the joists, the top layer is 90 degrees or at right angles to the joists. If the subfloor is at right angles to the joists, the top layer is usually parallel to the joists. A layer of building paper is placed between the two layers of flooring, to act as an insulation and to provide a resilient surface to take care of imperfections in the flooring. In Fig. 8-17, a small space is shown at the bottom of each seam. This space ensures that at floor level the boards will make good contact and provide a continuous surface without cracks. However, the angle is barely discernible, and on some softwood floorboards, it may be omitted.

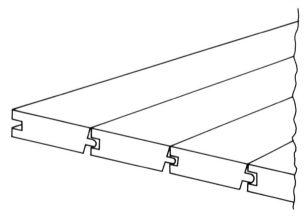

FIGURE 8-17. Tongue-and-Groove Flooring.

One advantage of tongue-and-groove flooring is that it permits invisible nailing. Each board is placed with its groove fitted to the tongue of the preceding board. Nails are placed along the tongue at an angle, as shown in Fig. 8-18. Each nail is countersunk by hitting with a nail set so that it doesn't interfere with the fit between the tongue and groove of the next board. There are special flooring nails, but any kind of small-headed or headless nails can be used. For floorboards about ¾ inch thick, the nails should be about 2½ inches long and spaced every 10 or 12 inches along the tongue.

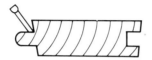

FIGURE 8-18. Nailing Flooring.

If a small section of the top flooring is gouged or otherwise damaged, you can replace it. To remove the damaged section, first mark it off carefully and then drill a large hole in each corner, as shown in Fig. 8-19. These holes should not penetrate the subfloor. With a chisel, split the section by cutting from hole to hole along the grain, as indicated by the dotted lines in the figure. Cut across the grain at the ends. Remove the damaged section by literally chopping it up with the chisel. Be careful not to damage the adjacent tongue and groove. A new board is cut to length to fit in the opening. The underside of the groove must be removed, as shown in Fig. 8-20, to get it into the space. For best results, plane off the bottom edge of the groove, but if you are careful, you can remove it with a chisel. Drill a pilot hole for a finishing nail in each corner of the new section, and drive in the nails.

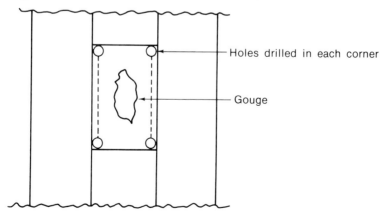

FIGURE 8-19. Removing Damaged Section of Flooring.

FIGURE 8-20. Cross-Section of Replacement Section.

Without pilot holes the nails could split the wood. Countersink the nails and cover heads with wood filler.

When a floor squeaks when you step on it, this is a sign of a space between the joist and subfloor or between the subfloor and top floor. If you can get underneath the floor, look for such a space between the joist and subfloor. This can be caused by a sagging joist or a loose nail in the subfloor. To cure the problem, you can wedge a thin piece of wood between the joist and the subfloor where the space occurs. To make sure that the wedge stays there, you can coat it with glue before inserting it. If the subfloor is firmly attached to the joist, but the top floor seems to move slightly on it, you can pull the top floor down to the subfloor, by inserting screws from below. Allowing about ¾ inch for each of the two floor layers, the screws should be at least 1 inch long and not more than 1¼ inches.

If you cannot get under the floor because there is a ceiling below it, you will have to drive nails into the floor itself to fasten it down. First, locate the joists. To do this take a small block of hardwood, place it on the floor, and tap it with a hammer. When the block is over a joist, there is a "solid" sound when you hammer on it. Between joists there is a hollow thud. Joists are spaced 16 inches apart, so that when you locate one, you should have no difficulty in finding the rest. The block is used to avoid damaging the floor with the hammerhead. After locating a joist, drive nails into the floor at the joist at an angle, alternating the angle at adjacent nails. Use 2½-inch or longer finishing nails or threaded flooring nails. If the squeak is between joists, indicating a space between the floor and subfloor, just drive nails at an angle at the point of the squeak to push the top floor down. In all cases, countersink the nails with a nail set so that the heads are below the surface of the floor. Use a wood filler to hide the nailheads.

When a house is old, floors may sag noticeably. This may be caused by the shrinkage of joists or other supporting members or by a gradual sinking into the ground. If a sag is noticed on the first floor of the house, it can usually be corrected easily by using a jack post to prop up the supporting timber. Jack posts look like oversized automobile jacks and are available at building suppliers. Some special tools are needed to install a jack post, but they are inexpensive. At the point on the basement floor directly below the beam that is to be supported, it is necessary to attach a base plate to prevent the jack post from moving sideways. You will need a star drill or a masonry bit to make holes in the cement or concrete in the basement; these are described in Section 7-7. Make holes at least 1 inch deep for the bolts to hold down the metal base plate. Use the plate itself as a template to locate the positions of the holes. Lead expansion anchors are placed in the holes. These expand when bolts are driven into them, and the pressure holds the bolts in place.

The jack post is set on the base plate and extended until its top plate just touches the timber to be supported. Use a level to make certain that the post is vertical. Then fasten the top plate to the timber with nails or screws to prevent slipping. Turn the screw on the jack post about one quarter turn and let it set for a day. Then turn it up *only one half turn per week*, until the sag is not noticeable. If you try to jack up the beam faster than this you can damage the house frame and even break gas or water pipes. When you move in small increments, everything in the house stretches or settles between movements to adjust to the small pressure.

8-11. HOW TO INSTALL A NEW THRESHOLD

When a threshold is so worn that a visible gap appears under the door, even with weather stripping in place, it is time to replace the threshold. The first and hardest part of the job is removing the old threshold. Installing a new one is relatively simple.

It is best to remove the door to give yourself as much room as possible to get out the old threshold. Simply remove the pins in the hinges and lift the door out. To remove a pin, hold a wooden rod or an old screwdriver under the head of the pin, and hit it gently with a hammer. If the pin is stuck, drive it out with a punch through the hole in the bottom of the hinge. After the door is removed, pry off the door stop on both side jambs. Use an old chisel and pry off in small increments so as not to crack the stop. If you do split a stop, you can glue the pieces together again.

When the stops are out, you may be able to remove the old threshold in one piece. Slide it out if it protrudes under the jambs. If it cannot be removed, you can split it with a chisel to simplify removal. Use the old threshold as a pattern for a new one, if possible. If it is too badly damaged, measure the space for a new one. The new one should look something like the one shown in Fig. 8-21. Slide the new one under the jambs and into position. If you are replacing the threshold

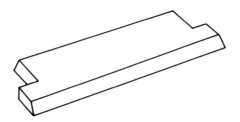

FIGURE 8-21. Threshold.

on an outside door, you should put a layer of roofing asphalt or linoleum cement under the threshold to make a waterproof and windproof
seal.

If you cannot slide the new threshold under the jambs, because it is
thicker than the old or the floor is uneven, cut scraps of wood to fit
the spaces under the jambs.   Then fit the new threshold flush with the
jambs instead of under them.   Similarly, if you cannot slide out the
old threshold, you can cut it off flush with the jambs, using a small
hand saw.   Then fit a new threshold into the space.

The new threshold should be made of hardwood, since it must
withstand much traffic.   This makes it more difficult to nail down.
Use pilot holes about 1/16 inch in diameter through the threshold to
avoid splitting the wood, and nail it in place with 2- or 2½-inch finishing nails.   Countersink the nail heads with a nail set and cover the
heads with wood filler.

8-12. HOW TO REFINISH WOOD FLOORS

When a floor has a few scratches in it, you can usually remove the damage without having to resort to a complete refinishing.   If the scratches
do not penetrate farther than the finish, they can be removed with
steel wool.   If there are stains as well as scratches, use a cleaning agent
with the steel wool.   Rub only in the direction of the grain.   When the
scratched finish is removed, smooth the surface with fine sandpaper or
fine steel wool, and apply a matching shellac or varnish.   Dilute
shellac slightly with alcohol; dilute varnish with turpentine.

If scratches are deep and penetrate the floor, remove the finish, as
indicated above, and smooth the wood.   Then fill the scratches with
wood filler or wood plastic to a level above the surface of the floor.
Remove excess with a putty knife.   When it is dry, sand it flush with
floor, using smooth sandpaper.   Finish with shellac or varnish as above.

Refinishing a floor completely is not a difficult job, but it requires special equipment, which can usually be rented. There are three steps in refinishing: (1) sanding off the old finish; (2) applying a finishing coat of varnish or shellac; and (3) applying a coat of wax to protect the finish.

Before beginning the sanding operation, remove all furniture from the room, including pictures, drapes, and venetian blinds. Sanding leaves a thin layer of dust on everything. Look carefully over the entire floor, and if you see any nailheads, drive them down with a nail set. This is a good time also to nail down any loose boards or squeaky spots in the floor. Open the windows, shut the doors, and you are ready to begin.

You will need to rent a drum sander and a disc sander. The drum sander is used first to cover all large areas in the room. Sand parallel to the grain. Follow the directions supplied with the machine, and you will find it amazingly simple to operate. The disc sander is for edges which are not accessible with the larger drum sander. With both sanders, you begin with a coarse paper to remove the finish and then progress to finer sandpaper in a second and third operation. Return the sanders.

After the sanding is completed, and before beginning the finishing, go over the *whole room* with a vacuum cleaner, including tops of doors, windows, and baseboards. Any dust left in the room can spoil the finish.

Finishes for floors fall into three categories. *Floor sealers* soak down into the wood and do not form a film or coating on the surface. *Varnishes, shellacs,* and some *synthetic* finishes form a surface coating which may be colored but is usually transparent so that the grain of the wood is visible. Floor *paints* cover the floor with an opaque coating. The choice depends on the type of finish desired. Sealers and transparent finishes are covered in this section, and painting a floor is discussed in Section 9–13.

If you want a matte finish on the floor, you should use a floor sealer. Apply the first coat with a brush or mop, or wipe it on with a cloth. If you wish to add color to the floor, you can get colored sealer. Let the sealer remain on the floor for about 15 or 20 minutes, and then wipe off the excess. Let it dry overnight, rent an electric buffer, and go over the floor. Now add a second coat of sealer in the same way. The sealer finish is usually scratchproof. Worn areas can be touched up simply by wiping on more sealer, with no danger of lap marks showing.

Varnish makes a pleasing finish, but it is slow drying and therefore awkward to use. So-called "quick-drying" varnishes should not be used, since they are not durable. Varnish can be put down over an old finish if the old finish is in good condition. For new wood or resanded wooded, use a sealer for the first coat. After it has dried overnight, apply the varnish. You should put on at least two coats of varnish, waiting at least 24 hours for each coat to dry. Alternatively, you can use a coat of thinned shellac as a sealer, and then two coats of varnish. Allow each coat to dry thoroughly before the next is applied. A varnish finish darkens with age.

Shellac is simple to apply and dries quickly. White shellac does not stain the wood, so that the natural grain is visible. Orange shellac also shows the grain but darkens the wood somewhat. Shellac should be applied in thin coats. Shellac as purchased should be thinned with alcohol. Ask your paint dealer to advise you how much to thin it, since dealers may mix their own shellac already thinned. For bare wood, plan on putting on three coats of shellac, allowing each coat to dry at least two hours before putting on the next. Shellac is not as water-resistant as varnish, but it is easier to apply, and worn areas can be touched up easily.

Synthetic or plastic finishes are the most durable. They *require no wax* and will last for years. They must be thinned with a special thinner and can then be brushed on easily. Two coats are sufficient. These materials are available in either a glossy or matte finish.

When your final finish is dry, you should wax the floor to protect the finish. Do not use a self-polishing liquid wax on a wood floor, since these waxes contain too much water, which can damage wood. Paste waxes and solvent-based liquid waxes (not self-polishing) are satisfactory. Apply with a soft cloth and let dry about 20 or 30 minutes. Then use the electric buffer to polish. Two thin coats, buffed separately, give a longer-lasting shine than one thick coat.

8–13. HOW TO LAY A WOOD FLOOR OVER CONCRETE

If you want to convert a basement room or a garage for "living" quarters, you may wish to have a wood floor laid over the concrete floor already there. You can do it yourself. The most important step is to make sure that you have a good vapor barrier under the floor. Waterproof mastic is excellent for this purpose. Spread it liberally over the concrete with a trowel or other flat-faced tool. A putty knife will do in a pinch. The mastic prevents moisture in the concrete from reaching the wood, where it can cause shrinking or warping of the floor.

You will not need a subfloor, but you will need *screeds* on which to nail the floorboards. Screeds are short sections of 2 x 4's, pressed right into the mastic and lapped, as shown in Fig. 8–22. The rows should be about 1 foot apart, and the overlap between screeds should be about 4 or 5 inches. The length of a screed is not critical; anything up to about 3 feet is satisfactory.

Tongue-and-groove flooring is laid perpendicular to the screeds. It is usually a good idea to buy the flooring as much as a week in advance and store it in a dry, warm place in your home. This will tend to remove any excessive moisture in the wood. Nail only on the tongue side of the board, as shown in Fig. 8–18 and described in Section 8–10. Nail each board to every screed it crosses. This not only makes the floor stronger but also holds the screeds together. After every three or four courses are laid (a course is one board or one line all across the room), place a scrap of flooring with its groove against the tongue of the last course, and hit the scrap with a hammer to drive the courses together.

When you get close to the opposite wall, you won't have enough room to drive nails into the tongue at an angle. You will have to drive nails into the face of the flooring. Make sure that you know the location of the screeds so that you nail the floorboards to them. It is best to drill pilot holes 1/16 inch in diameter in the floorboards before driving nails in the face, since hard woods can be split by nailing. When the flooring is all laid, nail a shoe molding all around the room to hide the cracks between the walls and the floor.

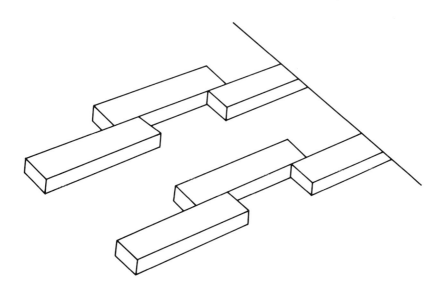

FIGURE 8–22. Screeds.

8–14. HOW TO LAY FLEXIBLE TILES

Tiling a floor is a boring job but one that is very simple to do. If you have a radio going while you are doing the work, the time can pass quickly, and you save the cost of a tile layer. Flexible tiles are available in vinyl, asbestos, cork, rubber, linoleum, asphalt, and combinations of these materials. For durability, vinyl tiles are best, or some combination of vinyl such as vinyl-asphalt or vinyl-asbestos. Use some form of vinyl tile in areas where you expect a lot of traffic. Linoleum rubber and asphalt are all grease-resistant, and, therefore, one of these should be selected for kitchens and other cooking areas. Cork is pretty but is the least durable.

Most tiles are available in 9- by 9-inch squares. Occasionally, you may find 12 x 12, 9 x 18, and other odd sizes. With 9 x 9 tiles, figure on buying two tiles per square foot of area in your room. With 12 x 12 or 9 x 18, buy 11 tiles for every 10 square feet. The extra tiles are necessary, because room dimensions are not usually divisable by tile sizes, and you must make allowance for some waste. In very large areas, there will be much less waste than in small rooms.

No matter what kind of tiles you will put down, the first step is to prepare the floor. Remember that any irregularities in the floor will show up in the tiles. If you are putting the tiles on a wood floor that is in good condition, just check that no nailheads are protruding. Countersink any nails that are visible. If the floor has small irregularities, you can sand or plane them smooth. Before laying the tiles, make certain that the floor is swept clean.

If tiles are to be laid on a concrete floor, the concrete should not be painted, nor should it have any cracks. Fill cracks with any filler material that sets hard. If the concrete has a coat of paint, you have to cover it with an underlayment of thin plywood or hardboard panels. Cover the concrete floor with a layer of waterproof mastic as a vapor barrier, and press the underlayment into the mastic. Joints in the underlayment should have cracks about 1/32 inch wide to allow for expansion of the material. The tiles will be placed to cover the cracks. Clean the floor before applying tiles.

If the wooden floor on which the tiles will be laid is rough or irregular, you should use an underlayment of plywood or hardboard sheets. Leave 1/32-inch cracks between adjacent sheets to allow for expansion. Nail the underlayment to the wooden floor. Sweep clean before laying the tiles.

The best way to plan how to lay the tiles is to use squared paper with each square representing a tile. You may want all the tiles the same color, or you may want a pattern. Use colored pencils or crayons to plan the floor on paper first.

Find the center of the room. To do this, measure the center points on two opposite walls, and connect them with a chalk line. Do the same with the other two walls. The center of the room is at the point where the chalk lines intersect. Lay out two crossing rows of tiles along the chalk lines from the center to the walls. These are not cemented down but are put down as a kind of first fitting. The space between the wall and the tile nearest it should be at least 2 inches. If necessary, move the chalk lines so that there is no space smaller than this.

Beginning at the chalkline, coat half the room with mastic or adhesive. A special adhesive is needed on concrete floors. Also, a special adhesive is needed with asphalt tiles. Follow the instructions on the can. Some adhesives must be allowed to dry before applying the tile. The adhesive is spread with a special grooved trowel, as illustrated in Fig. 8–23. When the mastic is tacky (or as indicated in the instructions), start to lay the tile. Do not slide the tiles to their positions, but try to place them correctly the first time. Put the first tile with its edges along the two chalk lines. Then place tiles next to three sides of the first tile. Continue, placing each new tile next to a tile already down until half the room is covered, except for the small space next to the wall. Then cover the other half of the room in the same manner. You will have to cut tiles to make them fit in the smaller spaces next to the wall. First you mark the tile to cut, as shown in Fig. 8–24. One tile is placed exactly over the tile laid nearest the wall. This is tile A in the figure. A second tile, B in the figure, is placed with its edge against the wall and is used as a guide to make a line on A. Cut tile A on the line, and the piece cut off will fit the space exactly. Most tiles can be cut with ordinary scissors or a linoleum knife. Tiles are easier to cut if the temperature is above 70°F. As-

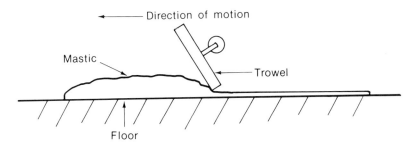

FIGURE 8–23. Applying Mastic.

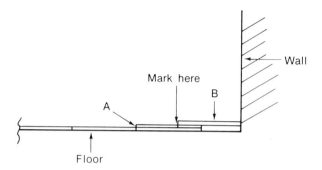

FIGURE 8-24. Marking Tile for Cutting.

phalt tiles must be scored, and then can be snapped along the scored line.

You need a few special tools to lay tiles or linoleum, including a special trowel, a linoleum knife, and chalk lines. You can buy these in one handy kit, with complete instructions, from mail-order houses and most building-supply stores. The kit is very inexpensive.

Some vinyl-asbestos tiles are available with an adhesive backing; these are simple to install. After the floor is prepared, just peel the backing off the tile and press the tile in place. No mastic is necessary. The adhesive will stick to concrete as well as wood.

When one or more tiles in a tile floor are damaged, pry them loose and replace them with new ones. To remove an old tile, heat it by putting an ordinary electric iron on it for a few seconds. This softens the old mastic. Use a linoleum knife to pry out the old tile. If the old mastic is tacky, you don't have to apply new mastic. Just put your new tile in place, and it will stick. If the old mastic is dry, scrape it out, and add new mastic before laying the new tile.

8-15. HOW TO LAY LINOLEUM

Linoleum is available in the form of tiles, in strips, and in room-sized pieces. The same general rules for floor preparation as were discussed in Section 8-14 apply here. Make sure that the floor is clean. Linoleum can be laid on top of an old worn linoleum if the old layer is not chopped up.

As with tiles, a paste is spread first and the linoleum laid on that. Sometimes the paste can be omitted when laying a linoleum covering in one large piece, but if two or more pieces are used, you must use paste, especially where the pieces join.

If an old linoleum has a worn-out spot, you can replace just the spot without having to replace the whole covering. Cut out the worn section of the old linoleum with a linoleum knife or scissors, and cut an exact piece to fit. Use the old section as a pattern. If the new linoleum is thinner than the old, use newspaper to shim it up. Apply paste to both sides of paper, or if no paper is used, apply the paste to the floor. Press the patch into position. Hold it down with weights until the cement dries. If edges are uneven, hammer them down or sand them.

8-16. HOW TO LAY CERAMIC TILES

At one time, laying ceramic tiles was a job for a professional, but manufacturers with an eye on the do-it-yourself market have simplified procedures. With special adhesives and even adhesive-backed tiles, you can lay ceramic tiles as easily as the flexible tiles described in Section 8-15. The floor must be smooth and clean. Follow the manufacturer's instructions as to how to put on the adhesive and the tiles. Ceramic tile floors are more expensive than other materials, but they last indefinitely and require almost no maintenance.

One form of ceramic tile is an arrangement of very small tiles, usually referred to as *mosaic*. A mosaic floor is easy to put down. The tiles are furnished with their faces stuck on a piece of paper about 1 foot square. The "square," as it is called, is put down as one unit on the mastic, which has been spread on the floor. First, the square is placed with the paper side up, and after the mastic has dried, the paper is washed off by soaking it with water. The mosaic tiles are spaced on the paper, and squares are put down with similar spaces between adjacent tiles. These spaces must be filled with grout. Simply push it into the joints with a trowel or putty knife, and after a few minutes wipe off the excess.

A tile entryway is both pleasing and functional, since this portion of the house gets a lot of traffic. If the front door of your house opens into a large hallway, you might consider putting a tile floor over the first 6 or 8 feet from the door. You can begin right at the threshold, or you can lift the threshold first and have the tile begin at a point under the threshold. Then the threshold is replaced and conceals the joint between the tiles and the wooden floor, as shown in Fig. 8-25. You may have to plane off part of the underside of the threshold to keep it from interfering with the door.

As with other tiles, kits are available that contain all the necessary tools and complete instructions. The cost of a kit is very small com-

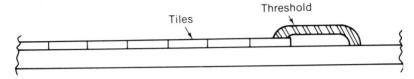

FIGURE 8–25. Threshold Covering Joint.

pared to the cost of the materials and is well worth purchasing when you undertake this job.

8-17. WALLS AND CEILINGS

At one time, most interior walls and ceilings were made of plaster and covered with paint or wallpaper. Although plaster is cheap, it is not a good material, since it absorbs moisture. When temperatures rise, the water in the plaster evaporates back into the room where it can be harmful to finishes on walls, floor, and furniture. If you have plaster walls however, you should not replace them as long as they are in good condition. You can repair cracks and dents in plaster walls easily. If you are planning a *new* wall or partition, do not use plaster.

Modern wall finishes include plywood, wood paneling, fiberboard, plasterboard, wallboard, plastics, tiles and many others. The characteristics of some of the many wall surfaces are given in Table 8-1. Remember that the characteristics shown apply to the bare materials. When the wall is covered with paint, paper, or tiles, it is much easier to clean and resists moisture better than the bare material. Hardboard is available with many different decorative finishes, in-

Table 8–1. Characteristics of Wall Materials

Material	Moisture Resistance	Ease in Application	Ease in Cleaning	Durability
Unfinished plywood	Fair	Easy	Difficult	Good
Finished plywood	Fair	Easy	Easy	Good
Bare plaster	Poor	Difficult	Difficult	Poor
Fiberboard	Fair	Easy	Difficult	Fair
Gypsum wallboard	Fair	Easy	Difficult	Good
Plasterboard	Poor	Easy	Difficult	Fair
Plastic sheets	Excellent	Moderate	Easy	Excellent
Hardboard	Excellent	Easy	Easy	Excellent

cluding simulated leather, wood paneling, and painted surfaces in a variety of colors. All the materials can be used on ceilings as well as walls.

If you plan to cover the wall with paint, wallpaper, tiles, or linoleum, your best bet for the base is unfinished plywood. A good second choice is gypsum wallboard.

8-18. HOW TO PATCH PLASTER

Holes in plaster, from small cracks to openings large enough to put your hand through, are usually repaired with spackling compound. This comes in powder form and is mixed with water as needed to make a smooth paste. The ratio of powder to water is not critical. The paste must be smooth—but stiff enough to remain where it is spread without running, and soft enough to spread easily. Spackling compound in paste form, that is, already mixed, is also available.

Before applying the spackling paste to the job, wet the plaster around the hole or on both sides of the crack with a sponge or damp cloth. Plaster tends to absorb moisture, and if the spackling compound is placed on dry plaster, the moisture from the compound will be drawn out too rapidly to make a good bond.

For small holes or hairline cracks, just apply the spackling compound to the spot to be filled with a large putty knife. Use only a little more compound than is necessary to fill the opening, and smooth it to a feather edge, removing any excess with the putty knife. For larger openings, first scrape away any loose plaster in the crack. Use a screwdriver, beer-can opener, or any pointed tool to do this. To make a good bond, it is generally supposed that the crack should be wider inside the wall than at the surface, as shown in Fig. 8-26(a). However, ideally the crack should be undercut on both sides, as shown in Fig. 8-26(b). Practically, it doesn't make too much difference. Open the crack wide enough to clean out all loose plaster, and then apply the spackle. If the opening is large, allow a first coat to dry and then apply a second.

(a) Wider inside   (b) Wider on both sides

FIGURE 8-26. Undercutting Crack in Plaster.

When the job is finished, the wall can be covered with paint, wall-paper, or whatever you wish.

If there is a lot of loose plaster, chisel away any edges which arouse the least suspicion of fault. If you cut away too much, you can patch up the hole, but if you leave some crumbly plaster, the whole job will be spoiled later.

When a large opening is to be plastered over, as when an electric fixture is removed, you will have to furnish a base for the spackling compound. One way to do this is to cut a piece of plaster board to fit into the opening and nail it to the studs or joists behind the plaster. When it is in place, the plasterboard should be about ⅛ inch below the outer surface of the plaster. Now you need only a ⅛-inch layer of spackling compound to finish the job. If you do not have any plasterboard or similar material, you can do an adequate job by stuffing the hole with newspaper crammed in about ⅛-inch below the plaster surface. Then finish with spackling compound as before.

8–19. HOW TO BUILD A WALL

Building a wall to divide a large room in two or to wall in a basement playroom is not as difficult as it might seem. Such a wall has no structural importance, since it does not have to support anything above it, and thus it can be quite simple. Before starting the job, you will have to plan it thoroughly, however, being certain to take into consideration such things as ventilation, light, heat, and possibly plumbing.

First, you must build a framework, as shown in Fig. 8–27. The lumber in the framework can be 2 x 3 stock joined with 3-inch nails. Begin by nailing the bottom plate to the floor from wall to wall. If

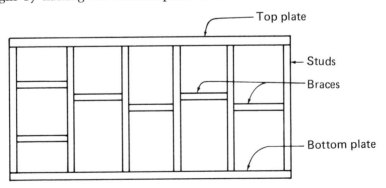

FIGURE 8-27. Framework for Wall.

the floor is wooden, nail the plate to the floor with nails every 20 to 24 inches. If the floor is concrete, you will have to drill holes in the plate and the concrete and insert special plugs, and then screw the plate to the concrete. Since many different types of fasteners for this purpose are available, ask your hardware or building-supply dealer to recommend a kind he carries and to tell you what size of holes to drill. If you plan a doorway in the new wall, do not drive any nails or other fasteners into the plate where the door will be located.

The top plate is fastened to the ceiling next. It must be placed directly over the bottom plate. You can use a plumb line to locate it accurately or a straight board and a level. The top plate should be perpendicular to the joists above, and it can be nailed directly on to the joists. If you must run the wall parallel to the joists, you should locate the top plate directly on a joist. In this case, put up the top plate first, and place the bottom plate directly below it. This may mean moving the location of the wall a few inches from your original plan.

Studs are added next. They should be cut to length to fit between the plates. The studs at each end are flush with the side walls. All studs are toenailed to the plates from both sides. Use nails about 2½ inches long. In standard construction, studs are usually spaced 16 inches apart between centers, but since this is merely a partition, it is quite all right to have larger spaces, even up to 2 feet. Short lengths of 2 x 3 stock are cut to fit between studs as braces. Note that in Fig. 8–27 these are staggered so that nails can be driven through the studs into the braces. For most walls you should use two braces between adjacent studs, as shown between the two studs at the left of the figure. However, for lightweight wall coverings, a single brace between adjacent studs is sufficient.

If you lay out and plan your work accurately, you can cut the braces first and use them to locate the position of each stud from the preceding one. This eliminates the need to worry about positioning the stud exactly vertical.

If you plan a doorway, the framework must have an opening for the door, as shown in Fig. 8–28. In this case the end studs are placed first and then the studs on each side of the doorway. Allow 1¾ inches on each side for the rough doorway framework plus an additional 1 inch on each side and top for the door frame, if a frame is to be used. The rest of the studs can be spaced conveniently between the door studs and the end studs.

The doorway itself is shown in Fig. 8–29. First, cut out the bottom plate with a saw between the studs on each side of the doorway. Nail a shorter stud to the studs on each side. These shorter studs extend from the floor to the height of the doorway. Be sure to nail them onto

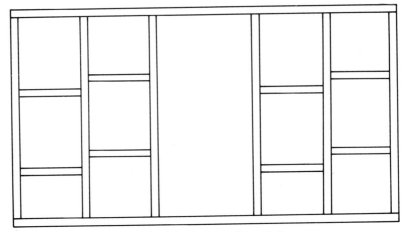

FIGURE 8–28. Framework with Doorway.

the floor plate as well as onto the studs. In the figure, you will note two boards above the doorway. These are two 2 x 3's nailed together to form a lintel. A short piece of 2 x 3 is added between the lintel and the ceiling plate. If the door will have a threshold, don't forget to consider the thickness of the threshold in planning the height of the door.

If the wall will have other openings, as for windows, they are surrounded by double thicknesses of 2 x 3 stock in the same manner. Short sections of 2 x 3 stock are nailed to the side studs first. Then double thicknesses of 2 x 3's are nailed above and below. For wide windows, add the supporting vertical braces between the horizontal members and the plates.

FIGURE 8–29. Doorway.

If you are building a basement playroom or other area where two new walls are to meet at right angles, you will need a corner post. Make your own post by nailing three 2 x 3's together, as shown in Fig. 8–30. Each 2 x 3 is cut to extend from floor to ceiling plates, and the post is toenailed to the plates.

Before covering the wall, install wiring and plumbing as required. This is one reason why these must be considered in the original plans. It is easier to install them before the wall is covered than to have to cut openings in the finished wall.

Gypsum wallboard and hardboard are the two favorites for covering the wall, although any of the materials listed in Table 8–1 can be used, as well as newer materials that are constantly being developed. When you select a wall material from the many available, make sure that you buy the recommended nails to fasten the sheets to the studs. You will also need something to cover joints between sheets and nailheads. For some materials, a joint cement must be spread into the joint with a putty knife. The same cement is used to cover nailheads. For others, decorative adhesive strips are fastened over joints and nailheads.

For decorative purposes, you may want to conceal the joints where the wall meets the floor and ceiling. This is usually done with some kind of molding nailed along the joint. At floor level, a simple base-board nailed along the wall may be sufficient. At ceiling level, any of the moldings shown in Fig. 7–3(a) may be used, as well as large variety of special ceiling moldings stocked at most building-supply houses.

8–20. HOW TO FUR A WALL

When you wish to cover an existing wall with some sort of finished sheeting (such as finished plywood or decorative hardboard, for

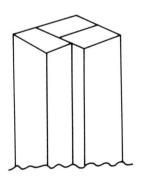

FIGURE 8–30. Corner Post.

example), the wall must be flat.   If the wall is irregular, as a stone wall or broken plaster wall, some sort of flat surface must be added to the wall before applying the finishing.   The usual method is to fur the wall.   Furring material consists of flat boards 1 inch thick and at least 2 inches wide.   These are nailed flat to the wall at convenient intervals, usually about 16 inches apart.   They are mounted horizontally and are nailed directly to the studs.   Large, finished wallboards can then be nailed to the furring.

If there are irregularities in the wall, the furring strips can be gouged out with a chisel to go over a projection or can be shimmed with wood scraps to go over a hollow.   Use a level or plumb line to check that the furring is flat.   Furring can be nailed directly to concrete walls using nails specially made for this purpose.

Furring can also be used for new ceilings.   When a ceiling is badly damaged, instead of trying to fix it, nail furring strips across the joists, right over the old ceiling.   Then fasten wallboard to the furring.

8-21. HOW TO TILE A WALL

Wall tiles are available in vinyl, plastic, metal, ceramic, and, in fact, in all the materials used for floor tiles.   Whereas floor tiles are usually 9 x 9, most wall tiles are 4½ x 4½, but aside from this the methods of applying the tiles are essentially the same.

As with floor tiles, you will need a few special tools for wall tiles.   These include a spreader for the mastic and something to cut the tile.   Plastic tiles can be cut with a small finishing saw or smooth hacksaw.   Metal tile can be cut with tin snips or a hacksaw.   Ceramic tiles can be cut to fit by nibbling bits out with ordinary slip-joint pliers.   When you buy tiles, you can also buy a kit of tools to use specifically with the kind of tile you will use.   These kits are very inexpensive.

If you are tiling from some point above the floor, draw a line on all walls at the lowest level.   Start tiling from this line.   Use a level to make sure the line is horizontal.   Do not trust your eyes for this.

Patch the wall before laying the tiles.   Make sure the wall is smooth and clean.   When laying a tile, try to place it down where it belongs.   Do not slide it to its position.   Most tiles require mastic, but some plastic wall tiles come with adhesive backing which will stick to plaster, wood, and most wallboards.

You can use ceramic floor tiles to make a mosaic wall.   Apply them to the wall in the same manner described in Section 8-16 for laying them on the floor.   Ceramic tiles require grouting after they are laid.   A ceramic wall requires almost no maintenance and is very easy to keep cleaned.

When a tile must be cut to fit into a space next to the wall, measure it in exactly the same manner as described for floor tiles. This is illustrated in Fig. 8–24.

If a fixture is already fastened to the wall and cannot be moved, you can tile around it. If possible, however, try to attach fixtures later. Leave a space for the fixture, and fasten the fixture to the wall so that its flange overlaps the tiles all around the space. In this way you avoid having to cut a tile. Alternately, you can tile the whole wall and use fixtures that are fastened to the tiles by strong adhesives.

8–22. HOW TO REPAIR A TILED WALL

When one or more tiles in a wall are cracked, they are usually ignored. However, if the wall is in the bathroom, water vapor can enter the cracks and cause damage to the wall under the tiles. The broken tiles should be removed and replaced with new ones. To remove the old tile, first scrape away the grout around it. You can use a beer-can opener or a cold chisel to loosen the grout. Pry out the cracked tile or tiles with an old chisel or screwdriver, but be careful not to mar any of the adjacent tiles. Do not worry if the cracked tiles break up further.

After the old tile is removed, replace it with a new one as you would on a bare wall. Make sure that the wall underneath is clean. Add mastic and press in the new tile. Then apply grout around the tile.

When an opening appears around the tub in the bathroom at the junction of the wall, it is usually caused by settling. If the opening is small, clean out old grout with any handy tool, and recaulk the opening. Special silicone grouting is available in tubes and is very simple to apply. If the opening is too large for grouting, it can usually be covered with edging tiles made of ceramic or other materials to match your walls. These are tiles designed to attach to the tub and the wall and cover the crack.

8–23. HOW TO INSTALL SHELVES

Although a shelf can simply be nailed to a vertical member, this is undesirable, because the nails must support the entire weight on the shelf. The joint should be reinforced. Some methods of doing this are shown in Fig. 8–31. In Fig. 8–31(a), spacers are used between shelves to absorb and support the weight. This method makes very strong shelves. In Fig. 8–31(b), cleats are used. These are nailed to the uprights, and the shelves are nailed to them.

For decorative purposes, the cleats can be quarter-round moldings or any other shape instead of rectangular. The channel, shown in Fig. 8–31(c), is simple to install and useful in that shelves can be removed easily when desirable. The channel is usually made of aluminum, although channels are available in brass, galvanized iron, and other metals as well.

For a neat, professional-looking job you may want to use one or more of the joints discussed in Section 7–3. Two of these are shown in Fig. 8–31(d). The rabbet is used for the top shelf, and dadoes for lower shelves. Doweling and other joints can also be used.

8–24. WALLPAPER

Walls made of plaster or wallboard need some sort of finish to make them presentable. The simplest finish is paint, but wallpaper is eco-

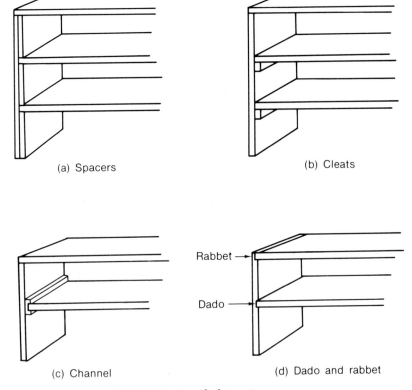

(a) Spacers   (b) Cleats

(c) Channel   (d) Dado and rabbet

FIGURE 8–31. Shelving Supports.

nomical and more decorative. Wallpaper comes in a great variety of colors, designs, and materials. In addition to paper, wall materials include vinyl, canvas, and other fabrics. All are usually referred to as *wallpaper* or *wall coverings*. Most of the wall materials, including paper, are water-resistant so that there is little danger of tearing wet paper when hanging them, and because they resist moisture, they are easily washed and can even be scrubbed. Many patterns and materials are available with adhesive backing, so that the messy job of mixing and applying paste is eliminated.

When you choose a wallpaper, you will be influenced by price. However, the first problem is to select a pattern that is acceptable. A common mistake is to choose a paper with a "cute" pattern that becomes boring after seeing it every day. Since it is much easier to work with prepasted paper, try to select a pattern in the prepasted materials carried by your dealer. Price is affected by quality, but it is also influenced by the design. Stripes, flowers, scenery, and other simple patterns are usually less expensive than designs which simulate wood, velvet, or other materials.

The easiest way to find out how much paper to buy is to measure the room and then take the dimensions to your wallpaper dealer, and let him do the estimating. Remember to measure doors, windows, and other openings that won't be covered, and subtract these areas from the overall area of the walls. The dealer will usually allow you to return unstarted rolls, so it is a good idea to buy one or two extra in case you made a mistake.

Before hanging paper, make sure that the wall is sound. Patch all holes and cracks. If the wall has a coat of smooth paint or enamel on it, rub it with sandpaper to roughen it slightly. The wall should feel smooth, but paper will not cling as well to surfaces which are too smooth. Although it is preferable to remove the old paper, new wallpaper can be hung right over old wallpaper if the old surface is not torn or peeling. In this case, try to have the seams between sheets come between old seams, since if seams are lined up on top of each other, they become more noticeable.

8-25. HOW TO REMOVE OLD WALLPAPER

If the old wallpaper is torn, blistered, or peeling, it should be removed before applying new paper. It is possible to scrape off old paper, but the quickest and best way in the long run is to steam it off with a wallpaper steamer. You can rent a steamer from your wallpaper dealer and finish the job in a fraction of the time it would take to scrape off the old paper. The rental cost is quite small compared to the cost of the wallpaper, so that it adds only a small percentage to the overall cost of the job.

A steaming machine has a boiler in which water is heated by electricity in small units or by kerosene in larger ones. The steam from the boiling water is fed through a hose to a perforated plate which is held against the old wallpaper. The steam soaks into the paper, softening the paper and the paste holding it to the wall. The paper can then be stripped off the wall with a putty knife or any flat tool. A special tool for the purpose, called a *wall scraper*, looks like a very wide putty knife.

When using the machine, begin at the bottom of a wall, since the hot steam tends to rise and will soften the paper above the plate as well as directly under it. Move the plate upward slowly with one hand while you strip the paper below with the other. Make sure that the room is well ventilated to prevent the room from filling up with steam.

The steamer can also be used to remove wallpaper from a papered ceiling. However, if paper is to be removed only from walls and it is desired to leave the old paper on a ceiling, you cannot use a steamer. The rising steam would loosen the ceiling paper. In this case, you will have to soak the paper on the wall by hand, preferably applying hot water with a large paintbrush or mop. You can also use a paint roller. When the paper is soaked, you will be able to strip it off with a flat tool.

Canvas-backed wallpaper is the easiest to remove; plastic-coated papers are the most difficult. In order to make the steam penetrate the plastic, it may be necessary to rub down the wall with coarse sandpaper. This scratches the plastic coating and lets the steam reach the paper below.

When you are finished removing the old paper, wipe up all excess moisture as soon as possible. Patch the wall where necessary to make a smooth surface for the new paper.

8-26. HOW TO HANG WALLPAPER

Before you begin, make sure you have the necessary tools. You will need a smoothing brush, a seam roller, sponge, and a sharp razor blade mounted in a handle. You can buy a wallpaper tool kit which includes these tools as well as a wall scraper for removing old paper. These kits are inexpensive. A seam roller looks like a caster from a living-room chair, and, in fact, if you don't have a seam roller, you can use a caster instead. If you use prepasted paper, you will not have to mix paste and apply it. If not, you will need a paste brush and paste bucket in addition to the other tools.

The first step is to cut the paper into strips reaching from floor to ceiling, taking into consideration the necessity of fitting the pattern from one strip to the adjacent one. Allow 2 or 3 inches extra at each end of the strip. This excess will be cut off later. You should buy pre-trimmed paper, which has the edges trimmed and is all ready for hanging. Pile up the strips, pattern side down, with the first strip to be hung on top of the pile and the strips arranged in the order in which they will be hung.

If you are using prepasted paper, this next step is eliminated, but if not, now is the time to apply paste. Paste is applied to one strip, and that strip is hung. Then paste is applied to the next, and so on. When using prepasted strips, follow the manufacturer's directions. The strips are usually soaked in a bathtub full of water or, if you want to be fancy, in a special wallpaper tank. One roll is soaked at a time. To apply paste to the unpasted paper, it is necessary to have a long table. A 5-foot length of plywood on a bridge table makes a good temporary table. Place the strip on the table with the bottom end hanging off the end of the table. Apply paste with the brush to the part of the strip on the table. (Follow the manufacturer's directions as to mixing the paste.) Now fold the bottom of the strip over toward the center, without creasing the paper, so that pasted surface is against pasted surface. Slide the paper along the table so that the rest of the paper can now be pasted. You can now place the paper on the wall with its top at the ceiling. The bottom will be tucked under, making it easier to move the strip.

Begin next to a doorway. As you proceed around a room, the last strip will not have its pattern exactly matched to that of the first strip, but if the discontinuity is behind you as you enter the room, it is less noticeable. If there are large windows in the room, you can begin at a window edge, since the window becomes a discontinuity in the pattern.

Hang the first strip by placing the top half against the wall with its top edge 2 or 3 inches above the junction of wall and ceiling. Use a plumb line or vertical chalk line for the first strip. When the paper is properly lined up with the chalk line, smooth the upper half to the wall with the smoothing brush. Now pull down the portion that is tucked under, and smooth this to the wall, also. When all the bubbles are removed by smoothing, cut off the excess 2 or 3 inches at top and bottom with your razor.

If the first strip is to go around a corner, have only about 1 inch of

width on one wall and the rest on the next wall. Line up the edge
that is farther away from the corner with a plumb line. Walls do not
always remain perpendicular to the floor and to each other, and it is
possible that the 1-inch width on the other wall will not be plumb to
the floor. Every time you go around a corner, follow the same procedure of lining up the far edge with a true vertical.

After each strip is hung, sponge off the surface, being careful to
remove all traces of paste. Also remove paste from floor and ceiling.
After every two or three strips are hung, run the seam roller along the
seams to press them firmly to the wall. With some papers, the manufacturer advises *not* using a seam roller. With these you can press
seams to the wall with a damp sponge.

9

Painting

A coat of paint quickly brightens a dull room or a drab house. It is simple and inexpensive, yet completely effective. Although you may think of paint as a beautifying agent, its most important function is protection. A properly applied coat of paint prolongs the life of a house, protecting the surface from the elements, as well as keeping moisture from penetrating and rotting interior members of the structure. Inside the house, paint or varnish protects floors from wear, walls and ceilings from moisture, and woodwork from abuse.

To most people, the word "paint" includes all finishes normally applied with a paintbrush, such as varnish, enamel, stain, and calcimine, as well as paint. All these are discussed in this chapter as types of paint.

9-1. TYPES OF PAINT

The material in paint which gives paint its color is called *pigment*. Pigments also seal the surface against moisture and protect it from wear. However, it would be difficult to spread dry pigment on a surface, so it is suspended in a liquid *carrier* or *vehicle*. The vehicle evaporates, leaving the pigment as a smooth layer on the surface. Common vehicles are alkyd, oil, latex, and varnish. At one time the most common pigment was white lead, and it is still used, but titanium and other chemicals have better characteristics and are used in more expensive paints. Some pigments containing lead, mercury, or chromium are poisonous.

Stains are "paints" which dye the wood itself rather than cover it. Lacquers and varnishes cover the surface with a transparent, hard coating, so that the wood grain is visible but protected. These may be clear or colored.

Alkyd is a synthetic resin. Alkyd paints dry quickly and produce a strong, hard finish. They are available in enamels or flats.

Enamels use varnish in place of oil or alkyd as a vehicle. An undercoat is usually necessary with an enamel, and the undercoat must be matched to the final finish. Enamels are available with a high gloss or semigloss.

Latex paints are by far the most popular for the home handyman, because they are water-thinned. This means that brushes and equipment can be cleaned with ordinary soap and water. Latex paint produces a strong hard finish and dries quickly. It can be used on almost any surface.

Calcimine and whitewash are inexpensive water-based paints used for temporary coatings or where cost is important. They are easily renewed when necessary but do not wear well. Calcimine is frequently used on ceilings, and whitewash on fences.

Special paints are designed for specific tasks such as painting concrete or stucco, varnishing floors, or painting shingles. Paints may also contain ingredients to kill fungi, prevent rust, resist moisture, or increase durability.

9-2. CHOICE OF PAINT

The worst part of painting is cleaning up when the job is finished. Too often in the past, a handyman has put off a small painting job, because cleaning would take longer than applying the paint. With the introduction of latex paints, cleaning up is much easier, since the paint can be washed out of brushes with ordinary soap and water.

The relative ease or difficulty of cleaning your painting tools when the job is done is certainly a consideration when selecting a paint for the job.

Another consideration is drying speed and how this affects the method of application. All paints can be applied with a brush or a spray, but some dry too fast to be applied with a roller.

For outdoor paints, resistance to the elements is an important criterion. For interior paints, you will probably want to know if fingerprints and dirt can be washed off easily.

Floor paints must withstand the expected traffic. Paints to be used in bathrooms and kitchens must be moisture-resistant.

Latex paints are the outstanding choice for most paint jobs around the home. They can be used on almost any surface, and, in fact, latex paint can be applied directly to fresh plaster. You can use a brush, roller, or spray to apply it, and clean your tools with water when you are finished.

A latex surface is washable. The paint dries fast, so that a second coat can be applied in about three hours after the first. When you apply latex, lap marks disappear, so that anyone can do a professional-looking job.

Alkyd paint dries to a tough, strong finish which is more moisture resistant than latex finishes. Thus, alkyd might be preferred for kitchens and bathrooms. It is also frequently used on woodwork. Manufacturers supply both alkyd and latex in matching colors so that latex can be used on walls and alkyd on woodwork. Alkyd can be applied by brush, roller, or spray and dries in about a day. Tools must be cleaned in turpentine or an equivalent solvent.

Alkyd is available in flat, high-gloss enamel, and semigloss enamel. Latex is available in flat and semigloss. Although alkyd has greater moisture resistance, latex may still be your choice for a kitchen or bathroom if you want the relative simplicity of cleaning up afterward. However, an alkyd job will outlast latex in a moist environment.

Titanium as a pigment has the best covering power but is very expensive. Calcium carbonate is good and is frequently mixed with titanium and other pigments. Calcium carbonate forms a light powder on the painted surface, which then is washed off when it rains. Surface dirt is washed off with it, so that the painted area is practically self-cleaning. This process is called *chalking* and is a desirable feature of exterior paints, but it must not be too rapid.

Rubber-based and plastic-based paints, specially formulated for painting masonry, dry very rapidly, in about one hour. This is too fast for a roller, but these paints can be applied with a brush or a spray. No other paints have better weather resistance. Special solvents are required for thinning and cleaning.

Enamels are tougher than flat paints. Usually the higher the gloss, the better the finish will withstand wear and cleaning. Oil and alkyd enamels are very tough, but manufacturers now offer latex enamels in a semigloss which is more durable than a flat paint, although not as strong as conventional enamels.

Special undercoats or primers are required on some surfaces before a final coat can be applied. Latex paints do not need a special primer, so that in effect latex is its own primer. Two coats of the same latex paint are applied.

Alkyds and oil paints cannot be applied directly to porous surfaces. A first coat of special sealer is needed.

Paints that are preferred for specific applications are indicated in Table 9–1. Note that, when a latex paint is acceptable, you may prefer it to the "best" paint because of the ease of applying and cleaning up.

Choice of color is a matter of personal preference, but there are some basic relationships which you should be aware of before selecting a color. Some colors seem warm, some cool. Some make rooms seem larger. In general, pastel shades make rooms brighter and larger-looking. They tend to convey cheerfulness. Dark colors are the reverse, making rooms seem smaller and somber. Use lighter colors in very small rooms.

Combinations of colors can change the apparent size of a room. For example, if a ceiling is too high, it can be painted a darker color than the walls, and will then seem to be lower. In a long rectangular room, the end walls can appear to be closer if they are painted a darker color than the longer walls.

Paint colors look different when viewed in daylight and when seen under artificial lighting. It is best to get paint samples before you select colors, and examine them both at night and in the daytime.

The coverage of paint is usually expressed in square feet per gallon and varies both with the type of paint and type of surface. Thus, an oil-based paint will cover an area three times as big on wood than it will on masonry. A second coat of the same paint usually covers a larger area than the first. When buying paint, note the coverage, as indicated on the can. Your paint dealer will usually allow you to return unopened cans of paint, so it is better to buy an extra can if you're not sure of the amount.

TABLE 9-1. Paint Selection

Application	Preferred Paint	Acceptable Paint
Bathroom, kitchen, and laundry	High-gloss enamel	Latex semigloss
Other interior walls and ceilings	Latex flat	Alkyd flat
Woodwork, doors, trim (interior)	Enamel	Latex flat, latex semigloss
Wood floors	Varnish, alkyd floor enamel	Latex floor paint
Concrete floors	Latex floor paint	Alkyd floor enamel
Furniture	Varnish, enamel	Latex semigloss
Flexible tiles	Latex floor paint	
Wallpaper, bare plaster	Latex flat	
Wooden exterior	Latex house paint	Oil house paint
Shingles	Latex house paint	Shingle stain
Brick, stucco, cement block	Latex masonry	Special cement paints
Exterior Doors, windows, trim	Special trim paint	Oil house paint
Fences	Oil house paint	Latex house paint
Exterior wood floors	Deck enamel	Latex floor paint
Exterior concrete floors	Latex floor paint	Deck enamel

9-3. SAFETY

Before, during, and after painting, there are certain safety precautions which *must* be taken. The principal dangers are falls from ladders, chemical irritation, poisoning, and fire. At this point you may think that the risks of harm outweigh the potential economic gain of doing the job yourself, but actually there is little danger as long as you are aware of the hazards and take simple precautions.

Exterior painting usually involves the use of ladders. Safety on a ladder is covered in Section 3-7. Indoors, similar problems arise when you paint a ceiling or upper wall. Use a stepladder rather than a box or a chair. A common practice is to place a board across two chairs or two ladders so that a larger area can be painted without your having to go up and down too many times. This is safe as long as the board is solid enough and wide enough, and you don't lean too far.

Paint fumes may be toxic, especially if the paint contains lead or mercury. Fumes from solvents may also be toxic as well as flammable. To minimize the dangers, always provide as much ventilation as possible when mixing paints, painting, and when cleaning equipment afterward. When removing old paint with a scraper or blowtorch, paint dust may get into the air, and this can be very toxic if the paint contains lead. It is advisable to use a respirator when removing paint with a scraper or torch. This is not a danger when a chemical paint remover is used.

Paints and thinners can irritate the skin on contact. If you do get any solvent on your hands, remove it immediately. Better, wear plastic gloves when handling turpentine, naphtha, or other solvent, or any chemical paint remover. Rubber gloves may also be used with most chemicals but not with solvents for rubber-based paints. Plastic gloves are cheap and can be thrown away after each use.

Avoid the risk of fire by using nonflammable thinners and cleaners wherever possible. If a flammable substance is used, dispose of rags in a tightly sealed metal container. Do not leave oily rags lying loose as they can ignite by spontaneous combustion.

When pouring paints or thinners, take care that there is no splashing which can irritate the skin or, worse, get in your eyes. It is not necessary to wear safety glasses when painting, but do take care not to touch your eyes or get anything in them.

Many of these precautions are unnecessary when you use water-soluble paints. You can also avoid the dangers of lead poisoning by using nontoxic paints. On children's toys and walls of children's rooms you should *always* use lead-free paints.

9-4. PAINTING TOOLS

If you have the proper tools, painting is a cinch and can be very enjoyable, since you immediately see a marked improvement as you proceed. If you don't have all the necessary equipment handy, painting can be a frustrating experience.

Good painting requires good brushes. Originally, a good brush was made only of natural bristles from hog hair. These bristles could be dipped in most caustic solvents without deterioration, whereas cheap brushes rarely lasted for more than one job. However, new synthetic bristles, especially those made of nylon, are supplanting the hog-hair bristles among home handymen. Nylon brushes resist solvents as well as natural bristles and are better for latex paints. Also, nylon brushes are easier to clean than hog-hair brushes.

A good brush holds more paint, thus making painting faster and easier, and lets you apply the paint smoothly without spattering. These are some of the things a professional painter looks for when he buys a brush:

1. *Flagged* bristles. That is, the ends of some of the bristles should be split. Flagged bristles hold more paint and enable you to spread the paint evenly. Not all bristles are flagged, but the more flags, the better the brush.

2. *Tapered* bristles. In a good brush, bristles are thicker at the base than at the tip. Tapered bristles provide an even flow of paint but are particularly important for accuracy when painting in corners or on edges.

3. *Fullness.* There should be a full set of bristles in the brush. Cheaper brushes sometimes have a hollow space in the center, which makes it difficult to paint smoothly.

4. *Variable length.* If bristles are of different lengths, the brush should paint more evenly.

5. *Springiness.* Brush the bristles against your hand. They should feel elastic.

6. *A strong setting.* The bristles should be bonded firmly to the handle. A weak setting allows bristles to fall out. A strong setting increases the life of the brush, improves the shape of the brush, and makes the brush easier to clean.

Your paint-supply dealer can recommend what brushes to use. Remember, good brushes cost more than poor ones but are worth the money. The difference in price is negligible compared to the cost of the paint, and good brushes can last a lifetime. Some typical brushes are shown in Fig. 9–1.

The larger the brush, the more paint it will hold, and the faster you can spread the paint. Therefore, you should use the widest brush that you can. However, to paint a molding or table leg that is 1 inch wide, a 4-inch brush would be impractical. Thus, the brush size should be tailored to the job. For large, flat surfaces, such as walls or ceilings, a 4-inch brush, shown in Fig. 9–1(a), is preferred—if you want to use a brush. However, you may decide to use a roller instead. A smaller

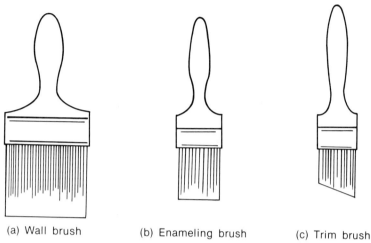

(a) Wall brush   (b) Enameling brush   (c) Trim brush

FIGURE 9-1. Brushes.

brush, about 2 inches wide, is used for wood work and trim. Special brushes are made for enamel and varnish, and if you plan to use these finishes, get a 2-inch enamel brush, shown in Fig. 9-1(b). It is thinner than the brush used for paints. Also, you will need a small trim or finishing brush, shown in Fig. 9-1(c). The bristles are cut on a bevel, and the brush is used to "cut in"; that is, to paint in tight corners where the surface you are painting joins another.

A useful tool is a metal comb for brushes, shown in Fig. 9-2. After a brush is cleaned, you should comb the bristles before putting it away. Combing straightens bristles, especially those in the interior and helps to maintain the shape of the brush.

If you are going to paint large areas, such as walls or ceilings, you will find it easier to use a roller. In fact, with a roller, you will never have need for a large brush. You will still need a small brush, about 2 inches wide, both to get into corners, where the roller can't reach, and to do woodwork and windows.

A paint roller, as its name implies, rolls paint onto surfaces in

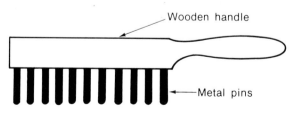

Wooden handle

Metal pins

FIGURE 9-2. Metal Comb.

place of brushing it on. Two rollers are illustrated in Fig. 9-3. The short-handled roller, shown in Fig. 9-3(a), is used for side walls; the long-handled model in Fig. 9-3(b) is for ceilings or floors.

The roller has a sleeve which is held on the handle by a wing nut, so that it can be removed quickly. An extra sleeve permits quick color changes without your having to stop and wash the equipment. The roller sleeve is covered with a fiber cover which may be made of natural or synthetic fibers. Synthetic-fiber covers are best for latex paints and are usable with oil-based paints as well, although natural fiber covers, usually wool, are recommended for oil-based paints and varnish. A new cover, containing a blend of natural and synthetic fibers combines the best features of both and can be used with any finish. However, if you use only latex paints, you should choose the synthetic-fiber roller, because it is cheaper and does the job well.

The pile of a standard roller is a nap of about 3/8 inch. This is recommended for most indoor painting and all smooth surfaces outdoors. A high nap, about 1 inch, is used for rough surfaces, such as masonry, stucco, and rough metal. Special naps are also available for special effects, such as a carpet weave for a stipple effect. In general,

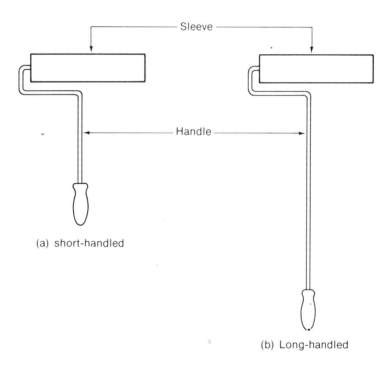

(a) short-handled

(b) Long-handled

FIGURE 9-3. Paint Rollers.

the shorter the nap, the smoother will be the finish. Thus, for glossy enamels, a very short nap is recommended, and rollers with naps of only 1/4 inch are available for this purpose.

The standard width of roller is 9 inches, but special sizes are available for special jobs. A 3-inch roller is available for painting trim and can be used for most of the cutting-in jobs that usually require a trim brush.

The pan used with the paint roller is shown in Fig. 9–4. It has a tilted bottom so that paint occupies the deep end only. The roller is dipped in the paint, and the excess is pressed out on the exposed end of the bottom. Ridges in the bottom aid in squeezing out excess paint.

When you buy a roller, do not look for bargains. Make sure that you can remove the sleeve from the handle easily and quickly. The core of the sleeve should be of a durable material that won't fall apart with repeated use and cleaning.

Do not use a roller with finishes that dry too rapidly, such as lacquers and fast-drying enamels. Read the label on the paint can. If a roller can be used with the finish, there will be instructions on how much to thin the paint when using a roller. Paints generally should be thinner when applied with a roller than when applied by brush.

Another way of applying paint is by spraying. For small jobs, paint can be purchased in a spray can for quick touchups or a complete paint job. There is no cleaning up afterward. For larger jobs, a spray gun is used. You can usually rent a spray gun from the dealer who sells you your paint.

Paints must be thinned with appropriate solvents before spraying, but once the mixture is in the gun, spraying is one of the easiest methods of painting. You can spray latex paint, enamel, lacquer, rubber-based paint, or almost any finish. Further, you can apply it to almost any surface, including cloth, leather, paper, metal, plastic, masonry, as well as wood. For picket fences and odd-shaped pieces of furniture, spraying is by far the fastest way to paint.

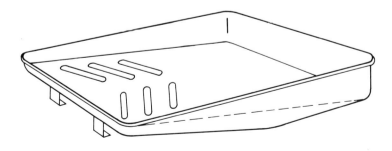

FIGURE 9–4. Pan.

If spraying is so wonderful, why not use it for everything? It does have some drawbacks. There must be adequate ventilation. Even outdoors, you should wear a mask. Since it is impossible to restrict the spray to the surface being painted, surrounding objects must be protected more thoroughly than when using a brush or roller. But with proper precautions spraying is fast, economical, and efficient. For example, it is almost the only method of satisfactorily painting wicker furniture.

Another item in the family of painting tools is the paint glider, shown in Fig. 9-5. This has a fiber pad similar to the material on a paint roller. The pad is dipped into the paint and is then drawn over the surface by pulling the handle while the pad is in contact with the surface to be painted. The glider can be used on both horizontal and vertical surfaces. The short handle limits the reach but makes it very convenient for painting stairs and woodwork. The pad is removable for ease in cleaning.

9-5. OTHER EQUIPMENT NEEDED

No matter which method of painting you select—brush, roller, or spray—you will need auxiliary equipment in order to avoid frustrations and simplify your work. To some extent the extra equipment and materials will vary with the type of job, but you will know what you need if you think of the paint job as a whole. The job begins with preparation of the surface. If there is heavy furniture in a room where you are painting, the furniture must be protected, as must the floor. Outdoors, plants and lawns must be protected. If you smear paint accidently where it doesn't belong, you want to be able to wipe it up immediately. Finally, you have to clean your painting equipment when you are through.

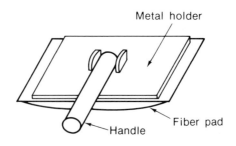

FIGURE 9-5. Paint Glider.

Wherever you are painting, you need a drop cloth to protect plants, floors, or furniture from dripping paint. Drop cloths are available in paper, plastic, or cloth. In a pinch you can use an old sheet or spread newspapers, but drop cloths made of plastic or specially treated paper are very inexpensive. Although, if you are very careful, you may be able to paint without dripping, you will be able to paint much faster if you have a drop cloth and don't have to worry about floors and furniture.

To pick up drops of paint that spatter accidently, you need a supply of clean rags. These should be lintless, but pieces of torn sheets, old underwear, or almost anything clean will do. When you are painting close to a line of demarcation, you will want a guide to ensure that the paint does not get beyond the line. A piece of cardboard makes a good shield, or you can buy an inexpensive metal shield in your paint store. Some people prefer masking tape. When painting a window sash, for example, masking tape is placed on the glass adjacent to the rails and stiles of the window. Then when you paint the sash, you don't have to be careful about keeping paint off the glass. When you are finished, strip off the masking tape, and the excess paint will come off with it. If you find masking too much of a chore, you can use a shield instead, as shown in Fig. 9–6.

When painting walls, you must first prepare the surface. But sometimes you miss a spot. You should have available a hammer and nail

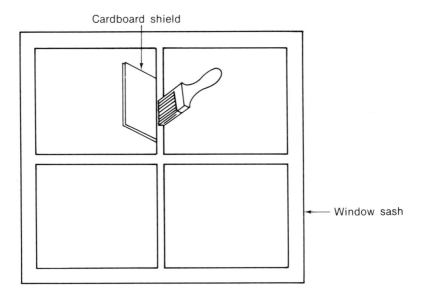

FIGURE 9–6. Using Shield.

set to drive in any nailheads that you overlooked, and you will need putty to cover them. For plaster walls you need spackling compound or wall-patch compound and a putty knife, in case you have to repair a crack. Sandpaper and clean dustcloths may be necessary and should be available.

Indoors you need a stepladder, outdoors an extension ladder. You also need some means of fastening your pail or tray to the ladder, since a spilled bucket of paint is a traumatic experience. Special pail hooks are available, or you can bend a wire clothes hanger to support a pail of paint from a rung on the ladder. You can rest a paint pail on the shelf of a stepladder if you're careful. A roller tray is more precarious there. It is better to place your tray on the seat of a chair or firm box and use a handle on your roller long enough to reach the tray without your having to descend the ladder. Naturally, you must protect the chair with some sort of drop cloth.

You will need solvents to clean brushes and to thin paints. If a special thinner is specified, as for rubber-based paints, buy that. Water-based paints require only soap and water for cleaning. Turpentine is usually used with enamel, varnish, and oil-based paints. Lacquer thinners are available for lacquer. Shellac is usually thinned with alcohol.

You will need containers for solvents when you are cleaning brushes. You will also need containers for mixing paints. You can use old coffee cans and jars for solvents. Old paint cans are reusable both for mixing paints and for holding solvents when you are cleaning brushes. If you want to save old paint cans for this purpose, clean them with the appropriate solvent as soon as you have used up the paint. Cans from latex paints can be washed in soap and water. An old paint can is useful for holding paint while you are painting, since it has a handle to carry it. If you fill the can only half full of paint, you will find it easier to move than a full pail. If you want to avoid a large part of the cleaning process, don't save old cans. Buy inexpensive cardboard paint buckets. Use them as you need them and throw them away when you finish the job.

When you finish painting, you invariably have some paint on your hands. This can be washed off with the same thinner used for the paint, but some people find the paint solvents irritating to their skins. It is better to use special cream cleansers rather than washing your hands with potentially irritating solvents. Protective creams are available which are rubbed on the hands before painting and wash off with all paint smears in ordinary soap and water. You can also use plastic gloves.

9-6. HOW TO PREPARE THE SURFACE

Paint is not permanent. Eventually a painted surface wears or shows flaws or appears dingy, and the homeowner then decides to repaint. If care is taken in preparing the surface before painting, the time between paint jobs can be lengthened. Surface preparation is the most important aspect of a paint job. A properly prepared surface will hold its paint without flaws three or four times as long as paint applied with little or careless preparation. The steps you must take in getting the surface ready for painting depend on the type of paint used, the type of surface, and whether the surface is inside or outside the house. A brief explanation of the types of paint flaws and their causes will help you understand the need for preparation and the indicated preventive measures.

The most noticeable fault is *peeling.* Do not blame this on poor paint. Peeling is caused either by poor surface preparation or by excessive moisture in the wall under the paint. If paint peels off to the bare wood on exterior walls, it is almost certainly caused by moisture entering the wall through an improperly calked seam or from leaky gutters, flashings, shingles, or masonry. Peeling on interior walls is usually caused by poor adhesion resulting from painting over dust or oil. *Blistering* is a prelude to peeling and is usually caused by moisture in the wall under the paint. If an exterior wall is insulated but has no vapor barrier (see Section 5-6), water vapor from inside the house will seep through the wall and cause blistering outside. Blistering and peeling can be prevented by starting with a clean surface and by preventing moisture from reaching the wood behind the paint.

Checking is the appearance of hairline cracks on the surface of the paint. Checking may be caused by expansion and contraction of the wood under the paint or may result when a finishing coat is applied before the undercoat is completely dry. To prevent checking, the surface must be smooth and covered with an undercoat compatible with the finishing coat.

Cracking is an advanced form of checking in which the cracks are wider and deeper, extending down to the bare wood. *Alligatoring* is also a form of checking in which the surface is covered with interlacing lines so that the paint film looks like an alligator skin. In both cases, the paint will eventually peel off. Cracking and alligatoring may be caused by insufficient drying time between coats of paint, use of the wrong undercoat, or painting over an oily surface. When either cracking or alligatoring occurs, the paint must be scraped off, and the surface should be repainted.

Crawling is the formation of drops of paint on the surface. *Running* or *sagging* is, as the name implies, a flow of paint perpendicular to the horizontal brush strokes. Both may be caused by applying paint to a surface that is too smooth, too cold, or too greasy.

Wrinkling is akin to running and crawling, in that it can be caused by applying paint to a cold surface or during cold weather. Wrinkling occurs when the surface of the paint dries first, forming a skin over soft paint beneath.

Bleeding is the appearance of stains caused by resins in the wood. The resin frequently is exuded around knots but may also appear on bare wood. To prevent bleeding, bare wood should be treated with sealer before painting.

Chalking is the wearing away of the pigment as a light chalk-like dust. When you rub your hand on the painted surface, the chalk comes off on your hand. Chalking is a desirable characteristic of exterior paints, since it helps keep the paint surface clean. Rain washes away the chalk and, with it, the dirt on the surface. The thickness of the paint film is decreased as chalking takes place, so that in effect the paint is wearing away. But this, too, is desirable, since if layers of paint were added without this wear, the coating would become so thick that it would crack or peel of its own weight. Chalking should begin about two years after a coat of paint is applied, and may start earlier if the paint contains titanium. Undesirable chalking occurs shortly after the paint is applied and is usually caused by poor surface preparation or by rain or mist on the paint before the paint has dried. *Flaking* is a type of undesirable chalking where the paint brushes off in flakes rather than dust.

Staining is discoloration in the paint from foreign materials, such as rusty nailheads below the surface or corrosion of metallic gutters or pipes. The rust stains or water stains from moisture embedded in the wood show through the surface paint. This can be prevented by covering metal parts and countersunk nailheads with the proper rust-preventing sealer or primer before painting.

Mildew is a fungus but looks just like dirt on the painted surface. However, dirt can be washed off, whereas mildew cannot. If left on the surface, mildew can severely damage the paint film. Mildew can be bleached out with ordinary household bleach. Paint dealers sell kits to enable the homeowner to check whether a dirty surface is covered with mildew or just plain dirt, but you can make just as good a check with water and bleach. If water removes the dirt, it was just dirt. If water is ineffective, but bleach works, it is mildew. Mildew must be cleaned off as soon as it is discovered, by scrubbing with a mixture of TSP, bleach, and warm water, as described in Section 3–6. To prevent mildew from recurring, apply a mildew-resistant paint after the surface is completely dry.

From this list of painting flaws and their causes, you can see that moisture is a culprit in many instances, as are dirt and grease. Surfaces must be smooth but not so hard and shiny that paint won't cling. Cracks should be calked on exterior walls, patched on inside surfaces. Don't try to close gaps by painting over them with paint. Loose wallpaper must be stripped off. Loose paint must be scraped away. Dust, dirt, oil, and grease must be removed from the surfaces.

For inside walls that are in good condition, dusting and vacuuming may be sufficient preparation. Don't forget to dust the tops of doors and window ledges. Any dust in the room can settle on your wet walls before the paint dries and spoil the paint job. In kitchens, make sure to wash grease off walls with soap or detergent and warm water. Shiny enamel finishes which are going to be repainted must be dulled, since the new paint will not adhere well to the hard enamel. This can be done by sanding or rubbing with steel wool or by washing with a mild solution of washing soda.

Patch any holes in walls, ceilings, or floors. Use spackling compound, as described in Section 8–18, for plaster or plasterboard, and use putty or wood filler for other surfaces.

Drive in all protruding nails and countersink the heads. Cover with putty. After patches are dry, sand them smooth, and the dust should be cleaned off. Note that latex paints can be put over a plaster patch that is not completely dry, but oil paints cannot.

If you are painting over wallpaper, make sure the paper is fastened firmly to the wall. If it is peeling, it is better to strip off loose paper than to try to make it stick with paint. Similarly, if the old paint is cracked or peeling, it is better to remove it by scraping or by a chemical paint remover than to paint over it.

On exterior walls, scrape away all loose paint with a paint scraper. Use a wire brush to remove loose paint from corners and rounded projections. If paint has been removed to the bare wood, use a primer recommended for the paint that will be used as the final coat. Calk all openings to prevent moisture from getting in behind the paint. Check gutters and flashings for leaks. Fasten loose boards and countersink nailheads. If there are any rust spots on the surface, remove them with steel wool. Cover nailheads with aluminum paint or other rust-preventing sealer.

Make sure that the putty around windows is in good condition. If the putty is dried out, now is a good time to replace it. Putty should be used to fill any small cracks in the wood. Masonry surfaces should also be touched up with patching cement or special plastic patching materials.

Clean everything before you begin. Remove mildew if you find it, as described in Section 3-6. Hose down the house, and use detergent and warm water for stubborn spots. Walls must be dry before you paint.

If old paint must be removed, there are several ways to do this. Professionals sometimes use a torch to burn off the paint, but this method is not recommended for the inexperienced. For most jobs, it is sufficient to scrape off loose paint with a scraper, leaving some good paint still attached. If large areas of paint must be removed, a chemical paint remover is better. It is also the best for removing paint or varnish from curved or irregular surfaces. When a chemical remover is used, all traces of it must be eliminated before adding a new coat of paint. This is done by washing the surface with a rag soaked in alcohol, turpentine, or special solvent. Adequate ventilation must be provided when using most chemical paint removers, since they are highly flammable.

On fine furniture, paint can be removed by sanding, but it is a difficult procedure and mistakes can be costly. For the home handyman, chemical removers may be preferable, since they are easier to use. Chemicals are always preferred on intricate designs and in tight corners.

Some walls need a primer or sealer before paint is applied. New plaster walls must be thoroughly dry before putting on the primer. Allow at least two months for drying, and six months is not too long. Use a primer recommended for the particular paint you will use. Repaired plaster spots do not need a long drying time. In fact, latex can be used almost immediately. Cover the spackled spot with paint. Then when the paint dries, paint the whole wall. Alkyd and oil-based paints usually require an undercoat when they are to be used on bare wood. The instructions on the can usually specify preferred undercoats. Latex paint can be its own undercoat. As a general rule, if you are painting over an old paint layer, you don't need a primer, but if you are painting on a new surface, especially one that is porous, the surface should be sealed first.

9-7. HOW TO HANDLE PAINTS

Paint is a mixture of pigment in a vehicle or carrier, such as oil or water. The pigment is not dissolved in the vehicle but is held in suspension. When a can of paint remains unused for an extended period of time, the pigment settles to the bottom of the can. Before the paint can be used, it must be mixed thoroughly so that the pigment is in suspension again. When paint is left in the can overnight, the pigment settles again, and the paint again must be mixed. If the paint is not mixed thoroughly, the color on the painted surface will vary. Also, the pigment will be distributed unevenly so that its protective property will vary from place to place.

When you buy paint, the dealer will mix it for you on a machine if you intend to use it the same day. The mechanical shaker agitates the can so that the pigment and vehicle are thoroughly mixed. Alkyd and oil paints can be used immediately after shaking; latex paints should stand unopened about an hour before using. WARNING: Never shake varnish.

If you must mix paint yourself, because you want to finish a partially used can for example, you can ensure a thorough blending by following these steps. When you open the paint can you will note that the oil has risen to the top. Pour off the surface oil into a clean, empty container such as another paint can or a cardboard mixing pail. Stir the remaining oil and pigment with a wooden paddle until they are thoroughly blended. Gradually pour oil back into the mixed paint, stirring as you do so. Finally pour the mixed paint back and forth between the two pails several times.

Try to have enough mixed paint available to do the complete job, or at least a whole wall. Different cans of paint even from the same batch number may have slight differences in color. If you change cans when you go from one wall to another, the color change will not be noticeable, but if you change in the middle of a wall, it will.

If you add a thinner, as is usually required when you use a roller, make sure that the thinner is right for the paint. Read the label. Do not add too much thinner. Here again, the thinner causes a slight change in color and you must add exactly the same amount of thinner to each can of paint. Thinner is added in the same way paint is mixed. Add a little at a time, stirring constantly. Finally pour the mixture back and forth between two containers.

The paint can tends to get messy as you work. The groove that holds the lid usually gets filled with paint, and the outside of the can is frequently wet with paint. As you put the lid back on the can when you are finished, the paint in the groove can splash out and make a mess. One way of avoiding this is to punch holes in the bottom of the groove with a hammer and nail. Then most of the paint in the groove will flow through the holes back into the can. The lid seals the holes when it is place. To replace the lid, put it over the groove, and cover the whole can with a cloth. Then tap on the lid with a hammer. Any paint that splatters will soil the cloth but nothing else. Another way to avoid the mess is to crimp aluminum foil all around the top edge of the paint can. When you are through, discard the aluminum, and the paint mess will go with it, leaving the groove free of paint.

Old paint is usually lumpy and should be strained before using. Cheesecloth or an old nylon stocking can be used as a strainer. Place the cloth over a clean container, and pour the paint through it. Discard the cloth and the lumps.

If you must stop painting for a moment, as to answer the telephone, it is all right to leave your brush or roller resting in the paint. For a longer break, as for lunch, the brush should not rest on its bristles. Before you start, you should drill a hole through the paintbrush so that it can be supported by a wire through the hole resting on the top of the can. The bristles will then not reach the bottom. This is shown in Fig. 9–7.

When a paint job is to be continued the next day, the paint must be poured back into the can and the can sealed. Be careful about splashing paint when sealing. When the can is reopened, note if a film has formed on the paint. If so, remove and discard the film *before* stirring the paint. You should clean out the brushes and leave them in thinner overnight.

When you are painting, you will want newspaper under the can to catch drippings. A better method is to glue a paper plate to the bottom of the can so that this drip catcher will move with the can.

When a job is completed, the equipment must be cleaned. If you used latex paint, simply wash everything in soap and water. Shake out all water from brushes or rollers, and wrap them in newspaper to

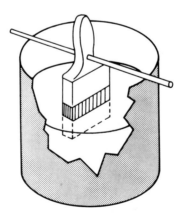

FIGURE 9–7. Wire to Support Brush.

keep them free of dust. If you use turpentine or other thinners to clean your tools, pour the thinner into a shallow pan and put your tools in the pan also. Work the thinner into every part of the brush until all traces of pigment are out. Then wash your tools in soap and water to remove the thinner, comb out the brushes, and wrap them in newspaper.

Save the dirty thinner. Pour it into a jar or coffee can that can be sealed with a plastic cover. After a few days, the paint will settle, leaving clear thinner that can be poured off and used over again. Store the clean thinner in a suitably labeled container. If it is flammable, put that on the label also.

9-8. HOW TO USE A BRUSH

Everyone knows how to use a paintbrush, and, in fact, almost any way you use it, the results will be satisfactory. However, if you take care of your brush and use it properly, it will last longer, and most important, the paint surface will last longer and have fewer flaws.

Before you use a new brush for the first time, it should be properly conditioned. Remove loose bristles, and shake out dust by tapping the bristles against the palm of your hand. If there are any "wild" bristles coming off at an angle to the rest, cut them off with a sharp razor blade. Suspend the new brush in linseed oil so that the bristles do not touch the bottom of the jar, and leave the brush in the oil at least overnight, but preferably for 24 hours. Squeeze out the linseed oil from the brush, and wash the brush in turpentine to remove any oil remaining. Brushes conditioned in this way will hold more paint than unconditioned brushes. If the brush is to be used with water-based paint, wash out the turpentine with soap and water. For oil-based paints, this last step is not necessary. Note that this is a one-time operation. After a brush has been used, it is not necessary to condition it.

The part of the bristles nearest the ferrule is called the *heel*. Paint in the heel is difficult to wash out and restricts the flexibility of the bristles. Therefore, when you dip a brush into a can of paint, the paint should cover only half the length of the bristles or a little more, as indicated in Fig. 9-8.

For the same reason, the brush should be held with the bristles pointing downward as it is moved from the pail to the surface being painted. The brush is dipped, then excess paint is removed by touching the brush to the inside of the top of the paint can. The brush should hold paint without dripping as it is moved to the surface to be

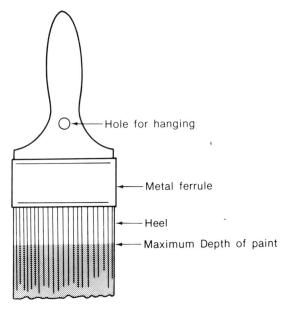

FIGURE 9-8. Maximum Depth.

painted.   Also shown in Fig. 9-8 is a hole in the brush for hanging the brush on a wire, as shown in Fig. 9-7.   It is a good idea to drill a hole like this in every brush you own.

Each time a full brush is brought to the surface being painted, daub paint on several spots first.   Then use long strokes to spread the paint evenly.   Always brush with the grain of the wood, if it is visible, but alternate the direction of the strokes.   If you stroke across the grain, the paint may have a rippled effect when it dries.   Do not end a stroke abruptly, since the brush may leave a large blob of paint if you do.   Instead, try to lift the brush off gradually at the end of each stroke. You will do this intuitively if you lift the brush before reversing direction.

If a loose bristle sticks on the painted surface, pick it up with the brush.   Then brush over the spot with a small amount of paint on the brush.   Never use a dry brush to try to correct missed spots.   Always use the flat side of the brush, never the edge.   When you paint with the edge, you distort the shape of the brush, which may be permanent.

If you neglect a brush, so that it becomes hard with paint or distorted, do not discard it.   A brush with distorted or wild bristles should be soaked in linseed oil for a few days so that the bristles become pliable.   Then the oil-soaked brush should be wrapped tightly in aluminum foil so that it is forced to the proper shape.   After a week, wash out the oil with turpentine, and the brush should be in good shape. A brush with dried paint should be soaked in a commercial brush cleaner for a week or more. Then comb out the bristles to remove old paint and clean the brush in turpentine. Finally, wash the brush with soap and water. Before putting the brush away, comb out the bristles with the comb shown in Fig. 9–2. Always store wrapped brushes flat.

9–9. HOW TO USE A ROLLER

A roller is much faster than a brush, and is preferred by most handymen for painting large, flat surfaces. However, a roller does not eliminate a brush, since the brush is needed at corners and in close quarters inaccessible to the roller. Ideally the work should be done by two people, one cutting in at corners with a brush, and the other painting the large surfaces with a roller. Use latex or alkyd paints, since they don't show lap marks where the rolled paint and brushed paint overlap.

Paints that dry too quickly cannot be applied by roller. This eliminates lacquers and some fast-drying enamels, but most other paints can be rolled on. If in doubt, read the label on the can. Latex paint is preferred because of the ease of cleaning up afterward. Whatever paint you use, be sure to read the label for any special instructions that apply to rolling. Many paints can be rolled as they come from the can, while others must be thinned. The type and needed amount of thinner is always specified on the label.

A new roller must be conditioned before use. Wash the cover in soap and water to remove all dirt. After rinsing, you can use the roller immediately with latex paint, since the roller should be wet applying water-based paints. For alkyd paints, let the cover dry thoroughly before using the roller.

The pan, as shown in Fig. 9–4, has a sloping bottom. Pour paint in so that about half the bottom is covered. To load the roller, dip it into the paint so that it is uniformly coated. Then smooth the load of paint by rolling the roller over the uncovered part of the bottom of the pan.

It is usually preferred to do the brushwork first. Cut in at all corners that cannot be reached with the roller. On your first stroke with the roller, begin by rolling upward so that excess paint is pushed ahead. Subsequent strokes should crisscross in random directions, as shown in Fig. 9–9. Note that each stroke is made in a more or less upward direction, and strokes do not cover the total area. Additional strokes

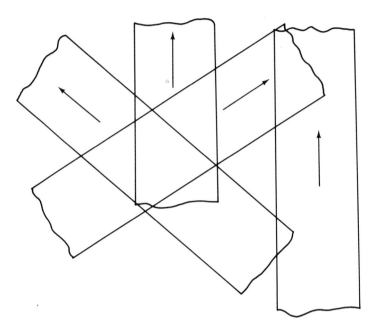

FIGURE 9–9. Random Roller Pattern.

will fill the gaps, and in general all strokes overlap others as much as 50 percent. If you roll too fast, you will throw paint ahead, so work slowly.

When you are finished, wash roller and pan immediately in the proper thinner: water for latex paint, turpentine for alkyds. Squeeze out as much moisture as possible, and wrap the roller in clear plastic sheet for an airtight seal. The roller can be stored moist or dry as long as it is clean.

9–10. HOW TO USE A SPRAY

Spraying is quick and easy, but extra precautions are necessary. It is almost impossible to control the "overspray," that is, spraying beyond the object being painted. Adequate ventilation is required, and even outdoors you should wear a mask.

Almost any kind of paint can be sprayed and on virtually any kind of surface. It is not necessary to buy a spray gun, since most paint shops will let you borrow or rent them as needed. For small jobs, aerosol cans of paint are the simplest to use.

Before spraying, make sure that the paint is thoroughly mixed and strained. Small particles of dirt or hardened pigment can clog the spray gun. Aerosol cans must be shaken vigorously for at least one minute to ensure proper mixing. If you are using a spray gun, mix and strain the paint before putting it in the gun.

The spray gun or can must be moved so that the spray is perpendicular to the surface being painted and so that the nozzle remains the same distance from the surface, as shown in Fig. 9–10. In Fig. 9–10(a), the path of movement remains constant. This is correct. In Fig. 9–10(b), the spray is moved on an arc so that the distance between spray gun and surface varies. This will result in an uneven paint layer. If the surface to be painted is curved, as, for example, the outside of a barrel, then the spray gun must follow a curved line to remain equidistant from the surface. This is shown in Fig. 9–11.

The tip of the nozzle should be about 8 inches from the surface. This may vary with different spray guns and different aerosol cans, so make it a point to read the label first before using the equipment. Before you begin painting the surface, you should practice on a piece of cardboard or wood scrap. As you move the gun over the surface, it should spray continuously. Do not start or stop the spray in the middle of a stroke. Thus, you start the spray with the gun pointing slightly off the surface. Then move the spray all the way across until the spray is off the surface at the other side. When coming back, always overlap your strokes. There will be no lap marks.

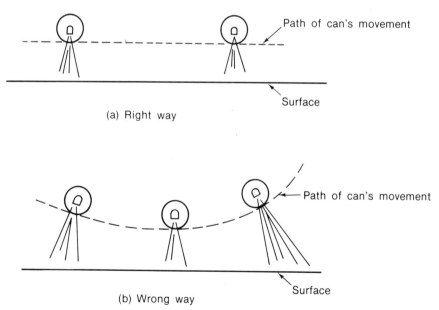

(a) Right way

(b) Wrong way

FIGURE 9–10. Movement of Spray.

Always save the best for the last. That is, when spraying furniture, start with the undersides of chairs and tables and other inconspicuous places. Finish on the best surface. The reason for this is that it is impossible to avoid some misting. If you did the top first, the misting from the rest of the job might cause the top to look sandy. Rubber-based paints have less misting than others.

9-11. HOW TO PAINT WALLS AND CEILINGS

Usually when you decide to paint a room, you will want to paint ceilings and walls. If you think that only the ceiling needs painting because the walls still look bright enough, you will find that after you paint the ceiling, the walls look dingy in comparison. The same thing happens in reverse when you paint only the walls. Therefore, wait until you feel up to painting walls *and* ceiling, and then everything will look bright.

When you paint a room, do the ceiling first, the walls next, and finish up with the woodwork, including doors and windows. Remove as much furniture as possible, and push the rest into the center of the room. Cover furniture and floor with drop cloths. Before you begin to paint, prepare *all* surfaces, patching, sanding, and dusting. Prime new surfaces, as needed. Latex paint is its own primer.

If calcimine was used on the ceiling previously, it must be removed completely. You cannot paint over calcimine, even with additional calcimine. When calcimine is removed from the ceiling, treat the ceiling as if it were new, priming or sealing it with a material compatible with the paint you will use.

To paint a wall or ceiling, you should use a roller or a 4-inch brush. The roller is preferred, since it is faster. However, the roller is somewhat difficult to use where ceiling and wall meet and on walls near the woodwork. Some positions are shown in Fig. 9-12. In Fig. 9-12(a),

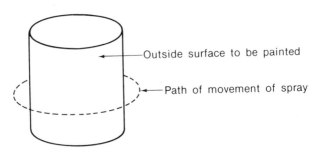

—Outside surface to be painted

—Path of movement of spray

FIGURE 9-11. Spraying on Curved Surface.

the roller is at the junction of wall and ceiling, touching both. Note that it cannot reach the junction line, and if it is used this way, there will be no paint at the top of the wall and at the edge of the ceiling. In Fig. 9–12(b), the roller is moved along the ceiling next to the wall. The ceiling will be painted right up to the wall. In Fig. 9–12(c), the roller is moved along the wall next to the ceiling. The wall will be painted right up to the ceiling. However, in a corner, at a junction of two walls and the ceiling, it is impossible to get the roller all the way into the corner. There you will have to cut in with a brush. Now, since you have to use a brush anyway, you might as well cut in every junction and save yourself some troublesome manipulation of the roller. In Fig. 9–13, paint is shown brushed on at the junction of each wall and the ceiling and also at the junction of each pair of walls. It should also be applied by brush on the wall next to door frames, window frames, and woodwork. Note that if the ceiling is to be a different color from the walls, you would apply paint with a brush on the ceiling next to the walls, being careful not to get paint on the walls. If both ceiling and walls are to be the same color, you don't have to be as careful and can apply paint with a brush to both sides of the junction simultaneously. It is best to do all the cutting in before starting to use the roller, but if two people are working together, one can do the cutting in while the other uses the roller at the same time.

If possible, get two ladders and put a plank across at a convenient level so that you will be able to do a larger area, without having to climb up and down as often. If the room is rectangular, it is better to go back and forth across the short dimension of the ceiling than to paint along the length. Place the ladder so that you are painting ahead of you rather than overhead. Place the pan firmly on a box at a convenient height so that you can dip the roller in it without coming down.

The first stroke with the roller loaded should be away from you.

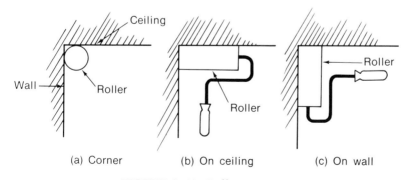

(a) Corner   (b) On ceiling   (c) On wall

FIGURE 9–12. Roller Positions.

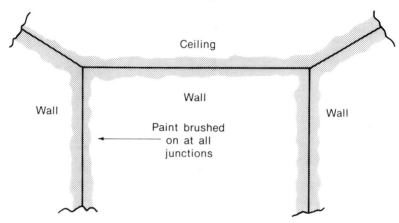

FIGURE 9-13. Cutting In.

Then paint a strip across from wall to wall overlapping the paint you put on by brush near the junction. Paint the next strip coming back overlapping the first and continue in this way until the whole ceiling is finished. Plan to paint the whole ceiling in one session. If you do part of it and allow it to dry, lap marks may show where you left off.

After the ceiling is finished, you can paint the walls. Begin near a corner at the top and paint a strip about 3 feet wide from top to bottom. The first stroke should be upward when the roller is full of paint, but then paint in random directions. The next strip overlaps the first. Try to finish a whole wall in one session. Lap marks in the corner will not show. Paint the woodwork last. You can use a roller on the woodwork also, unless it has a very intricate design. The junctions of woodwork and walls should have been cut in earlier. Try to use an enamel for woodwork, especially windowsills, since fingerprints wash off more easily from enamel than from a flat paint. You can use latex enamel if you want the ease of cleanup of a water-based paint.

9-12. HOW TO PAINT DOORS AND WINDOWS

When you paint a door or a window, you must remember to paint every part and to paint in such a way that wet paint on one part does not interfere with your painting another. Painting a window requires care, and in order not to have to lean over painted surfaces, it is preferable to paint the window frame after the window is finished. Doors do not present quite the same problem, and you can paint the door frame before or after you paint the door, at your own convenience.

If a door is one unbroken surface, there is not much problem on deciding the order of painting. Remove doorknobs and other hardware. Paint the edges first with a brush. For interior doors, you can omit the bottom edge, since no one sees it, but for doors to the outside, the bottom edge should be painted to protect the door from moisture seeping under it. Remove the door from the hinges, and paint the bottom edge with any quick drying coating. Then rehang the door and paint the other edges. Finally, paint the surface of the door with a roller or brush.

If a door has panels, there is a preferred order of painting the parts to minimize the possibility of lap marks. This order is indicated in Fig. 9–14. First, the edges are painted; second, the moldings around each panel. Both of these are done with brush or roller. Third, the panels are painted; fourth, the horizontal members or rails; and fifth, the vertical members or stiles. After painting, leave the door ajar until the paint has dried. Then put back the doorknobs and other hardware.

The order of painting the parts of a double-hung window is indicated in Fig. 9–15. All parts are painted with a brush. First, raise the lower sash as high as it will go and lower the upper sash part way. Now begin by painting the check rail on the top sash. This is the bottom horizontal member. Second, paint the horizontal and vertical bars that divide the sash into small panes. Some windows have such bars

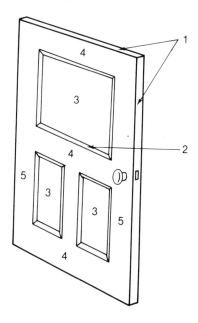

FIGURE 9–14. Order of Painting Door.

in one or both sashes, while others may have one large pane in each sash, in which case, this step is omitted. The vertical members (stiles) of the sashes are painted next. Throughout the foregoing procedures, it is necessary to raise and lower the sashes to get at the surfaces. You can grasp the horizontal rails of the sashes to do this, since they are painted last.

When painting a window, you have to be careful to keep the paint off the glass. You can mask the windowpanes before painting or use a shield, as shown in Fig. 9-6. Or you can just try to be careful. Don't worry too much if you get a little paint on the glass. Let it dry, and then remove it with a razor blade. If a door has a glass pane in it, paint the molding around the pane before painting the rest of the door. Use the same precautions to keep paint off the glass, or scrape it off later, after it dries.

9-13. HOW TO PAINT FLOORS

Interior floors are usually finished with a transparent coating, as described in Section 8-12, so that the natural grain of the wood shows through. Paint is opaque and hides the beauty of the wood. On the other hand, paint also hides any flaws and blemishes in the floor. Outdoor floors, on decks and porches, for example, are usually painted, and some poor-quality wood floors are also painted. Paint is some-times used on concrete floors.

Any good quality paint will protect a floor, but specially designed floor paints will resist wear longer. The simplest to use is latex floor paint. You can apply this paint over a damp surface, since it is water-solvent. It dries in about an hour. However, you should wait until the next day to apply the second coat. Two coats are usually suffi-cient, but on bare wood, a third coat is necessary. You can apply the paint with a roller or a wide brush.

Oil-based and alkyd floor enamels are the most common floor paints. They are more durable than latex paints. However, the cleanup process is more involved. Also, these paints cannot be put down on a damp surface.

Rubber-based paints are best for concrete floors, although the other floor paints are also quite satisfactory. Rubber-based paints should not be used on wood floors. Since gasoline attacks rubber-based paints, do not use these paints on a garage floor. Rubber-based paints cannot be applied with a roller, because they dry too rapidly. Although these paints have excellent durability on concrete and masonry surfaces, the average homeowner should not use them, because they are more difficult to apply and require special solvents for cleaning the equipment after the job.

Latex or alkyd floor paints can be applied with a roller or a brush. Latex paints are usually applied as they come from the can, but alkyd paint may be thinned with turpentine. Follow the instructions on the can. For concrete floors, a simple but effective method is to pour some paint directly on the floor and spread it with a stiff push broom.

9-14. HOW TO PAINT EXTERIORS

Painting the outside of a house is *not* a job for a handyman. Even if you do everything right, the amount saved by doing the job yourself is not enough to justify the risks. Some of the problems, such as unexpected costs and health hazards, are hinted at in Chapter 1. A good exterior paint job should last five years, and the potential savings by doing it yourself, amortized over the five-year period, is too small to justify it.

Nevertheless, you may want to tackle the job yourself, feeling that any saving justifies it. If the house is more than one story high, you will be climbing up and down ladders, and even if you did nothing else, the climbing alone could tire you. Review the rules for safety on ladders, presented in Section 3-7. For a bungalow or ranch type of home, most of the work can be done from ground level, so that you don't need quite the same physical fitness as for a taller house. As a compromise, when you have to paint a larger house, hire professionals for the upper floors, and do the bottom yourself.

The first step is preparation of the surface, as described for exteriors in Section 10-4. It is very important to protect against moisture. A leak in a gutter or flashing can allow water to enter underneath the paint, which can then cause blistering or peeling. Before painting, protect shrubbery and lawns by covering them with drop cloths. Remove all removable hardware and fixtures. Mix paint thoroughly, and you are ready to begin.

You can use a brush, a roller, or a spray to paint the outside of a house. Spraying would be fastest if you didn't have to worry about masking windows and other areas you don't want to paint. Also, spraying is impossible on windy days. For the amateur, the brush and roller are thus preferred. Your best bet is latex house paint, no matter how you intend to apply it. Latex, being water-based, can be applied even when the walls are not completely dry. Cleanup afterward is very simple, since everything can be cleaned in soap and water. Spray guns should be cleaned before returning them to the dealer. Latex paint may require special primers on some surfaces. Read the instructions on the can.

A roller with a long handle saves climbing up and down ladders and permits you to paint a larger area from one spot, be it on a ladder or on the ground. Before using a roller, you should cut in at edges and corners. Then roll out to overlap the painted edge strip.

In general, you work from the top down. Start with overhangs and gables. Then paint the walls. Try to finish a complete surface at each painting session so that lap marks won't show. Gutters, downspouts, windows, and doors can be painted in any convenient order. For metal parts, including railings, windows, gutters, and downspouts, see Section 9–15. Shutters and trim are usually painted last. Masonry and stucco require special treatment, explained in Section 10–4.

Do not paint if it is too hot or too cold. The surface should be between approximately 50 and 90°F. Do not paint if it is too windy, since dust may be blown on the wet paint. Do not paint if someone is burning leaves or trash in the vicinity, since the smoke can dirty the wet paint.

Allow about three days between coats, if a second coat is to be applied. In general, two thin coats will last longer than one thick one. If a primer is used, one coat of paint on top of the primer is usually sufficient.

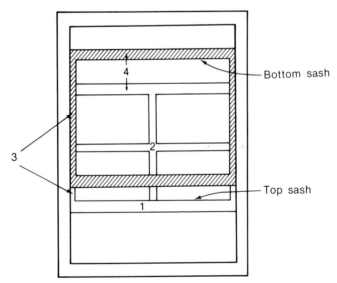

FIGURE 9–15. Order of Painting Window.

9-15. HOW TO PAINT METAL

The secret of a good paint job on metal is proper surface preparation. If the surface is clean and a proper primer is used, painting is easy, and the paint job will last for years. If the surface is not prepared correctly, nothing you do after that will help.

First, it is most important to remove all dirt and grease from the metal surface. Paint just will not adhere well to an oily surface. To remove grease, use a detergent with water or a nonflammable solvent. Any loose flakes of old paint or loose rust must also be scraped away. Solid rust, however, can remain. After cleaning, the surface may be treated, depending on the metal. Then a primer is applied. The primer has two purposes. In the first place, it is a coating that will adhere strongly to the metal and to which paint will adhere. Therefore, paints that would not ordinarily adhere to the metal surface can be used if the correct primer is used between the paint and the metal. Second, primers used on metals that tend to corrode have anticorrosion properties so that they react chemically with corrosive elements, neutralizing them. The type of primer depends on the type of metal.

Iron and steel tend to rust, forming a loose coating that flakes off. Even when covered by paint, the corrosion continues under the coating unless a suitable primer is used. Nonferrous metals, such as copper, tin, brass, and aluminum do not rust but do become tarnished or oxidized if left exposed to the air. These metals take paint better after oxidation. Galvanized iron is iron coated with zinc. Paint will not adhere to a new galvanized surface but will adhere to one that is weathered.

Iron or steel with little or no rust should be touched up with emery cloth or steel wool to remove all traces of corrosion. Then it is cleaned to remove all grease and oil. For a primer, use red lead or zinc chromate. (Careful, both are poisonous!) The next day, paint with enamel or aluminum paint.

Iron or steel that is severely rusted needs a different treatment. With a wire brush, scrape off all loose rust, and sand any pits in the metal. Clean with detergent and water to remove grease. Prime with a special anticorrosion paint. Use the same anticorrosion paint for the second coat.

Copper, brass, and aluminum should be allowed to weather for two or three months until they lose their gloss. After cleaning off grease, coat with a zinc chromate primer. Finish with a coat of any good exterior paint or enamel or aluminum paint. Galvanized iron should weather for at least six months before painting. Clean off grease, and prime with special primer for galvanized surfaces. Finish with a good exterior paint or enamel.

9–16 HOW TO PAINT MASONRY

Walls made of stone, brick, or stucco can be painted as easily as wood. Again, the most important part of the job is preparation of the surface. The surface can be cleaned of dirt and loose paint by using a wire brush. The primer and paint can be applied by brush, roller, or spray, unless the instructions on the can specifically forbid it. That is, some paints cannot be rolled, but that is a function of the paint, not of the surface.

There are many different kinds of masonry paints, and they are not usually compatible. If you are going to use the same type of paint that was used before, it is sufficient to clean the surface of dirt and loose paint and simply paint over it with the new paint. If the new paint is different from the old, you may have to remove all traces of the old paint.

Latex masonry paints are the simplest to use, because they thin with water. Latex paint dries quickly and is very durable when used on unpainted brick or stucco. It cannot be used over old layers of oil-based paint. Nor can it be used on any old paint that is chalking. However, suitable primers are available that solve both problems.

Cement water paints are the cheapest. They come in powder form and must be mixed with water. One of the main ingredients of cement water paint is portland cement. The walls must be *wet* when this paint is applied. The second coat should be applied before the first is completely dry. Cement water paint is especially suited to walls that tend to get damp. It dries to a hard, but brittle finish. It is tricky to apply, and therefore of little interest to the average handyman.

Oil-based masonry paints give a durable finish on old masonry surfaces but adhere poorly to surfaces less than a year old. They fare poorly on damp walls. At least one week of clear weather is needed before applying an oil-based paint, to ensure that the masonry is completely dry. Because of this, and also because of the need for special solvents for thinning and cleaning up, home handymen usually do not use oil-based masonry paints.

Rubber-based paints adhere exceptionally well on new masonry, and they cover in one coat. They do not adhere on some old painted surfaces. Check the instructions on the can for compatibility.

If the desired new paint cannot be used over the old existing paint, one solution is to sandblast the old paint off the surface. This is a costly procedure and not one for a handyman to tackle. Usually a suitable primer can be found that will make a good bond to both paints. One coat of primer followed by one coat of desired paint will be enough for most masonry surfaces, especially if the primer is the same color as the finishing coat.

As with other exterior surfaces, begin painting at the top and work down. If you use a roller, you will have to cut in with a brush at edges and corners. Try to finish a complete surface each time you paint so that lap marks are nonexistent.

9-17. HOW TO FINISH FURNITURE

If you build furniture or buy ready-to-paint furniture, you can save money by finishing it yourself. "Finishing," when applied to furniture, means covering the object with paint, varnish, lacquer, or other film, for protection of the surface as well as for the sake of appearance. A piece of ready-to-paint furniture is about 20 to 30 percent cheaper than the same piece finished. However, except for painting, finishing is a long, slow process. Although each coat may be put on quickly, the surface should be allowed to dry at least 24 hours between coats, and at least four coats are usually required. In addition, the surface must be sanded or rubbed several times during the process. You must decide whether the saving by buying ready-to-paint pieces justifies the additional work.

If a piece of furniture is functional rather than decorative, such as for use in a kitchen or playroom, you may decide that it need only be painted. Paint covers the wood completely so that the grain is not seen. By the same token, paint covers blemishes and permits you to build furniture out of odd scraps of wood with grains or patterns that don't match. This would be impossible if you wanted a transparent finish such as varnish, shellac, or lacquer. The transparent finishes are used when the natural beauty of the wood should be visible through the finish.

Before beginning any finishing job, plan your work. Remove all hardware, such as locks, metal knobs, and handles, before beginning. Drawers should be removed from chests or cabinets and stood on end with the front, the surface to be painted, in a horizontal position. Plan to coat the inside corners and hard-to-reach areas first. Save the easily accessible surfaces for last.

Painting is very simple. Any good enamel can be used. First, the surface must be dusted thoroughly. Then, use a 2-inch brush to apply an undercoat to the bare wood. This is usually a white enamel under-coat compatible with the final coat, but it can also be tinted. If you use latex enamel, the same enamel can be used for both undercoat and final coat. Only the two coats are necessary. The undercoat should be allowed to dry at least 24 hours. Then the surface is sanded with fine sandpaper until it is smooth. Dust the surface thoroughly to remove all traces of dirt and grit. Then apply the final coat. After another 24 hours the piece of furniture is ready for use. Paint should not be used on expensive, beautiful woods, since it hides the natural beauty.

Varnish is tricky to apply. The biggest problem is air bubbles appearing on the surface, preventing a smooth finish. Bubbles form and cannot be removed if the can is shaken or stirred vigorously, so handle with care. Dip the brush in the varnish so that only one third of the length of the bristles is below the surface. Instead of wiping the excess off by drawing across the lip of the can, tap the brush against the edge of the can, as shown in Fig. 9–16. This minimizes air bubbles. Pressing down too hard with the brush also causes air bubbles, so use a light pressure on the surface. Flow the varnish on with long strokes. Special brushes for varnishing are available. These are very soft, with many flagged bristles to hold more varnish and fewer air bubbles.

The first coat of varnish may be thinned with one part turpentine to nine or ten parts varnish. Succeeding coats are not thinned. Each coat should dry at least 24 hours and is then sanded smooth with very

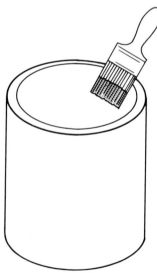

FIGURE 9–16. Tapping Off Excess Varnish.

fine sandpaper. When sanding, always rub with the grain so that minute sanding marks do not show. Remove all dust before starting and after each sanding, before applying the next coat. Formerly, the final coat needed to be rubbed by hand to produce a satin finish rather than what was considered an objectionable mirror-like surface. Now semigloss and flat varnishes are available for the final coat and need no rubbing. The glossy varnishes are tougher and are used for two or three coats first. Then a "satiny" varnish is used for the top coat.

If you want something to protect the wood and are not too particular about looks, apply one or two coats of shellac. Shellac may also be used on good woods, since the grain shows through. For a fine finish on dark woods, you can apply about four coats of shellac, sanding each coat with very fine sandpaper. However, do not use shellac on tabletops that may be subject to water, since water stains shellac.

Stain is used to color the wood without hiding the grain. It is easy to apply. However, on soft wood, stain soaks into the ends more than on flat surfaces, causing the ends to be darker. This can be prevented by first coating the ends with a thin layer of shellac. Stains can be brushed on easily, since they do not show brush marks.

When the wood is stained to the desired tone, the stain finish can be protected by covering it with clear lacquer. The only problem with applying lacquer is that it dries very fast, so you must work as fast as possible, without retracing your steps. Apply in long strokes from one side of the surface to the other, and have each stroke overlap the preceding slightly. One problem is that the lacquer is clear, and thus you can't see whether you've missed a spot until it has dried. You can go back then and touch up these missed areas. You should apply at least three coats of lacquer, and five is preferable. After each coat is dry (except the final coat), rub the surface smooth with a ball of very fine steel wool. Dust the surface before applying the next coat.

Refinishing furniture involves removing the old finish and then finishing by one of the methods described above. If you plan to use paint, however, it is not necessary to remove the old finish so long as it is hard. In fact, you may be able to get by with only one coat of enamel, since the old finish can act as an undercoat.

Removing the old finish is accomplished easily with new chemical removers. Buy one that is nontoxic and nonflammable. Pour it freely over the surface, and spread with a piece of wood or cardboard. For irregular surfaces, use an old brush. Let it stand 5 to 10 minutes and then scrape off the paint with a dull knife. Repeat if necessary. After the old finish is removed, wash the wood with ordinary water to remove all traces of the chemical. When the wood is dry, you are ready for refinishing.

Before refinishing, make sure that the surface is in good condition. If it is scratched, the scratches should be covered. If it has screw holes, knot holes, or cracks, fill them with a wood filler. The filler can be stained to match the wood. Light scratches can be removed by rubbing with furniture polish thinned with rubbing alcohol. Scratches in walnut can be stained by rubbing them with a piece of walnut meat. Scratches in mahogany can be touched up with iodine. Matching oil stains for most woods are available. After the surface is fixed up and dusted, finish as desired.

Kits are available for special finishes for furniture. Plastic and wood veneer laminates with adhesive backing can be applied directly to surfaces, even to surfaces built up out of scraps of wood. Antiquing kits enable you to make a new piece of furniture look like a genuine antique. Gold leaf and other special effects are all easily applied with kits on sale in building-supply stores and mail-order houses.

10

*Outside
The House*

Most of the big jobs connected with a house have to do with the exterior, such as putting on a new roof, painting a house, or building a chimney. These are all jobs for professionals. The savings in doing it yourself, amortized over the expected life of the project, is too small to justify the time and risk. Nevertheless, there are many exterior tasks you can do yourself that *will* save you money. If you tackle the routine maintenance jobs mentioned in Chapter 3, you will save money simply by prolonging the time before a big job is necessary. Some homeowners do nothing else themselves. However, there is no need to pay a serviceman to do a small job you can do with little effort and no risk.

10-1. ROOF REPAIRS

Acrophobia is fear of high places, and is a good excuse for not tackling roof jobs yourself. If, in fact, you really are afraid of high places, it isn't worth the risk for you to do your own roof repairs. If you are not afraid of heights but don't want to fix the roof, you can always claim acrophobia, anyway.

Although you should usually have a new roof installed by a professional roofer, there are many small roof jobs well within your capabilities. However, if the roof is still covered by a guarantee or if you are insured for the damage, as from windstorm for example, always let a professional handle the job. If you are not covered by insurance or a guarantee, then you can tackle such jobs as fixing small leaks, loose or broken shingles, damaged flashings, and wrinkled or blistered roofing.

Before beginning a roofing job, read the paragraphs on ladder safety in Section 3-7. If you must walk on the roof, especially one with a steep slope, wear shoes with soles that will grip (preferably, soft rubber). Try to walk on the roof as little as possible, since shoes can damage shingles. Do not go up on the roof when it is wet or when there is a high wind. It is a good idea to have someone hold the ladder firmly while you are on the roof and to stay in the vicinity of the ladder. Then if you slip, the ladder will stop you from falling off the roof. On very steep roofs, you can place a short ladder flat on the roof, tying it to a tree on the other side, as shown in Fig. 10-1. This gives you a firm footing.

The first sign of a leak in the roof may be a damp spot on a ceiling or wall or a drip inside the house. The first problem is finding the location of the leak. This is not always simple to do. When water enters a hole in the roof, it can travel several feet along the inside before it drips off. Then the damp spot on the ceiling will be far from the actual hole. If the attic is unfinished, you can examine the inside of the roof closely and determine where the water is entering. Drive a nail up through the roof from the inside at the leak so that you can find the exact spot on the top. If you cannot examine the inside of the roof, you will have to examine the top carefully to find a possible source of the leak. Begin approximately above the damp spot inside the house and check shingles and nails in all directions from this spot until you find the defect. Look for broken shingles or shingles that have bent up away from the roof. Look for loose nails that are raised so that water can enter the nail hole and travel along the nail to the inside. Frequently, a leak is caused by cracked or pitted flashing, so you should examine all flashings for defects, including rust. On roofs covered with rolled roofing, look for cracks or dried areas as well as loose nails.

Most leaks can be fixed with asphalt cement or some other roofing compound available in hardware stores specifically for this purpose. It is usually applied with a small trowel, but you can use a putty knife or even a flat piece of scrap wood. If a shingle is raised, apply roofing compound under it liberally and push it down flat. You cannot use too much compound. If the shingle tends to curl up again, nail it down with flat-headed roofing nails and apply more compound over the heads of the nails. Likewise, any loose nails should be hammered in again, and their heads should be covered with the compound.

When a shingle is broken, the cure depends on the type of shingle.

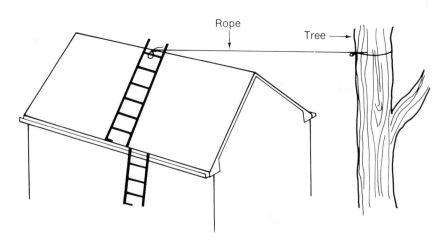

FIGURE 10-1. Ladder on Roof for Footing.

Broken tile shingles can be fixed with asphalt cement. Broken wood shingles should be replaced. Shingles are usually laid in such a way that each shingle overlaps the nails holding the lower shingle, as shown in Fig. 10–2. To remove a broken shingle, it is necessary to insert a hacksaw blade under it to cut the nails holding it. Then the shingle can be pulled out. Apply roofing compound liberally and slide in a new shingle. Nail it down and cover the nailheads with more roofing compound. It may not look as pretty as the rest of the roofing, but it won't leak.

If an asbestos shingle has a small break, you can patch it with

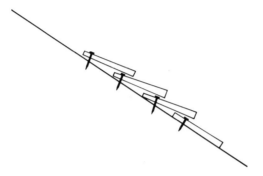

FIGURE 10–2. Nails Holding Shingles.

roofing compound. First, apply compound liberally under the edges all around the break, and then nail down the edges with flat-headed roofing nails, as shown in Fig. 10–3. Smear more compound over the entire broken area, making sure that you cover all the nailheads. Then cut a patch out of an old shingle or piece of rolled roofing, and cover the whole break with the patch.

If the leak is on the hip of the roof—the peak where two slopes meet—cover the whole hip with new asphalt shingles. First, apply roofing compound liberally, and then beginning at the lowest point, nail the shingles over the hip, each one overlapping the one just below it, as shown it Fig. 10–4. Cover all nail holes with the compound and also spread the compound on each shingle where the next shingle will overlap it.

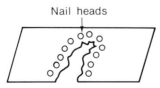

Nail heads

FIGURE 10–3. Broken Asbestos Shingle.

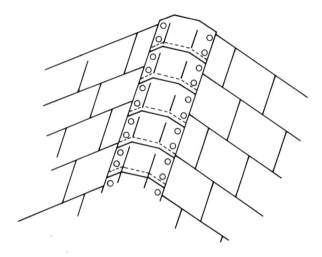

FIGURE 10–4. Patching Hip of Roof.

On flat roofs, rolled roofing is usually used instead of shingles. If a crack occurs, fix it in much the same way as a crack in an asbestos shingle, shown in Fig. 10–3. First shove a lot of roofing compound under the edges of the crack. Then nail all around the crack, as shown in Fig. 10–5(a). Coat the nailheads and the whole area of the crack with more compound, and apply a patch over it, as shown in Fig. 10–5(b). The patch can be cut from an asbestos shingle or a scrap of rolled roofing.

Defects in flashing are more difficult to fix. If a flashing is badly cracked or corroded, call in a professional roofer to replace it. However, you can make *temporary* repairs on small cracks, and sometimes the temporary repairs outlast the rest of the flashing. Buy a special roofing cement for the purpose, and apply a heavy layer over the defective part of the flashing. Make sure that the flashing is clean and

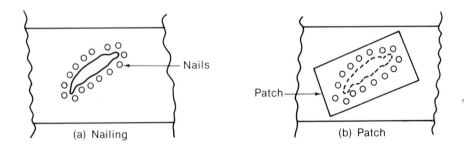

FIGURE 10–5. Crack in Rolled Roofing.

smooth so that the cement will adhere to it. For extra strength, cover the cement with a layer of roofing paper or roofing felt, and cover that with another layer of cement.

The best way to fix leaks is to prevent them from occurring in the first place. Look at your roof occasionally, especially after a windstorm. If you spot loose shingles, exposed or loose nails, broken shingles, or other defects, fix them before leaks develop. Use the techniques described in this section.

Rolled roofing on flat roofs tends to expand when the sun is hot and contract at night. The continued expansion and contraction causes it to wrinkle and blister.

Wrinkles and blisters are signs that the roofing has worked loose and are potential sources of leaks. If you see such a spot, fix it before a leak develops. With a sharp knife cut two cross cuts on a blister or wrinkle. Then pry up the four corners, and apply roofing compound liberally under them. Press them down and nail them, as shown in Fig. 10-6. Finally, cover them with more compound and a patch, as in Fig. 10-5(b).

10-2. SNOW ON THE ROOF

After a snowstorm your roof should be covered with a blanket of snow. If it melts as fast as it lands, it is usually a sign that heat is being lost through the roof as the result of improper insulation. A layer of insulation under the roof will lower your heating bill. Assuming your roof is properly insulated so that there is a blanket of snow there, additional problems can arise, depending on whether the roof has a steep slope or a gentle one.

In very cold climates, snow on a gently sloping roof may melt slightly under the heat of noonday sun, but the water may freeze again before it reaches the gutter. This happens because the water drains under the snow where the blanket of snow keeps off the cold air. But as soon as the water emerges near the roof edge and before it reaches the gutter, the cold air, especially on windy days, freezes it,

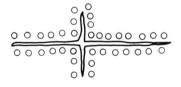

FIGURE 10-6. Nailing Corners of Blister.

so that a ring of ice is built up just above the gutters. This ring of ice forms a barrier so that water from more melting snow backs up under the blanket and may be forced up under shingles, causing leaks. This is not likely to happen in moderate climates, since the sun is usually hot enough to melt the ice barrier during the day. If you have been troubled with an ice barrier before, you can prevent one from forming by placing an electric heating cable on the roof. These cables are available at mail-order houses and building-supply stores. Run a cable in a zigzag pattern along the edge of the roof. It does not have to melt all the ice, but as long as it melts a few channels through the ice barrier, the water will drain off.

On steep roofs, ice barriers are not a problem, since the water runs off rapidly before it can refreeze. The main problem here is the danger of an avalanche of snow sliding off the roof in large quantities. Snow-slides can be prevented by installing snow guards on the roof. These are simply metal fingers protruding from the roof and are easy to install. Complete instructions for installation are furnished with the snow guards as well as information for determining how many guards are needed for your roof. The steeper the roof, the more guards you will need.

10-3. GUTTERS AND DOWNSPOUTS

Gutters and downspouts are necessary to drain thousands of gallons of water away from your house every year. Without this drainage system, water from rain and melting snow would flow down the walls of your home and cause damage both inside and out.

It is important to keep gutter and downspouts in good condition, and the life of this drainage system can be prolonged by following the maintenance recommendations in Section 3-7.

If the straps and clamps holding gutters come loose or are bent, they can be straightened and attached to the house again. It may be necessary to use plastic wood or other filler in the nail holes so that the nails will not come loose again. If straps have rusted through or are broken, replace with new ones.

Sometimes a gutter is forced out of line by a heavy snow or a ladder pushed against it so that it no longer slopes toward the downspout. Then water can overflow the gutter instead of draining properly. If you notice an incorrect slope, don't wait for a rainstorm to prove it. Pour some water into the gutter and if it flows the wrong way, fix it by bending straps and claps or attaching new ones so that the gutter slopes toward the downspout. The slope should be at least a ¼-inch drop for every 4 feet of gutter length. It can be as much as ¼ inch per foot.

If leaks develop, you can fix them or replace the whole gutter. Before tackling a leak, examine the gutter carefully to see if it is worth fixing. A rusted-out spot in a gutter may be the beginning of large-scale deterioration. However, if there are only a few leaks and the gutter is otherwise in good condition, you can fix it easily with a special plastic repair kit available at most hardware dealers. The kit contains fiberglas cloth for patches and a special resin in which the cloth is soaked before it is applied. These patches will outlast the metal in the gutter. The same repair kit can be used to fix downspouts as well as gutters, and works well on wood and all types of metal. The patch can be painted to match the gutter so that it is inconspicuous. Before using the patch, make sure that the gutter is clean and smooth. The resin is very strong but will not adhere well to dirt or rust. Use steel wool, if necessary, to clean off rust.

If a gutter is damaged beyond repair, it must be replaced. With new aluminum gutters, this is a relatively simple job. Aluminum gutters are available at lumberyards and building-supply stores. They come in 10-foot lengths and are easily cut with a fine-toothed hacksaw. Special connectors allow connecting gutter to gutter and gutter to downspout without special tools. Downspout leaders and corners are usually attached to a length of gutter while it is on the ground, and then the whole thing is lifted and nailed in place.

If you live in an area that has snow, the outer edge of the gutter should be below the roof line, as shown in Fig. 10–7, so that snow can

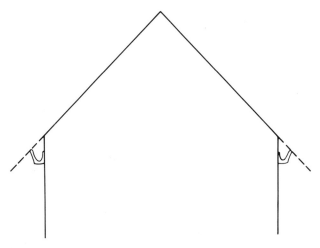

FIGURE 10–7. Gutter Below Line of Roof.

slide off without hitting the gutter. You can determine this by laying a yardstick or other straightedge on the roof and attaching the gutter below the stick. The gutter must, of course, extend beyond the edge of the roof horizontally so that rain or melted snow flowing off will drain into the gutter. To hang the gutter, a hole is drilled through front and back, and an aluminum ferrule is inserted, as shown in Fig. 10-8. Then a spike is driven through the holes and ferrule and hammered into the cornice or other convenient board under the eaves. Spikes should be spaced 24 to 30 inches apart. The gutter must slope toward the downspout with a drop of at least ¼ inch for every 4 feet.

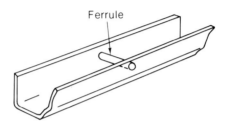

FIGURE 10-8. Holes for Hanging Gutter.

On long runs of about 40 feet or more, the gutter should be highest at the center and should slope to a downspout at each end. If you are alone when you hang the gutter, drive a few spikes under the eaves as temporary supports, and hang the gutter by strings attached to these spikes. By adjusting the strings, you can bring the gutter to its approximately correct position. After the gutter is attached, remove the spikes and strings.

10-4. WALLS

The outside layer of the exterior walls of a home is usually decorative rather than structural. Thus, if this covering is damaged, whether it is made of stucco, clapboard, or shingle or other siding, the house won't fall apart. Consequently, many homeowners tend to ignore cracks, broken shingles, or damaged siding. However, these must be attended to promptly, since any opening, even a hairline crack, can be an entryway for moisture, which can cause paint to peel and even structural damage due to rotting of the wood.

Openings around windows, door frames, water pipes, and other joints should have been caulked, as described in Section 5-8. When the old caulking dries out, it should be renewed. This and other maintenance procedures should be routine. However, all exteriors should be checked again whenever a repair job is undertaken, since it is so easy to do this.

If the exterior walls of your house are covered with asbestos or wood shingles, you should check at least once a year to make sure that no shingles are missing or broken. Shingles are usually installed with the lower part of one shingle overlapping the upper part of the one below. Wood shingles sometimes are installed with an additional wood strip under each row of shingles so that the shingles are raised from the surface to give a shadow effect. These arrangements are shown in Fig. 10–9. For illustrative purposes, the nails are shown only partially driven. In practice, of course, they would be hammered all the way in. In Fig. 10–9(a), each shingle is laid overlapping the lower one. Notice that nails are driven in near the bottom of the upper shingle only. The upper edge of each shingle is not nailed down until the next one is placed above it. This arrangement is used for all types of shingles, including wood and asbestos. The shadow effect, in Fig. 10–9(b), is used for wood shingles. The extra strip, near the bottom of each shingle, moves the bottom of the shingle outward. However, as in Fig. 10–9(a), nails are placed only near the bottom of the upper shingle, and in this case, the nail penetrates the shadow strip as well as the top of the lower shingle.

When a shingle has a slight crack, you may be able to fill it with wood putty. If the crack is not large, or if the shingle is split in two with both pieces still in place, it is usually not necessary to replace

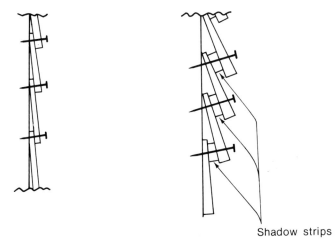

Shadow strips

(a) Plain shingles   (b) Shadow effect

FIGURE 10–9. Shingle Arrangements.

the shingle. Slide a piece of roofing paper or roofing felt under the shingle so that the paper is under the whole split. Then hammer nails into the shingle at each side of the crack at the bottom, as shown in Fig. 10-10. Be careful not to hit the shingle too hard with the hammer, or you might crack it. If the shingle is too brittle from age, you should drill small holes for the nails first, to avoid splitting the shingle.

If a shingle is badly damaged, it must be replaced. The first part of the job is removing the old shingle. This means first removing the nails from the shingle above it, as well as those along the bottom of the damaged shingle. Referring to Fig. 10-9, you can see how these nails are positioned. Slide a hacksaw blade under the upper shingle, and cut off the nails. Alternatively, you can drill right through the nailheads. A third method is to gouge the wood around the nailheads so that you can get a grip on the nails with pliers and pull them out. Once the upper nails are removed, you can pull the damaged shingle forward at the bottom to pry out its nails. Now slide out the damaged shingle and slide in a new one, nailing it in place. Use rustproof nails, preferably the threaded type, which are less apt to loosen.

If shingles are loose or nails have come loose, add a few extra nails and fasten the shingles down again. A loose nail is a sign of a worn nail hole, so new nails should not be placed in the same holes. If a nail has any sign of rust on it when it comes loose, discard it and use only new rustproof nails.

Clapboard siding, like shingles, is installed with each board overlapping the board below it. The arrangement shown in Fig. 10-9(a) could also be an end view of clapboards. Clapboards are usually installed over a layer of waterproof tar paper.

When a board is split or cracked along the grain, you can repair it without removing it from the wall. First, pry open the crack and fill

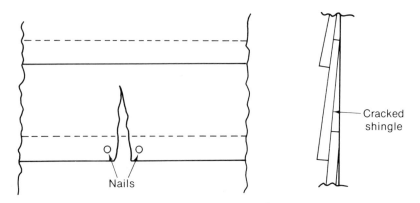

Nails

Cracked shingle

FIGURE 10-10. Cracked Shingle.

it with waterproof glue. Drive a few large finishing nails into the board below, just under the bottom of the edge of the cracked board, and bend these nails upward so that they force the crack shut, as shown in Fig. 10–11. When the glue is dry, remove these nails, and fill the holes with putty or plastic wood.

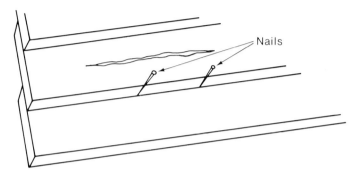

FIGURE 10–11. Cracked Clapboard.

If a board has pulled loose anywhere along its length, nail it back. However, for a better job, drill pilot holes and screw the board back with flat-head screws. Cover the screw heads with putty.

If a board is badly damaged, it is not necessary to replace the whole board. First, cut out the damaged section with a chisel or a small saw. If you put wedges under the damaged board, as shown in Fig. 10–12, you can cut it with a saw without damaging the board below. To be safe, you can tape small scraps of wood on the board below to protect it from the saw. Use wedges to pry up the board above so that

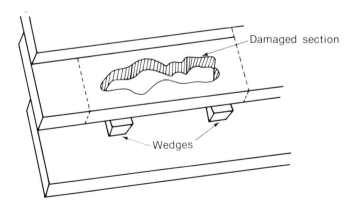

FIGURE 10–12. Damaged Clapboard.

you can get under it to remove the damaged section. It may be necessary to cut nails with a hacksaw blade to get the damaged section out. Be careful not to tear the tar paper. Cut a section of new board to fit the opening. Before sliding it in, repair the tar paper (which always gets torn no matter how careful you are), by smearing roofing compound over any holes. Then push the new board in place. Use a small block below it to protect the new section from the hammer, and hammer the board up to its proper location, as shown in Fig. 10–13.

Cracks in a stucco wall can be patched with a mixture of 1 part Portland cement to 2½ or 3 parts clean sand. You can buy the cement and sand separately, or you can get ready-mixed preparations. The ready-mixed materials for home handymen sometimes have lime added to make the mortar easier to work. Whatever mixture you use, simply add water to make a stiff mortar. If the mortar holds its shape but is pliable enough to be spread on with a trowel, it is just right. Incidentally, the same ready-mix can be used for repairing plaster or mortar as well as stucco.

To repair a small crack or small broken section, first remove all loose cement and dirt. Use an old chisel to dig out crumbly edges. Don't be afraid of making the crack wider. In fact, you should open the crack to a width at least equal to the depth of the stucco, and preferably twice this. Undercut the edges so that the opening is wider at the inside than it is at the outer surface. This makes the bond better. Again, clean off all loose particles. Wet the edges of the crack thoroughly and apply mortar with a trowel or putty knife, overlapping the outside surface by about 1 inch.

If a large area is broken, you must rip out the whole damaged section down to the metal lathing. If the wire mesh looks rusted, remove that too, and examine the wood below for damage. Replace damaged wood in the same way that damaged siding is replaced. However, if there is sign of termite activity, you will have to call in an

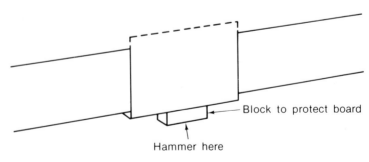

FIGURE 10–13. Installing New Section.

exterminator. Assuming the wood is in good condition, it is first covered with building paper, which is held on with large-headed rustproof nails. Then metal lathing is nailed on with special double-headed nails that hold the mesh a short distance off the wall. When the mortar is applied, there is some on each side of the mesh, and when the mortar dries, the mesh supports it.

Stucco is applied in three coats, with a lot of waiting in between. Wet the edges of the hole, and apply enough mortar to fill the hole to about half its depth. The mortar must be pushed through the metal mesh so that it fills the space between the wall and the mesh. After the first coat has stiffened for about an hour, it must be *scratched* so that the next coat will adhere to it. Scratching is usually done with a *scratching tool*, shown in Fig. 10-14. You can make your own tool

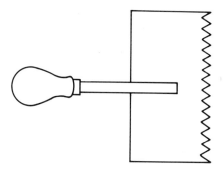

FIGURE 10-14. Scratching Tool.

from a flat piece of metal or you can even scratch the surface with a scrap of wire mesh. The purpose is simply to make the surface irregular. Allow about a week for the first coat to harden, and again wet the whole surface by sprinkling with a fine mist. Now apply a second coat and smooth it level with the surface. To get a sand texture, let the mortar get dry for 15 or 20 minutes, and then rub it in a circular motion with a float, shown in Fig. 10-15. Make your own float

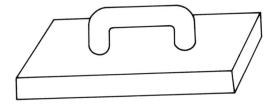

FIGURE 10-15. Float.

from a flat piece of wood with a handle attached. Finally, to get a spattered finish, add more water to the mortar to thin it and sprinkle it on with a whisk broom. If the original stucco is colored, you can buy a colored mixture for the repairs.

10-5. DAMPNESS IN THE BASEMENT

Although the basement is inside the house, dampness in the basement is usually caused by moisture leaking or seeping through the walls from the outside, and thus this problem is treated in this chapter. To be sure, dampness can be due to condensation. Water condensing on the walls inside the basement looks just like water seeping through the walls, and your first problem is to determine exactly the source of the dampness. A simple test is to attach a piece of glass or small mirror to the basement wall and leave it overnight. In the morning, check to see if the glass is fogged, indicating condensation. If the glass is clear, but the wall itself is damp, then moisture is seeping in through the wall.

If condensation is the problem, the cellar air must be kept dry. Do not hang wet laundry in the basement. Make sure that clothes dryers are vented so that the moist air is blown outside. Provide additional ventilation, if necessary, by installing an exhaust fan. You can also buy electric or chemical dehumidifiers to dry the air.

Leakage and seepage both apply to water entering the basement *through* the walls. *Leakage* is the term used for water flowing in through a defect in the wall. The flow of water is visible. *Seepage* is slower and may be due to a porosity in the masonry. The walls are damp, but no visible flow is evident. Generally, the ground outside the house contains excess water, which is forced through openings and porosities in the wall. Thus, most seepage is below ground level. Large openings above ground level may admit rain, but these openings are easily detected. Since excess water in the soil can cause a damp basement, you should make sure that water from the roof runs away from the house. Gutters must empty into downspouts, and downspouts in turn should terminate in an elbow directing the water away from the house. A splash pan may also be used, as shown in Fig. 10-16, to feed the water to a garden or other area where watering is required. If the water is not needed for a garden, the ideal situation is to have each downspout terminate in an underground dry well. This is a large undertaking which you may wish to avoid by trying all other remedies first.

The best way to make the basement walls waterproof is to apply a waterproof coating on the outside of the walls. First, you must dig a trench to work in, down to the footing, so that you can get at the wall. Then, the wall must be scrubbed clean. The waterproof coating consists of several layers, as shown in Fig. 10–17. A heavy layer of asphalt or hot tar is applied first and is covered with a layer of roofing felt. Another layer of tar is applied. For best results, add more roofing felt and more tar or asphalt. If you can replace the soil carefully, that's all you need. However, it is too easy to damage the waterproof coating when replacing the dirt, so it is advisable to apply a coat of cement plaster to the wall before replacing the dirt.

The method just described is also a lot of work, and often the damp basement can be cured from the inside. A special heavy-duty cement is used. It is available in powder form and must be mixed with water to form a thick, creamy paste, which is then brushed on with a special fiber brush. The wall must be cleaned and large holes patched. Then it is wet down and the cement is applied on the inside.

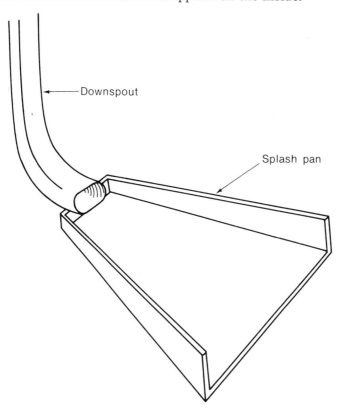

Downspout

Splash pan

FIGURE 10–16. Splash Pan.

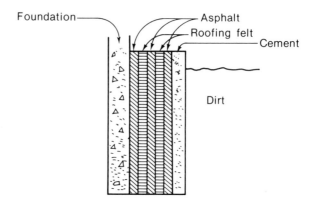

FIGURE 10–17. Waterproof Coating.

Another method involves the use of a special liquid patching solution. A small hole is dug next to the foundation on the outside about 6 to 8 inches deep. This should be close to the spot where water is seeping in. The liquid solution is poured into the hole and seeps into and through the foundation through the same cracks that admit water. As the solution hardens, it patches the cracks and porosities. This is illustrated in Fig. 10–18.

Sometimes water seeps under the foundation wall and enters an open joint between the floor and the wall, as shown in Fig. 10–19. If

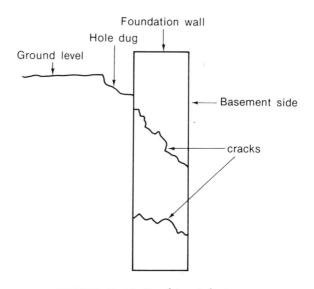

FIGURE 10–18. Patching Solution.

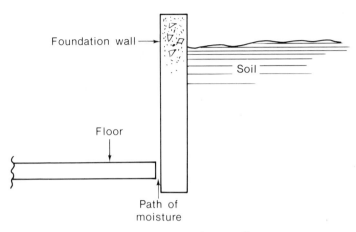

FIGURE 10-19. Defective Floor-Wall Joint.

you find large cracks between wall and floor, these should be closed. First, fill the crack with asphalt or tar, and then build a cove or curb out of concrete, as shown in Fig. 10-20.

New materials for sealing cracks and porosities in foundations are continually being developed. Check with your hardware dealer for the latest developments before committing yourself to any particular method. Epoxy sealers that are applied with a brush are effective in many instances. No matter what sealer or method of sealing you use, remember that it is important to have the surface clean.

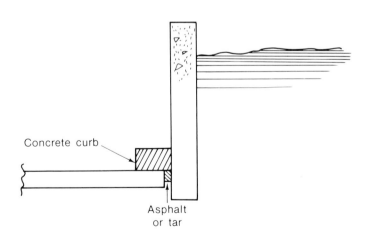

FIGURE 10-20. Curb to Seal Opening.

10-6. MASONRY

Building a wall of concrete, brick, or stone is a job for a professional.
A poorly built wall can collapse from improper footing, improper mixing of cement or mortar, or improper construction, and the amount
saved by doing it yourself does not justify the risk. A well-built wall
lasts for years with virtually no maintenance, whereas a poorly built
one needs constant refinishing and patching. However, even a well-
built masonry wall needs attention at times. Mortar joints eventually
crack and crumble. Concrete walls and floors may crack from a
settling of the house or even from a slight earthquake. Repairs on
masonry are relatively simple and well within the capabilities of the
average homeowner.

The basic materials for masonry repairs are portland cement, sand,
lime, gravel, and water. *Portland cement* is a manufactured material
which is mixed with the other ingredients to form *cement, mortar, or
concrete.* Cement is a mixture of 1 part portland cement to 3 parts
sand to which water is added to form a thick paste. Cement is used
for patching cracks and small openings in masonry walls and floors
and also in stucco. Mortar is cement to which hydrated lime has been
added. This makes the paste more workable. Mortar is used in laying bricks or repointing brick walls. It is also used for patching in
place of cement. Concrete is a mixture of 1 part portland cement, 2
parts sand, and 3 parts gravel, with enough water to form a thick paste.
Concrete is used for foundation walls, floors, sidewalks, patios, and
for special purposes, such as setting posts in the ground. You can buy
the individual ingredients and mix them yourself, but the dry materials must be mixed thoroughly and uniformly. For the average handyman, it is better to buy premixed concrete or premixed mortar which
requires only the addition of water. For small jobs, you need only take
a small amount of the premixed material from the bag and mix it
with water, without worrying about blending several ingredients in
the correct proportions. For large jobs, such as building a patio, you
can buy concrete already mixed with water and have it poured directly
into your forms, thus saving a lot of work with very little extra expense.

For general all-round patching, you should use premixed mortar.
To patch cracks or small openings on concrete floors, walls, or sidewalks, first open the crack with a cold chisel and undercut the cracks
so that they are wider at the bottom than at the surface. Brush off
all loose particles and dust with a wire brush. Wet the surface near

the crack and wet all edges of the crack. If you fail to do this, the old concrete will draw water out of the new mortar before the new mortar sets properly. Mix mortar according to directions on the bag. It is not necessary to use the whole bag at once. Now pack the mortar into the crack with a small trowel. The preferred tool is a triangular trowel, but even a putty knife can be used. Make sure that the mortar is packed in solidly so that there are no air bubbles that could weaken the joint. The longer it takes to dry, the harder the joint will be. To prevent the mortar from drying too fast, sprinkle it at least twice a day for two or three days, or cover it with wet burlap.

To replace large sections of broken concrete, use ready-mix concrete and mix it with water according to the directions on the package. As with small cracks, the edges of the opening must be clean and solid. Undercut the opening. If the hole does not go all the way through the old concrete, make sure it is at least 1 inch deep. Roughen the concrete at the bottom so that the new concrete will adhere better. Wet the exposed areas, and pack in the new concrete. Level off the new concrete by drawing a long board across it. Remove the excess now, since you won't be able to remove it when it is dry. Smooth the surface with a trowel or a float. The float, shown in Fig. 10–15, packs down the concrete, but at the same time it pushes the heavier gravel to the bottom and allows the sand and portland cement to float to the top, making a smoother surface.

When working with large amounts of concrete or mortar, the mix is prepared in a convenient location, and then small amounts are carried to the job as needed. Professionals use a tool called a *hawk*, which is simply a flat piece of wood with a handle attached, as shown in Fig. 10-21. You can get by with a flat piece of plywood about 10 to 12 inches square. Wet the surface of the hawk, pile some mortar on it, and carry it to the location of the crack to be filled. Push off hunks of mortar into the crack with a trowel or even a metal rod.

To repoint mortar joints, that is, to repair mortar in a brick wall,

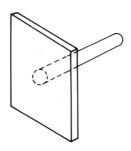

FIGURE 10–21. Hawk.

use mortar mix, and add water according to the directions on the bag. Clean out the old crumbling mortar with a cold chisel and a wire brush. Wet the bricks on each side of the joint. Now apply the mortar. You can use a pointed trowel for this. Professionals use a joint filler, shown in Fig. 10-22. This is simply a bent metal rod. Its use

FIGURE 10–22. Joint Filler.

is illustrated in Fig. 10-23. The mortar is pushed off the hawk with the joint filler, which shapes the mortar as well as packing it down. After the mortar has set for about 15 minutes, use a trowel or round rod to shape the joint to match existing joints.

10–7. BLACKTOP DRIVEWAYS

Blacktop driveways eventually develop cracks. Then water seeping into the cracks causes more cracks and breaks in the surface. Repairing damaged driveways is simple, but prevention is also simple. To prevent water from damaging the blacktop, the surface should be sealed against moisture. Sealing materials are sold in cans in most hardware stores and building-supply shops. A 5-gallon can will cover at least 200 square feet of blacktop. Pour the sealer right from the can onto the driveway, and spread it thinly with a push broom. The sealer

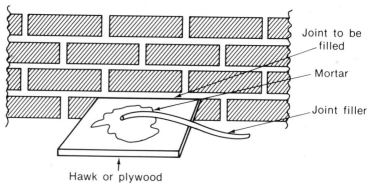

FIGURE 10–23. Filling a Mortar Joint.

forms a tough coating which fills small cracks and holes and protects the surface from oil and gasoline as well as from moisture. For large cracks mix the sealer with sand to form a thick paste, and push the paste into the cracks with a trowel. After it is dry, seal the whole surface.

When a driveway has large holes, cold-mix asphalt is the simplest patching compound. It is available in large bags and can be used as it comes out of the bag. WARNING: If the bag is stored, place several layers of paper under it, since it may stain the floor. To use the asphalt, first make sure the hole is clean, with no loose dirt or crumbled pieces of blacktop in it. For very deep holes, cover the bottom with gravel and tamp it down to furnish a solid bed for the asphalt. You can use a 2 by 4 to tamp down the bed. Fill the hole with asphalt to within 1 inch of the top. Air bubbles must be removed. This is done by chopping into the asphalt with a shovel or hoe. Now use the same 2 by 4 to tamp down the asphalt. Finally, pour on more asphalt to a height of about ½ inch more than the surrounding surface. Drive your car back and forth over the patch to flatten it down.

After patching a driveway, you should seal it to prevent further damage. Make sure the surface is clean, and apply sealer with a push broom, as described at the beginning of this section. If you would prefer a cement finish, you can seal the blacktop with ordinary portland cement. First, wet the surface thoroughly, and then sprinkle the powdered cement over the surface by hand. Now spread the cement evenly with a push broom. You may have to add more water as you go along. The cement coating makes the blacktop look like a concrete pavement.

10-8. FENCES

A well-built fence last for many years with little maintenance. A poorly built fence needs constant repair. Rather than keep mending a badly constructed fence, it is better to tear it down and have a new one built correctly.

Eventually even a good fence needs some repairs. Frost in the ground can push posts upward so that they become loose. Wind blowing continually on one side of a large fence can cause it to lean over. Moisture can cause nails and hardware to rust and pull loose, and moisture also causes wood to rot. Many of these problems can be anticipated, and preventive measures can be taken. If posts are set in concrete, they will be less apt to work loose. A fence that has openings in it is not likely to be blown over or be affected by the wind. There are many fence designs that provide openings for the wind and still maintain privacy. Rustproof nails and hardware are less affected by moisture, but even these should be covered with antirust coatings. Some woods, such as cedar and redwood, resist rot and stand exposure with little deterioration. These are excellent for fence posts and in fact for all parts of a fence. Other woods that are not inherently moisture-resistant can be treated chemically to withstand rot. Chemicals for this purpose, such as pentachlorophenol, are available at home-supply stores. Posts and parts of the fence that will touch the ground should be soaked in the chemical solution for several hours. Other parts should be dipped in the solution for a few minutes or simply painted with the solution. Boards should be treated before they are attached to the fence so that unexposed parts also get treated.

Before you start to build a new fence, check your local building code. Usually a maximum height is specified, and a minimum distance from the property line may be required. You may also need a permit. After passing these hurdles, decide what kind of fence you want. Lumberyards and building-supply stores have plans for many kinds of fences, and frequently sell the needed lumber in kits. The lumber should be pretreated for protection against termites and rot so that you don't have to soak it in chemicals. The lumber dealer can advise you on the spacing of posts for the fence you select.

Drive a stake in the ground at each end of the fence line and tie a cord to the stakes as a guideline. Drive additional stakes into the ground along the cord at the location of each post. Posts are set first, and once they are in, the difficult part of the job is done. Posts should be buried at least one third of their length. The best way to make sure that a post stands for a long time is to set it in concrete, especially if the ground is soft. A cross section of the hole is shown in Fig. 10–24. The hole should be dug with a post-hole digger to keep it to a small diameter. Its depth should be at least one third of the length of the post. Put a flat rock in the bottom, and rest the post on the rock. Some gravel is poured in and tamped down. If any water does get in, it drains through the gravel away from the end of the post. Before pouring the concrete, nail braces to the post and to stakes in the ground, as shown in Fig. 10–25. Make sure the post is vertical by holding a level against it on two sides. Now pour in concrete and tamp it down, using a trowel to chop out air bubbles. Shape the surface so that it slopes away from the post, as shown in Fig. 10–24, so that rain will flow off. Allow the concrete to dry at least four days. If there is an air space between the dry concrete and the post,

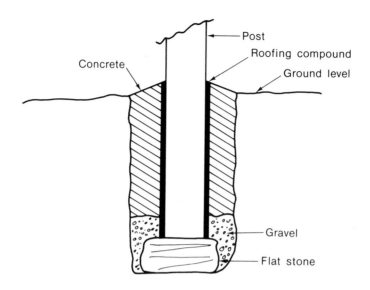

Concrete

Post

Roofing compound

Ground level

Gravel

Flat stone

FIGURE 10-24. Post Set in Concrete.

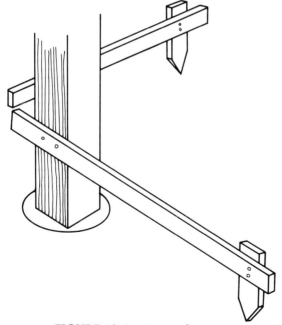

FIGURE 10-25. Braces for Post.

fill the space with roofing compound so that rain and moisture will not enter.

   If the soil is firm, such as adobe, you do not have to use concrete. The post can be set and held with earth, as shown in Fig. 10–26. As with concrete, a flat stone should be placed in the bottom of the hole, and a few inches of granite must be added to drain away water. Then put back the earth you removed, making sure to tamp it well. During this last step the post should be braced as shown in Fig. 10–25.

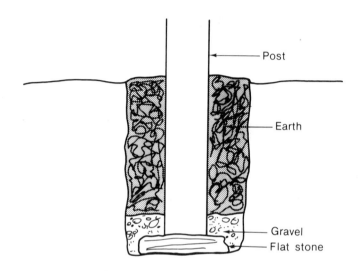

FIGURE 10–26. Post in Solid Earth.

   A wobbly or loose post in an existing fence can be cured by setting it in concrete. Dig a hole around the post at least 1 foot in diameter. The hole should reach almost to the bottom of the post. It is not a good idea to have concrete under the bottom of the post, since the concrete then forms a pocket that can trap water, which would eventually rot the end of the post. Fill the hole with concrete, tamping it down and chopping out air bubbles, and shape the top of the concrete as shown in Fig. 10–24. After the concrete has dried at least four days, fill any air space between post and concrete with roofing compound. If you do not wish to use concrete, you can brace the post with wood or metal reinforcements. Angle irons are shown in Fig. 10–27. These are set tightly against diagonally opposite corners of the post and are driven into the earth to a depth of at least 2 feet. If you have difficulty hammering on the end of the angle iron, use a piece of scrap iron as a driver. After the angle irons are in place, drill holes in them, and fasten them firmly to the post with long screws. Lengths of wooden 2 by 4's can be used instead of the angle irons. Use two, one on either side of the post. To facilitate driving them, cut a taper on the ends that go into the ground. Use a wood block on top of each 2 by 4 so that the hammer will not split the end. Drive them into the earth at least 2 feet, and fasten them to the post with long screws. The braces must be treated to prevent corrosion or rot. That is, angle irons should be aluminum or galvanized iron, and wooden braces should be chemically treated to prevent rot

The end grain of a board is the most susceptible point for water damage. If the fence is to be painted, make certain that all ends of boards are covered. If the fence is to remain natural, you can protect the ends with a coating of shellac.

If the end of a post has rotted, it cannot be braced simply by pouring in concrete. However, it is not necessary to replace the whole post. A new section must be added to which the remaining part of the post is firmly attached. Methods of doing this are shown in Fig. 10-28. In Fig. 2-28(a) two legs of lengths of 2 by 4 are attached to the post, and each leg is placed on a flat stone in the hole. In Fig. 2-28(b), a new piece of post is joined to the remaining post by bolts.

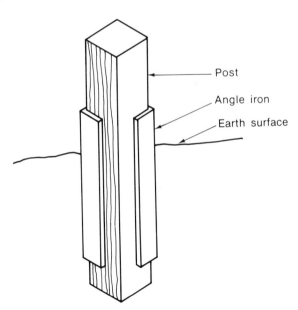

Post

Angle iron

Earth surface

FIGURE 10-27. Angle-Iron Braces.

In Fig. 2–28(a) the bottom of the post can be left irregular, whereas in Fig. 2–28(b) it is necessary to cut the post to form the joint. In either case, gravel is added and then concrete, as in putting in a new post. Make sure the post stands vertically and that all additional pieces are chemically treated to prevent rot. Screws and bolts must be rust-proof.

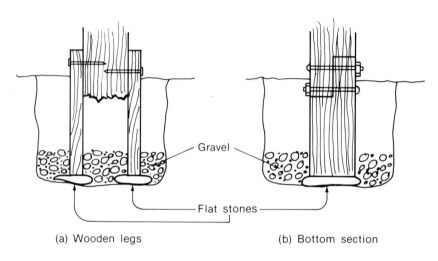

(a) Wooden legs   (b) Bottom section

FIGURE 10–28. Repairs for Rotted Post.

11

Stain Removal

In the normal course of events, stains appear around the house on floors and walls, on furniture, and on fabrics like rugs and drapes. This is expected and is not very disturbing. However, sudden stains can be as traumatic and aggravating as any major breakdown in the home. Imagine how you would feel in situations such as these. You have just laid white wall-to-wall carpeting in your living room and are having a party to celebrate. One of the guests drops her lipstick, and before it is retrieved, another guest steps on it, making a large red stain on the rug. Or perhaps your neighbor's pet dog urinates on the rug. Again, you cut your finger while carving the roast, leaving a trail of blood stains on rugs and floor between the dining room and bathroom and on the walls near the light switch. Also such things as children smearing walls with chocolate-covered fingers or leaving a lollipop on the floor, where someone steps on it, can be upsetting.

Although any of these situations can be as disturbing as a leaking roof or stopped plumbing, it is not a major catastrophe. No structural damage has occurred. In fact, you can be philosophical and say that the stain gives the house a "lived-in" look. However, if you are like most homeowners, you will want to remove the stain, both because it is unsightly and because it reminds you of an unpleasant occurrence.

The first rule in stain removal is: *Do it immediately.* An old stain is much harder to remove than a new one. In many cases, the spilled substance doesn't stain on contact but causes a stain later. For example, an acid may eat into the finish on a piece of furniture, but if it is removed in the first minute after being spilled, there will usually be no damage. Similarly, a colorless oil, spilled on a rug, does not show a stain. But dirt sticks to the oil more than to the rest of the rug, and in time a stain appears where the oil was spilled.

Treatment of a stain involves removing or disguising the staining material. Thus, if the staining substance can be dissolved, a solvent should be applied. However, you must be sure that the solvent will not harm the material or surface containing the stain. If no solvent can be found, perhaps the stain can be treated chemically. Again, if a bleach is used to make the stain transparent, the bleaching agent must not be injurious to the fabric. On floors and walls, it is sometimes simpler to apply a coat of paint to hide the stain.

It should be obvious that the stain remover must be suited to the stain. Thus, hot soapy water is excellent for removing greasy fingerprints on washable wallpaper but is worse than nothing in trying to remove raw egg from a carpet. However, hot soapy water cannot be used to remove the same type of grease stains from a woolen garment, since hot water shrinks wool and also causes it to turn yellow. The point here is that in addition to choosing a proper stain remover for the particular stain, it is important that the stain remover be suited to the material or surface containing the stain.

Solvents are used to dissolve the stain. Cold water is often the best solvent. Heat may set the stain, so hot water is not used unless the substance is specifically soluble in hot water. On materials that are harmed by water, rubbing alcohol can be used as a solvent. For oily stains, you may use cleaning fluid as a solvent. Do not use gasoline or other flammable cleaning fluids. Do not use carbon tetrachloride, since its fumes are highly poisonous. Carbon tetrachloride is one of the most effective solvents when used properly, but it does require expertise in handling. Almost as good, and much safer, are chemicals like trichlorethylene, which is sold as a nontoxic, nonflammable cleaning fluid under many trade names. Special problems require specific solvents.

Bleaches are used to make the stain colorless. Be careful. The bleach may take the color out of the fabric, too. Do not use poisonous bleaching agents. Safe bleaches are chlorine bleach, sodium perborate, and hydrogen peroxide. Chlorine is the strongest and fastest acting, but it should not be used on animal fabrics, such as silk or wool. The other two are safe on all materials. Hydrogen peroxide is the weakest but it is effective on scorch stains if the material is not damaged. Use whatever bleach you have in the house, but test it first on an inconspicuous part of the material. If it removes color from the fabric, it should be diluted. In general, chlorine bleach is left on the material for only five minutes and is then rinsed off with cold water. The other bleaches, being slower acting, may be left on longer, even for a few hours, before being washed out. Old stains can often be removed by bleaching.

Enzymes are used to soften old stains containing albumin, such as those caused by eggs, blood, glue, milk, and gelatin. Pepsin is a common enzyme available in powder form at most drugstores. To use it, the stain should be cleaned and left wet. Then the powdered pepsin is sprinkled on it. After about an hour, during which time you add more water to keep the stain damp, rinse off the pepsin with water. If it did its job, the stain will have been softened enough to come off with the rinse.

Washing agents such as soap and detergents help emulsify grease. Make sure that the soap or detergent you are using is safe for the fabric being cleaned. Read the labels. For stubborn dirt and stains, trisodium phosphate (TSP) can be used in place of soap. TSP may be purchased in hardware stores but is also the main ingredient of many household washing agents.

Acids are used to neutralize harmful alkalis. Ordinary white vinegar or lemon juice is effective for this purpose. *Alkalis* are used to neutralize acids. Baking soda or ammonia are both effective. Baking soda is sprinkled on the stain and moistened. When it stops effervescing, wash it off. Ammonia is not usually applied directly. The spot should be moistened and then held over an open bottle of ammonia so that the fumes can react with the acid.

11-1. FABRIC STAINS

Special problems requiring specific solvents are nail polish, lacquer, paint, and ink from a ballpoint pen. There are others, but these will illustrate the proper techniques. Nail polish and lacquer spills must be treated immediately, since they dry quickly. Use a rag to pick up as much of the spilled material as possible, being careful not to spread it to a larger area. Apply nail polish remover or lacquer thinner on the spot with a sponge to keep the spill from drying. Lacquer thinner is cheaper than nail polish remover, but you have to use what you have on hand. Either is effective. However, after the first dose of nail-polish remover, you will have time to buy some lacquer thinner to finish the job. Since lacquer thinner is flammable, open some windows, and don't smoke when you use it. In the same manner, paint is washed out with a paint thinner appropriate to the particular paint. If you use latex paints, you can clean up with plain water. Ballpoint ink is soluble in acetone or amyl acetate. Make sure that the material will not dissolve in the solvent. Acetate, for example, will be damaged by acetone but not by amyl acetate.

Oily stains, such as those caused by butter, grease, lipstick, salad dressings, and other fats, are treated immediately by surrounding and covering the spill with an absorbent powder to prevent the stain from spreading. As the powder is saturated, brush or scoop it off, and apply more. Repeat as needed until the spot is dry. Sponge the spot with a cleaning fluid. However, if the material is dark, the white absorbent powder may leave its own stain. Rather than have this happen, on dark fabrics pick up as much of the spill as possible with white paper towels, paper napkins, or anything absorbent. Finish with cleaning fluid.

If an acid is spilled on a rug or other fabric, neutralize it immediately by dusting with sodium bicarbonate (ordinary baking soda) and then moistening. The danger is not the stain but the possibility of the acid eating into the fabric. Acids also discolor the fabric, but frequently the color returns when the acid is neutralized. Citrus fruits, urine, and other acidic materials are neutralized in this way. The residue can then be washed out with water, or, if the fabric is not washable, with alcohol. A mild detergent can be added to the water to loosen any dirt in the stain.

If an alkali is spilled, neutralize it immediately with a mild acid such as white vinegar or lemon juice. Wash with water or alcohol, depending on the fabric.

Chocolate, egg, milk, gravy, blood, and sweat should be washed thoroughly with cold water. Heat will set the stain. You may have to repeat the treatment several times, adding detergent in later rinses. On nonwashable fabrics, use cool rubbing alcohol instead of water. Finish by applying cleaning fluid.

Coffee, tea, beer, soft drinks, and grass cause stains which are not set by heat. However, start by rinsing in cool water or alcohol, depending on the fabric. Soak in a mild detergent solution for several minutes to as long as an hour. Wash out with hot water if the fabric will stand it.

Wax, gum, shoe polish, adhesive tape, and other hard materials present special problems. Scrape off as much as possible without damaging the fabric. Then soak a cloth in cleaning fluid and apply it to the stain or wad of material. Cleaning fluid softens these materials so that they can be lifted off.

In all cases, if the treatment does not entirely remove the stain, you can use a bleach to finish the job. As mentioned above, chlorine is fast acting but may remove color from the fabric also. Before applying a bleach to a stain, try it on a piece of the material or on a corner where it won't show.

Remember that you know where the stain was and thus you will always be able to "see" the spot no matter how well you clean it up. However, it is unlikely that your friends will notice a difference unless you call attention to it.

11-2. FURNITURE STAINS

The most common type of stain on a table top is a ring left from a wet drinking glass. You can usually clear it up by rubbing it with a clean cloth dipped in a mixture of equal parts of olive oil and white vinegar. For larger, heavier rings that don't yield to this treatment, rub the area with a paste of pumice and oil. You can use light motor oil, linseed oil, or even ordinary cooking oil. Apply it with a lint-free cloth. Don't rub too hard, and stop when the ring is gone; otherwise you will rub off the finish. It may be necessary to rewax the finish when you have removed the ring.

If a hot plate or other hot object is left on a table, it causes a cloudy discoloration. You can remove this by rubbing lightly with spirits of camphor on a clean, lint-free cloth. The table top will need re-polishing when the stain is removed.

Alcohol stains on a table can be removed by rubbing gently with a paste made of cigar ash and a very light oil, such as castor oil. If you have no cigar ashes, use rottenstone instead—available in most hardware stores. You may have to polish the table top after the stain is removed.

Most other stains on furniture will respond to rubbing with the pumice-oil or the rottenstone-oil paste. Rottenstone is finer than pumice and causes less wear on the finish, but for heavy stains, pumice is preferred because it cuts faster.

If you try to use paper under a hot object to protect the table from the heat, you may find the paper stuck to the table. Damp newspaper will also stick to a table top as it dries. To loosen the stuck paper, soak it in olive oil, and when it is saturated, rub it off with a clean cloth.

If a table top has a cigarette burn, try to get the person who caused it to buy you a new table. Failing that, the burn spot must be rubbed off. You can get a very fine abrasive paper for the purpose, but it is simpler to cover just the burned area with silver polish, and rub it until all the charred surface is removed. Be careful not to scratch the undamaged area. After removing the stain, wipe the surface clean and coat it with polish or wax.

11–3. MARBLE STAINS

Most stains on marble surfaces caused by nongreasy substances, such as coffee, soft drinks, ink, and the like, can be removed by bleaching. Mix the bleach with an absorbent powder, such as talcum powder, so that it won't run off, and spread the resultant paste over the stain. You can't use too much. Add a few drops of ammonia. Cover the paste with a plastic sheet to hold in the moisture. After several hours, wash off the paste with ordinary water. Repeat if needed.

Grease stains should be treated with a special solvent available in hardware stores. Apply the solvent as a paste by mixing it with whiting or talcum powder. Let it stand several hours and then wash off with hot water. If the stain persists, use a bleach, as described in the preceding paragraph.

Rust stains can sometimes be removed just by rubbing with a piece of hard cloth. However, if the stain is old, it should be treated with a special reducing chemical available specifically for this purpose in most hardware stores as well as from marble dealers.

11-4. STAINS ON INSIDE WALLS

Most stains on walls are caused by grease. They cannot be covered by painting over them or papering, since grease can work through paint or wallpaper. It is important to seal in the stain before repainting or repapering. First, clean off as much as possible of the stain with a standard wall cleaner. Then cover the stain with a sealer. Shellac is one of the best sealers for this purpose. When the shellac is dry, you can paper the wall with no danger of the stain coming through. If you are going to paint, the shellacked area will look shinier than the rest of the wall. To prevent this, make a thin paste of spackle and spread it over the shellac with a brush. When it dries, paint the wall.

11-5. STAINS ON EXTERIOR WALLS

Exterior walls frequently get dirty from airborne dust. Sometimes dirt can be washed off by simply hosing down the house, but if dirt is oily, detergents will be needed. For especially dirty stains, TSP in hot water should do the job. There is nothing quite so good as a scrubbing brush and elbow grease. You can get brushes on the end of long poles to reach otherwise inaccessible areas.

Begin by soaking one wall. Then scrub with your detergent or TSP solution. Do not dip your hands in the TSP solution too often, or the natural skin oils will dissolve. You can avoid the risk by wearing rubber gloves. After one wall is scrubbed, wash it down with your hose. Repeat on other walls.

Metal stains can sometimes be bleached. Rust stains and copper stains yield to special solvents. These are available in hardware stores. The solvents are mixed with whiting, which is available in paint stores, to form a thick paste. This is applied to the stain and covered with a plastic sheet to keep it moist. After several hours, wash it off with your hose. Repeat if necessary.

Mildew stains look like dirt stains but do not wash off with ordinary scrubbing. Mildew stains can be bleached, and if TSP is added to the bleach solution, it is more effective (see Section 3-6).

Index

A

Acid stains, 307
Adhesive fasteners, 187
Adhesives, 184
Adjustable wrench, 42
Air cushion in pipes, 106
Alkali stains, 307
Alkyd-base paint, 239, 240
Allen wrench, 42
Alligatoring of paint, 251
All-purpose saw, 47
Alternating current, 157
Aluminum, 185
  channel, 186
  gutter, 283
  paint, 270
  shingles, 89
Ampere, 152
Anchor:
  molly, 187
  wall, 186
Anti-freeze valves, 66
Ants, flying, 77
Appliances, amperage of, 158
Asbestos shingles, 89
Asphalt:
  for driveways, 297
  shingles, 89
Attic:
  fan, 148
  insulation, 142
Auger, pipe, 113

B

Back saw, 45
Ballcock, 118
Basement, 91
  damp, 290
Basin, plugged, 111
Bits, 33

Black-top, 296
Bleeding:
  paint, 252
  radiators, 74
Blind mortise, 183
Blistering paint, 251
Blowtorch, 254
Board foot, 178
Boiler, 74
  draining, 74
  parts of, 135
Bounce, floor, 81
Box nails, 22
Box wrench, 41
Brace, 32
Bristles, 244
Brushes, paint, 244
  how to use, 257
Burner (*see* Furnace)
Butt joint, 181

C

Cable, jacketed, 166
Calcimine, 239
Calcium carbonate, 241
Care of tools, 58
Caulking, 146
Caustic drain cleaner, 112
C-clamps, 52
Ceiling:
  how to paint, 262
  maintenance, 82
Cement, 294
Central heating, 123
Ceramic tile, 223
Chalking, 241, 252
Checking of paint, 251
Checkups, routine, 80
Chimes, installation of, 171
Chisels, 48

cleaning, 73
maintenance, 72, 124
shutting down, 126
Furniture finishing, 271
Furring, 229
Fuse, 159, 160

G

Gain, hinge, 200
Gas furnace, maintenance, 126
Gauge:
steam, 135
water, 135
Glass, replacing, 193
Glazier's points, 194
Glider, paint, 248
Glue, 184
Grain in wood, 178
Gravity-feed hot-air heat, 128
Gravity-feed hot-water heat, 132
Grinding wheel, 60
Ground wire, 154
Grounding, 156, 160
Gutters, 282
maintenance, 90
repairs, 282
replacing, 283
Gypsum wallboard, 185, 224, 229

H

Hacksaw, 46
Hammer, 15
how to use, 17
Hammering in pipes, 105
Handsaw, 45
Hand-screw clamp, 52
Hardboard, 185, 224, 229
Hardwoods, 177
Hawk, 295
Heat loss, 76
Heater cord, 167

Heating cable, 282
Heating systems, 123
hot-air, 128
hot-water, 132
maintenance, 72, 124
radiant, 138
steam, 134
Heptachlor, 78
Hex wrench, 41
Hinge:
gain, 200
locating, 204
Hone, 60
Hot-air ducts, 128
Hot-air heating systems, 128
maintenance, 130
Hot-water heating systems, 132
maintenance, 133
Humidifier, 23
Humidity, 123

I

Ice barrier, 282
Insulation, 139
vapor barrier, 140

J

Jack plane, 50
Jack post, 214
Jamb, 200
Joint-filler, 296
Joints, wood, 181

K

Keyhole saw, 46
Kilowatt-hour, 157

L

Lacquer, 247
Lacquer thinner, 250

from marble, 309
from walls, 310
Staining of paint, 252
Stairs, 210
   repairs, 211
Star drill, 189
Steam gauge, 135
Steam heating system, 134
   maintenance, 136
Steamer, wallpaper, 233
Stiles, 199
Stillson wrench, 43
Stop:
   door, 200
   window, 196
Storage of tools, 58
Storm door, 142
Storm window, 87, 142
Striker plate, 201
Stringer, 210
Stucco, repairs, 288
Stuck window, 198
Stud, 227
SV cord, 166
Switches, 161, 163

T

Tack hammer, 16
Tang, 52
Tank, fuel, 127
Tank ball, 116
Tape, masking, 249
Tape measure, 55
Temperature, 123
Template for lock, 206
Tenon, 182
Termites, 77
   prevention, 77
Thermocouple, 126
Thermostat, 124
Thinner, 250, 255
Threaded nails, 24

Three-prong plug, 156
Three-way plug, 165
Three-way switch, 163
Three-wire outlet, 156
Threshold, 201
   installing new, 215
   maintenance, 81
Tiles, floor:
   ceramic, 223
   flexible, 220
Tiles, wall, 230
   repairing, 231
Tilting a radiator, 137
Titanium oxide, 241
Toenailing, 19
Toggle bolt, 187
Toilet tank, 115
   repairs, 117
Tongue-and-groove flooring, 212
   repairs, 213
Tools, 15 (*see also* specific items)
   care of, 58
   sharpening, 60
Torch, 96
Torque, 28
Traps, 107
   removing water from, 68
Tread, 211
Trim brush, 245
Trisodium phosphate, 75, 79, 88, 136, 310
Trowel, 295
Try square, 56
Try-cocks, 136
TSP, 75, 79, 88, 136, 310
Turpentine, 240
Twist drill, 33

U

Undercoat, 239
Underwriters' knot, 169
Union, pipe, 99

V

Valve, radiator:
 adjusting, 75
 cleaning, 75
 leaks, 137
Vapor barrier, 140
Varnish, 217, 239, 255
Varnish brush, 245
Vehicle, paint, 239
Venting radiator, 74, 134
Vents in drainage system, 108
Vise, 51
Voltage, 152

W

Wall, exterior:
 maintenance, 88, 284
 repairs, 285
Wall, interior:
 cracks, 83
 furring, 239
 how to build, 226
 how to paint, 262
 maintenance, 82
 materials, 224
Wall fasteners, 186
Wallboard, 185
Wallpaper, 232
 hanging, 234
 peeling, 83
 prepasted, 235
 removing, 233
Warped door, 210
Washer, drain, 114
Washer, faucet, replacing, 100
Waste pipe, 104, 107

Water:
 adding to boiler, 74
 damage, 71, 80
 how to shut off, 95
Water gauge, 135
Water hammer, 105
Water pump attachment, 38
Waterproof coating, 291
Watt, 156
Wax, floor, 80
Weatherstrip, 145
 installation, 146
Wheel, grinding, 60
Whetstone, 60
Whitewash, 239
Window:
 how to paint, 265
 maintenance, 86
 parts of, 195
 replacing glass, 193
 storm, 87
 stuck, 198
Window screens, painting, 87
Wiring, 157
Wood, 177
 floors, laying over concrete, 218
 grades, 178
 joints, 181
Wrenches, 41
 how to use, 44

Y

Yardstick, 55

Z

Zinc chromate, 269
Zipcord, 166